W9-CIG-530

The Last Survivor

The Last Survivor

Frank Krake

Translated by Haico Kaashoek

SEVEN DIALS

First published in Great Britain in 2021 by Seven Dials
an imprint of The Orion Publishing Group Ltd
Carmelite House, 50 Victoria Embankment
London EC4Y 0DZ

An Hachette UK Company

1 3 5 7 9 10 8 6 4 2

Copyright © Frank Krake / Uitgeverij Achtbaan 2018

The moral right of Frank Krake to be identified as
the author of this work has been asserted in accordance
with the Copyright, Designs and Patents Act of 1988.

All rights reserved. No part of this publication may be
reproduced, stored in a retrieval system, or transmitted
in any form or by any means, electronic, mechanical,
photocopying, recording, or otherwise, without the
prior permission of both the copyright owner and the
above publisher of this book.

This publication has been made possible with financial support from
the Dutch Foundation for Literature.

A CIP catalogue record for this book is
available from the British Library.

Map on page ix by Paul Scheurink

ISBN (Hardback) 978 1 8418 8525 4
ISBN (Export Trade Paperback) 978 1 8418 8527 8
ISBN (eBook) 978 1 8418 8528 5
ISBN (Audio) 978 1 8418 8529 2

Typeset by Input Data Services Ltd, Somerset

Printed and bound in Great Britain by Clays Ltd, Elcograf S.p.A.

MIX
Paper from
responsible sources
FSC® C104740
FSC
www.fsc.org

www.orionbooks.co.uk

For Jo

Contents

vii

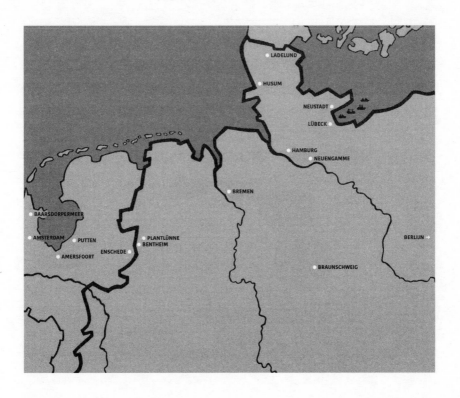

Prologue

Bay of Lübeck, Germany, 3 May 1945

The fighter planes appeared from the south, equipped with phosphorous bombs and rockets that they fired in bursts at the *Cap Arcona*. The majestic ocean liner, packed with five thousand concentration camp prisoners, was instantly transformed into a burning hell. The German flak guns were unable to fend off the wave of attacks, the rattling of machine guns and the uninterrupted explosions only completing the pandemonium. Emaciated inmates tried in vain to take cover.

Wim had to act quickly. He looked around. The luxurious ballroom was strewn with severed limbs. Dripping blood spattered the once so pristine white panelling and ornate ceilings. Everywhere soldiers, dead drunk and in blind panic, shot at anything that moved.

He crouched down and forced himself to keep thinking clearly.

After a few minutes, the Typhoons had disappeared as quickly as they'd come and an other-worldly silence fell over the battered though still floating ship. It gradually gave way to the screams of the bleeding wounded and the orders shouted by the German Volkssturm soldiers, who had stayed behind to guard the camp prisoners. Most of the SS members had weaselled their way out the previous night.

He must get away from here. Get off the ship as quickly as possible. That much was clear to Wim. He'd spent months in the worst German concentration camps, under inhuman conditions, where everyone around him had died of hunger, disease or maltreatment. The 'hell of Husum' they'd called it there. And then been worked to death in camp Neuengamme by sadistic SS officers, under the motto '*Vernichtung durch Arbeit.*' 'Extermination through labour.' They'd been murdered by exhaustion, despair and utter insanity. Don't ask how, but he'd survived it all. And was it now going to end like this, with freedom in sight?

He pulled himself together. Never.

Behind a pair of German prisoners, Wim fought his way upwards, to the deck and open air – though he wasn't the only one to do so. Hundreds of people trampled one another just to get away. That is, if you could still call such carcasses in rags people. On deck, they fought to the death for anything that might float. They dashed themselves against the ship's iron hull as it began to lean and steadily heat up. They were drilled by bullets from German soldiers, who shot at every prisoner they managed to get between their cross hairs.

Then the planes returned. They failed to notice the white flag the captain had raised, impossible to see through the smoke, and tore into the crippled ship. Shells exploded, machine gun bullets flew past Wim's ears. He fled to a small ladder, descending two steps at a time, and hid underneath a metal platform.

Trembling, he peered with one eye past the iron handrail

above. On deck, it was still the same sheer panic, the cursing and shooting soldiers. After this new wave of attacks had passed, he cautiously crept back out and looked around.

The sea was full of corpses. It reeked of death, a smell he'd come to know only too well since the Germans had first picked him up in a razzia – one of the Nazis' round-ups – and dragged him, by way of the torture chambers of Amsterdam, from camp to camp. Concentration camps in Nazi Germany without gas chambers: they existed. And they were no less effective. Inhumane places, encircled with barbed wire, where the chimney was your only escape. Tens of thousands of imprisoned civilians had been murdered there and had coloured the air around Neuengamme an ash grey for years, a constant sickly stench the legacy of their suffering. They came from Russia, the Netherlands, Poland and Denmark. From Germany, Italy, Belgium and France. Mostly young men in the prime of their lives.

Wim had narrowly survived. He weighed less than forty kilos but had an iron will to keep going. The advancing liberators had been within striking distance when the last survivors in the camp were herded together and put on a transport north – on foot or in cattle wagons – to the last remaining part of Nazi Germany, where the SS could continue their reign of terror. It was a journey that would cost many more innocent lives.

Wim felt the deck sinking underneath his feet while the ship shook from several explosions that seemed to come from the hold below. He looked at the grey-blue waves where, among the corpses, the fight for a single lifebuoy or simply a splintered plank just carried on.

The soldiers had now set their sights on the floating survivors, who were picked off one by one. The command from *Reichsführer-SS* Heinrich Himmler had been clear:

'No prisoners shall be allowed to fall into enemy hands alive.'

An order was still an order, so they shot. The exhausted prisoners who by some stroke of luck had managed to evade the bullets now succumbed to the temperature of the seawater, which froze their muscles and made them sink slowly to the bottom of the Bay of Lübeck.

'They were British. British!' pounded through Wim's head. He'd recognised the Typhoons' contours. It had been the liberators, so long awaited by everyone, who had sown murder and mayhem among the tattered, exhausted and undernourished crowd.

For the Royal Air Force, Operation Big Shipping Strike was a tremendous success. They believed they'd taken out the SS members and Nazi party leaders fleeing to Scandinavia. Johnny Baldwin, the famous and decorated leader of RAF No. 198 Squadron, which had carried out the attack, was now sitting 300 kilometres away with his co-pilots and a cold bottle of beer.

On the deck of the burning, glowing *Cap Arcona*, Wim was still fighting for his life. In a flash, his thoughts went out to his mother and sister in Amsterdam. He needed to see them again, tell them his story. He felt the hot air singeing his lungs.

Wim took another deep breath, closed his eyes – and jumped.

I

A child in hiding

Amsterdam, the Netherlands, 1932

'You little piece of shit! I know you're in here, you runt.'

Wim heard the footsteps coming closer. He pushed his face even further between his knees and pinched his nose shut, as he was scared of having to sneeze from all the dust. He was sitting safely behind the washstand, a plank five millimetres thick shielding him from discovery and a thrashing. For nothing. His stepfather was, as so often, completely wasted and in his evil drunkenness wanted yet again to vent all of his misery onto his nine-year-old stepson.

'Come on out, you runt, and then you'll see how we do things here.'

He listened to his torturer's heavy breathing and through a minuscule gap between the backboard and a plank, he could now see him standing there too. Hendrik Aloserij had to support himself with both hands so as not to fall over. He leaned against the washstand with his left hand and still held the door handle in his right.

That Saturday afternoon, Wim had been playing in the small kitchen when he heard the front door open. From the stumbling footfall on the stairs, he immediately knew it was time to pack up. 'Quick, get out of here,' his mother whispered.

He'd flown up the stairs to the attic. Under the rafters, he carefully stepped sideways over a thin beam along the ledge. He counted each step to himself. After exactly twenty-five steps, he reached the back of the washstand. In the pitch darkness, he felt his way to his favourite hiding spot, large enough to crouch on and wait with bated breath for his step-father's search to begin.

'Little piece of shit!'

Aloserij's favourite curse penetrated every fibre of Wim's slender body. He shuddered, only for a moment. The days when he'd have shaken like a leaf were far behind him. Nevertheless, he occasionally still woke up in the middle of the night, soaked in sweat, because of some bad dream in which he'd caught yet another beating.

He watched Aloserij's thin lips tremble with rage. His face was elongated, his head was bald and browned, his light eyes bulged. He had two oblong ears, so large that even in this precarious situation, Wim still had to smile. He was so happy that this wasn't his real father and that he could go through life with the modestly sized ears of another man. Add to that those beautiful waves in his hair, those finely shaped eyebrows and that always roguish look, which, despite him being so young, made him popular with the girls in his neighbourhood.

Aloserij moved his search to the bedroom across from the bathroom. Wim's older sister, Jo, had her own bed there, next to the one that Wim had to share with his half-brother Henk. When he couldn't find his stepson in that room either,

Aloserij, his words now approaching gibberish, headed for his own bed to sleep off the alcohol. Wim heard him shuffle towards the staircase and slowly descend. At least he wasn't as drunk as a few days before, when he'd bounced down the steep stairs on his rear end.

It wasn't spacious or luxurious inside their upstairs apartment at 78 Kleine Kattenburgerstraat, though compared to most of the other children on their small island on Amsterdam's east side, they couldn't complain. Three doors down, his friend Piet Klaver had to share a bedroom with four brothers. Their father had died in a work accident in the port and they needed to get by on welfare. Between all kinds of quick fixes and help from the neighbours, the family could just manage to survive. They only paid a guilder seventy-five each week for rent, which was why they, too, had come to live on the island.

In Wim's small house, the children heard everything. The interior walls were even thinner than the exterior bricks and those were just seven centimetres thick. In winter, heavy frost formed on the inside of the windows. When there was an easterly wind, you could feel the cold coming in through all the façade's pores. On days when the temperature outside dropped far below freezing, the difference inside their bedroom was marginal.

Wim's stepfather collected his pay on Saturdays. As a construction worker, he earned seventeen guilders a week. For that he spent ten hours a day, six days a week, scurrying up and down ladders, bags of cement and construction materials balanced on his neck. When, on Saturday afternoon, the week was over, he went straight to Café De Nieuwe Aanleg, an old bar on the corner of the Kleinestraat and Marinier-splein. He wouldn't come home until hours later.

That didn't always end well. A few months earlier, the children had been sitting with their mother around the paraffin stove in the kitchen, when they heard the front door open and then a hard, muffled bang. Wim's mother rushed downstairs and found Aloserij in a weird position, lying against the nearly vertical staircase, dead drunk. With a tenacity verging on primal force, she pushed him up the stairs, all the while yelling loudly into his ear to keep him awake. Upstairs, she dragged him into their bedroom, where she emptied his pockets and gathered together the last few guilders that were left of his pay, barely enough for the rent. She was beside herself and burst into tears. The children were silent, not knowing what to do.

After ten minutes, their mother had regained her compo-sure somewhat and sent Jo to the milkman to borrow some money. She came back with six guilders in her hand and a despondent look: six guilders that their mother would have to pay back over the following weeks as best she could. If Aloserij didn't drink away his pay, anyway.

For Wim, it was much worse if his stepfather came home not hammered but just heavily intoxicated. Drunk enough to be aggressive but not plastered enough to immediately fall asleep. It was at those moments that his hiding place offered the only salvation. Or he made sure he was out – far from home, wandering over the islands, together with Piet; playing marbles with the boys from Wittenburg, the next island over, or playfully ringing the doorbell of the crippled greengrocer on the Oostenburgergracht further down the canal.

Before moving to the island, they'd rented a beautiful new house in the Van Spilbergenstraat, all the way across town. Wim had never understood why his mother had insisted on going after Henk Aloserij, a man from Kattenburg.

'I'm your father,' he said, the first time they'd met, in an attempt to win over Wim.

'You're not my father,' Wim snapped.

The strange man looked at the boy with a friendly expression. He pulled out a dime from his pocket and tried to press it into his little fist. Wim's eyes flared fiercely.

'I don't want your money – and you're not my father.'

He turned around and ran outside, where he sat on a kerb. He'd never known his real father, who had died from one lung disease or another shortly before his birth. Jo had already told him that their mother was involved with another man. He'd already suspected as much. Usually, their family barely went to church, but for the last six months they'd gone almost every week. To the Sint Annakerk on the Wittenburgergracht, with those beautiful stained-glass windows, nearly as high as the trees that stood beside it. After Mass was over, the same bald man with a bronzed head and pale eyes would appear at his mother's side, the same man who had just introduced himself as his father.

Wim was so lost in thought he hadn't noticed that his sister had been sitting next to him for some time. Jo was more than a year older than him, but they were inseparable. Their mother made sure that Jo always dressed neatly, preferably in white dresses and with a matching ribbon in her dark hair. How she did it was a mystery, but with the few cents she had, she always managed to make her daughter shine. Wim was especially fond of Jo and enormously proud to be her younger brother; and from the same father at that. After school, they would always hang out together and there were no secrets between them – aside from his hiding spot upstairs.

2

Life on Kattenburg Island

Amsterdam 1935

During the latter half of the seventeenth century, three islands had been built on Amsterdam's east side, along the IJ river. Kattenburg was the most westerly; Wittenburg and Oostenburg lay right beside it. To the east, the Czaar Peterstraat separated them from the port. The residents of the small, often ramshackle workers' houses were proud of their neighbourhood: they called themselves 'Islanders', a nickname they'd made their own.

The entire area was dedicated to the shipping industry. At the time, its large shipyards were building hundreds of vessels for the Dutch East India Company. From Kattenburg it was only a short walk to the naval storehouse, the Marine Etablissement, once an important fortification for the city of Amsterdam. Café Het Gouden Hoofd, which was nearby, in turn bordered on the Mariniersplein. That was where the directors and managers of the many shipping companies lived, in houses that stood in sharp contrast to the humble workers' abodes throughout the rest of the neighbourhood. Nevertheless, the poorer Kattenburgers were prouder than they were jealous of this section of their island. The sense of belonging won out easily over the wealth divide.

Wim didn't have neighbours in this close-knit community but a great many aunts and uncles. In times of need, they helped one another out. Wim and his siblings witnessed this fact when their mother, who almost never got sick, found herself in bed with a high fever in the winter of 1935. As was usual, the neighbourhood jumped to her aid. Mr Adolfs, the butcher from across the street, walked in one Sunday afternoon with a pan-fried steak – real beef, which they never usually ate. Now and then they had enough money for a small cut of meat, but their mother would buy horse, which was much cheaper.

It was always bustling on Kattenburg. Vendors selling merchandise on cargo bikes would come along and loudly praise their wares. Mothers leaned from their windows to put their laundry out to dry and keep an eye on their brood. Sailors on shore leave and idle dock workers with little money and even less to do filled the streets of the island, which was connected to the rest of Amsterdam by a number of bridges. Wim scrounged together little bits and pieces everywhere he went: an apple from the greengrocer, a slice of ham from Adolfs the butcher – whom he loved to visit – or a roll of sweets for a few cents at the grocer's on the corner of the Tweede Kattenburgerdwarsstraat, just a stone's throw away. He usually saved the roll for his Sunday excursions with Jo. After going to church, they would first eat a couple of sandwiches at home before setting off, for everywhere and nowhere. Anywhere to get out of the house.

★

Wim's mother originally came from Maastricht, a vibrant and historic city at the southern tip of the Netherlands. She'd nearly got rid of her accent, though it still resurfaced when she was tired. She hadn't had an easy childhood. After her mother died, she'd been taken in by nuns, only to be kicked out again without warning when she was eighteen.

There had been nowhere she could go. At her wits' end, she turned to her mother's sister, Aunt Toos, for help. She was allowed to live with her aunt, but left again within a few weeks in a hurry. Her uncle, who was almost sixty years old, hadn't been able to keep his hands off her. After moving from place to place, she ended up in Rotterdam where, at the age of nineteen, she moved in with her boyfriend, Johannes Wijmans, Wim's real father.

When Hendrik Aloserij had married their mother, he'd adopted Wim and his younger half-brother Henk, and they'd carried his family name ever since. He hadn't adopted Jo though, since adopting girls was not something you did, Aloserij thought.

Wim and Jo didn't care much for Henk. In their eyes he was no good and their mother had never wanted to tell them who his father was. Before, when they'd lived on the Da Costakade in west Amsterdam, and Wim had been three or four years old, Mother had rented out rooms to make ends meet. They'd had different lodgers and Henk had been born in that period.

Henk was a real pest, particularly for Jo. On Saturdays they washed themselves in a large zinc basin on the tiles behind the house. They had just one towel for the three of them and Henk always wanted to go first, since then he had clean, warm water. After drying himself, he would 'accidentally' drop the towel into the basin and it was up to Jo and Wim to figure out how they were going to dry themselves off. In winter, this routine was genuine torture, since you couldn't just walk inside naked and dripping wet without getting into trouble. Their mother would give Henk a few cuffs around his ears, putting an end to this form of teasing, but he would only come up with something new.

And that was how the years passed on Kattenburg. For Wim, it was a reasonably carefree time. He'd learned to keep out of his stepfather's reach. Being invisible had become second nature to him. He moved like a shadow, kept his mouth shut at the dinner table, simply pretended not to be there and was always on his guard against a cuff or a swipe.

On a Sunday one summer, Hendrik Aloserij's hands were itching again. They'd all just come home from the morning Mass at the Sint Annakerk. Wim and Jo had stayed behind for a while; they'd first wanted to walk along the front pews, which were rented by the congregation members who were better off. Sometimes spare change, intended for the collection, would fall under them without being found. They picked up two cents: enough for some sweets on their walk. After a few minutes, they were chased out of the church by the sexton, the money deep in their pockets.

At lunch, Wim caught two cuffs before he could even get his first sandwich down. The first, supposedly, for eating noisily and the second for something he didn't catch and about which he didn't dare to ask. Just as Wim went to pick up a third sandwich, Aloserij snarled: 'You stuffing yourself again for that crapper?' With a scowl, he gestured upwards to where the toilet was. Wim didn't look at him and silently continued eating.

As soon as the chance arose, he and Jo left the table. They decided to go for a long walk, as far as possible from home.

'To the lake?' Jo asked.

'That works. We'll check out the beach.' After all, there was always a chance of running into nice girls there, though Wim didn't mention that. He was twelve now and becoming a real charmer. The girls hung on his every word whenever he started telling them about his adventures. It didn't matter to them that these took place in an area of just a couple of square kilometres on the islands.

Wim and Jo set off at a good pace. On the beach, just outside town, they shared the sweets they'd brought with them. A little further on, a sewage pipe emptied itself into the water.

The wind was coming from the wrong direction, meaning the beach wasn't busy. When the wind and current were in your favour, you could swim and paddle around wonderfully, completely free of charge, while the five-cent beach near Lake Nieuwe Diep honoured its name. They didn't have that kind of money.

But now it stank there terribly and the water looked murky. After ten minutes, the brother and sister packed it in and walked the whole way back. As they still didn't feel like going home, they continued along the IJ river and forgot everything and everyone around them. Hours later, they could see the Hembrug in the distance, spanning the North Sea Canal. They sat at the water's edge and watched the trains shuttling between Amsterdam and Zaandam over the bridge. They were tired from the long walk and the sultry summer weather. After finishing the last sweets, they lay back in the grass, closed their eyes for a moment and fell asleep.

When Wim awoke he had no idea what the time was, but the sun was already hanging low in the sky. He nudged his sister, who was still in dreamland.

'Mother's going be worried,' she said. 'And your shirt's all green.' Wim beat the grass and moss from his Sunday sailor's shirt as best as he could and they started the long walk home. That night, a little before one, they walked back into the Kleine Kattenburgerstraat. There were maybe twenty people standing outside their house, but it wasn't until they got closer that they finally spotted their mother. She was so short that she became lost among the excited neighbours. Her eyes were bloodshot and she threw her arms around them.

'I thought something had happened to you,' she whispered into Jo's ear.

'Nothing at all. We went to the Hembrug and fell asleep in the grass there.'

'The Hembrug – but that's more than five miles from here!'

The neighbours went back to their houses. For most of them, the night was already half over; they had to be up again at six o'clock. Hendrik Aloserij had paid little attention to all the commotion and, as usual, had coolly gone to bed at around nine o'clock as if nothing were wrong.

★

For a few days now, Wim had been as white as a sheet and moaning from stomach pain. It didn't matter what his mother gave him, nothing helped. He couldn't go to school and hadn't left his bed for two whole days. His mother, desperate for help, took the tram into town to the elegant Plantage Middenlaan, the street where Doctor Dasberg had his practice. He was a Jewish doctor whose patients included most of the wealthy residents of Amsterdam, though he also helped the sick in poorer neighbourhoods. Wim's mother had been to see him before, when she'd been married to Wim's real father.

Dasberg was a doctor you could count on in times of need and he promised to drop in after his afternoon rounds. After chatting briefly with Wim, who didn't say much in return, Dasberg palpated and massaged the area in question on his belly.

'Appendicitis,' was his diagnosis. He took a small white bottle of pills from his brown leather bag and handed it to Wim's mother. He also wrote a referral, so she could have Wim admitted to the hospital. An hour later, Dasberg returned to check whether his first diagnosis had been correct.

'Ninety-nine per cent certain that it's your appendix,' he said. 'That'll have to come out, but in a week or two, you'll be fine again.'

Wim got a firm handshake and a pat on his head. Two weeks later, he was playing again with the boys from the neighbourhood on the Kattenburgerplein as if nothing had happened. Exactly as Dasberg had predicted.

It was during this time that Aloserij very occasionally showed his human side. He visited Wim in the hospital and took him some fruit, or extra bread with jam, Wim's favourite. The boy didn't trust him though. Just a month prior to Wim's appendicitis, Aloserij had thrown him down the stairs. He'd been covered in bumps and bruises, his right arm completely banged up. Maybe his stepfather was feeling some regret, after all. If he could even remember what had happened.

3

An open casket

Amsterdam 1937

Wim's mother's belly kept getting bigger. She was nearly forty years old now and Wim was already fourteen. As the birds and the bees were never discussed in the Aloserij household, whenever their mother started talking about a stork, Wim and Jo would just look at each other. They'd discovered the book tucked in a drawer in her bedroom a long time ago and knew better.

But it was exciting. When would their new baby brother or sister be born? Wim knew only too well that the birth of his half-brother or half-sister would only further widen the distance between him and his stepfather. This was going to be Hendrik Aloserij's actual child.

Wim's stepfather's mother was looking forward to the birth too. Granny lived on the Kattenburgerachterstraat and she had a soft spot for Wim. He was the only one who was occasionally slipped something during visits – never Henk or Jo. She would then lift her overskirt and wiggle a penny out from the pocket sewn into her underskirt. Jo really didn't like her and was even a little afraid of their step-grandmother, but Wim enjoyed drinking a cup of tea at her home – in that way, he avoided her son, who seemed to be becoming crazier by the day.

From her living room on the third floor, you could see the entrance to the naval storehouse on the Kattenburgerstraat, where soldiers stood guard. Granny would then always draw his attention to the ornaments above the towering gate, framed in a large alcove that pointed skywards. That gate is from the seventeenth century, she would always say, as if she herself had been there in those days.

One late afternoon in April, Wim had just received a penny from Granny when he got an uneasy feeling. He said good-bye to his grandmother and hurried down the stairs. Dinner would be just about ready. He deftly passed between the small trucks, the mothers pushing prams and the vendors with their handcarts, and within five minutes he was home. There, a surprise awaited him. His mother wasn't in. She was in the hospital, Jo said. Something about her belly, she'd said, and Aloserij had gone with her. They could have dinner at Aunt Sjaan's, where they were already expected.

Around eight o'clock that evening, his stepfather knocked on the door, incredibly excited and with a sparkle in his eyes. He was sharp, worked up and – for once – sober.

'I've got a son! A son!' he yelled. 'Come on, we're going.'

Wim just managed to shout 'thanks!' to Aunt Sjaan as they left, their neighbour shaking her head and smiling broadly after them.

At the Wilhelmina Gasthuis Hospital, Wim got a fright when he saw his mother's drawn and deathly pale face. In no way did she still resemble the vital and energetic woman who, only that morning, had wished him a good day at school. The delivery had been extremely difficult and she seemed to have become a completely different person. A little creature lay on top of her stomach, wrapped in white towels with a beige hem.

'Bertus,' Aloserij proudly announced.

Wim didn't know whether to focus his attention on his mother or the baby. His youngest half-brother peered at him with tiny, watery eyes. Wim did find it funny, a baby, but he didn't dare to hold him yet. A penetrating smell hung in the air of the ward, one that he couldn't place but that made his head spin. After five minutes, he'd had enough. Bertus got a peck on his cheek. Jo came an hour later. At sixteen, she was already a young woman who simply couldn't get enough of the touching scene. On the contrary, Wim was eager to leave and walked through the endless white corridors towards the exit, mumbling 'Bertus' to himself again and again.

As Wim's mother was a bit older this time around, the recovery took much longer. She didn't come home from the hospital until three weeks later. That same evening, Reverend Brussel turned up on their doorstep to have a look at mother and son and to toast the happy outcome with the father. This wasn't the first time Brussel had come to visit them at home and he knew very well that Aloserij liked to keep his house stocked with a bottle of liquor. Usually, Jo would have to go and sit on the priest's lap, but now that she was sixteen, she avoided him conspicuously. She half hid herself behind a doorpost in the kitchen doorway, her eyes closely following the two men sitting in the small living room. Aloserij was expecting some kind of financial support from the Church and looked at the priest inquiringly.

'She's doing pretty good,' he said, 'but she could sure use a steak.'

'A steak? Well, I'm afraid she'll just have to make do with looking at one,' the priest said. He poured himself another drink.

For Jo, who was still listening in, Brussel's answer felt like a slap in the face. She realised there was a difference as large as life between what the priests preached about neighbourly love in church and what they actually practised. Their mother had arranged for her and Wim to be baptised when they were toddlers, and they'd also been confirmed, but Jo had had doubts about her churchgoing for some time now. These were only strengthened by the priest's behaviour.

Without anyone noticing, Wim had slipped outside and returned with a coal bucket. In the living room, he fed the stove. He moved like a shadow through the house and was soon back upstairs at his mother's bedside.

Aloserij wasn't able to enjoy his only son for very long. He rapidly fell to pieces from excessive drinking and his behaviour grew more erratic. He still came home wasted with some regularity, having guzzled away a large portion of his weekly salary, and on one occasion even splurged on a cab ride home. When he woke up sober again the next morning, Aloserij spent half an hour shouting 'Where's my wallet?' through the house. He'd probably left it in the cab but of course didn't want to admit it. A wild look in his eyes, he walked haltingly towards the scalding-hot cast-iron stove in the living room and went to grab hold of it with his bare hands. Wim's mother threw her mending work aside and sprang out of her chair, holding her husband back just in time.

'What do you think you're doing? You'll burn yourself if you grab the stove like that.'

A strange jolt went through Aloserij and he slowly sank to the floor. A few minutes later, he scrambled back to his feet and staggered into the kitchen, murmuring to himself. Wim's mother stayed behind uncertainly.

In the months that followed, he increasingly performed the strangest of antics. Wim's mother had already called for Doctor Dasberg several times. He'd given Wim's stepfather a full examination and referred him to the hospital. The only thing their mother would say about his situation was that his drinking had got the better of him. She had a card from the hospital on her bedside table with a number to call if things with her husband threatened to get completely out of hand.

It wouldn't take long. Winter was on its way and shrieking autumn storms ripped through the draughty houses on the island. Fortunately, these came in from the east, meaning that Aunt Sjaan's upstairs apartment kept the wind out of their living room. But their bedroom on the third floor stuck out over the buildings on the street and was exposed on all sides. To Wim, it felt as if the wind were blowing just as hard inside as it was outside and he crawled deep underneath his blankets. Henk was already asleep and Jo had just gone to bed.

Suddenly, a terrible scream from his mother shook him awake. Jo was already standing beside her bed, while Henk calmly continued snoring away. Brother and sister ran downstairs as fast as they could and just managed to see their mother, Bertus desperately clutched against her chest, pulling their stepfather away from the open window. The wind was howling through the bedroom and she shut the window with her left hand. It was as if Aloserij were in a trance; he spluttered gibberish and dazedly walked past them.

'That's it, I've got to call right now,' their mother said to Jo and Wim, remarkably calm. 'Jo, will you look after Bertus? Dad wanted to chuck him out of the window – I was just in time to stop him.'

Wim and Jo stood gaping at their mother, lost for words. The downstairs neighbours, the Tiekens, had a telephone and they'd already unlocked their door, having been woken up by the scream. Their mother rushed down, while Wim and Jo tensely waited in the living room.

Moments later, another giant scream. Only this time there was no panic in it – it was rage. Their mother ran out of the Tiekens' house and yelled her husband's name. Aloserij had opened their bedroom window again and, dropping his trousers to his ankles, had casually started taking a leak into the street.

She managed to calm him back down and sat with him until two nurses from the hospital came to pick him up a quarter of an hour later. They took him to Pavilion 3, the psychiatric ward, popularly referred to as the 'loony bin'.

Four weeks later, Hendrik Aloserij was lying in an open casket in their front room. His head was completely wrapped in bandages, Jo had told Wim. Wim wasn't allowed to look and didn't feel any need to. More than anything, everyone at home felt relieved. Not a trace of sadness, no emotion, no heart-wrenching scenes. It was all right.

It wasn't going to be easy, a single mother with four children – without work, an income, her body nowhere near up to strength. She was even too weak to push the pedal on the sewing machine, which was why Jo often couldn't go outside to play, instead having to help their mother put together nappies for their half-brother. But she really enjoyed the work, now that she'd finally been freed from the yoke of her stepfather.

Wim might have been the most relieved of all. After school, he went and played with Piet to avoid the casket in the front room. His stepfather may have finally been dead, but Wim still had to give him a wide berth. It didn't bother him. A week later, it was all behind him and peace returned.

Their mother spoke multiple times with workers from the social assistance service, and all kinds of strange people showed up at their house. One man just walked straight upstairs and had a look through their wardrobes, to see whether they owned too many things to qualify for welfare. He was known as the 'overseer of the poor'.

In the end, their mother would receive fifteen guilders a week, plus special coupons, from the municipality of Amsterdam. Not everything was to Wim's liking. He loathed the clothes he had to wear.

They couldn't pick these out themselves. Their mother had been given clothing coupons that were only valid at one store on the Prinsengracht, one of the main canals in the city's centre, and the whole street could see from a mile away where his new clothes were from. Wim tried to camouflage them with other pieces of clothing and that went well enough, but everyone at school could read the situation at home with a glance at Wim's black knee socks with the two red bands woven into them. He felt branded.

Fortunately, he wasn't the only one in his class. There were many fathers who were out of work and as a result, dependent on government assistance. This also had its advantages. With no less than fifteen other children from his class, Wim was allowed to go down into the school's basement. It was dimly lit and a dusty light bulb ensured he could just make out the boy standing in front of him in line. Here, the children from disadvantaged families were given porridge made from groats and buttermilk. He had his own little enamel pan; the bottom bore his scratched initials. That was how he came to find himself in line, his small pan in his hand and in clothes from social assistance, waiting for a few ladles of porridge.

Their mother bravely pushed her way through the difficult times too. She started to feel better and soon had some of her natural charm back. But all was not well for long, with Aloserij's brother – Uncle Guus – soon pursuing her.

One day, during a meal at the kitchen table, their mother cleared her throat and said: 'We're leaving.'

The children looked at her, their eyes questioning.

'We're leaving Kattenburg. I don't want anything to do with that whole family of your stepfather's. I'm going to look for a little house near Oosterpark. I still know some people there from before, back before I met him.'

4

Hard at work

Amsterdam 1938 – 1940

The family moved to 103 Tweede Oosterparkstraat, an upstairs apartment in a better neighbourhood, with the verdant Oosterpark around the corner. Wim still felt drawn to Kattenburg but had little time to actually go back and visit. On Sunday afternoons, he sometimes walked the few kilometres to be able to roam the streets with Piet, just like old times. Or he checked in on Granny, who was struggling to work through her son's tragic death. After a cup of tea at her place, he would bring his Kattenburg friends up to speed on his first job, as assistant wallpaper salesman at the Rath & Doodeheefver wallpaper factory.

There had been an ad in the newspaper, as the business was expanding quickly and needed new people. With his enthusiasm and tremendous energy, he was promptly hired for the advertising division, for six days a week. Each day, he had to go to 'The Wallpaper Palace', the elegant seven-storey main office on the Prinsengracht.

Wim quickly got into the swing of things. He sorted wallpaper samples for the sample books, which were sent by the factory on the Duivendrechtsekade to the main office. Most of all, though, he enjoyed going with the sales representative to clients in the wider area of Amsterdam. Wim then had to lug the heavy sample books. He wore a nice pair of trousers and a jacket – they were his pride and joy and he used them sparingly.

When he was allowed to go to the factory, he made sure to wear his old get-up; though by now, he'd stopped wearing the knee socks from social assistance. Of the three guilders he earned each week, he was allowed to keep thirty cents as pocket money; he gave the rest to his mother. She also let him buy new socks.

Wim felt privileged to have such a cushy job. Jo only earned two guilders fifty a week and had to work much harder than him. She'd got a position in the house of a professor with seven children and mainly worked in the kitchen. Cooking food, scrubbing and shining, and keeping the children busy after school. When she was peeling potatoes, her thoughts would sometimes drift to dreams of welcoming babies into the world as a midwife. But as soon as one of the professor's children called her name, she was jolted back to her harsh reality. Their mother allowed her to keep twenty-five cents as pocket money.

On his sixteenth birthday, Wim was finally allowed to attend dance classes. He'd been looking forward to them for a long time and had crossed off the months in an old school notebook. With that same energy with which he worked for his boss, he now swung across the dance floor on Saturday nights. He regularly came home with a chocolate bar and shared it with his half-brothers and sister. It had been stuffed into his jacket by one of his dance partners, just to get a leg up on the others.

He discussed his romances with Jo. There were still no secrets between them, despite her now going steady with someone for a few months. Wim also taught his sister the new dance moves from his weekly lessons. He would patiently demonstrate them for her in the middle of their living room and Jo had them down in no time, but in reverse. That's how two learned to dance for the price of one.

It pleased their mother to watch their Sunday morning ritual. She was proud of her children and happy they were free from Aloserij. She didn't even need to be strict with them, as they knew very well what was allowed and what was not. The only time she'd correct them was when they spoke in Amsterdam slang.

'Say that again in normal Dutch,' she'd immediately reply.

After the dance lessons with his sister, Wim, Henk and their mother went to church while Jo stayed home to take care of Bertus. Wim usually never listened to a word the pastor said. He only had eyes for the pews at the back, along the aisle, where a few of his dance partners and other young women would always be seated. He knew most of them at least by name. Whenever one of these girls' eyes met his own, he would give her a promising smile. He made a good impression in his neat, well-kept clothes and came across as a correct, pious young man.

Jo's boyfriend, Joop Ploeg, had been coming around more frequently, mostly at the weekends, since he lived some distance away in the town of Hoorn in Friesland. Jo had met him in the kitchen at the professor's house, where he'd come to deliver groceries. Together with his friend Ger, he brought fruit and vegetables from the countryside north of Amsterdam to the better-situated families in the capital, on a horse-drawn cart. Wim liked the guy – he was an exceptionally honest and nice man – but Wim was also aware that he was slowly losing his sister. He put the thought aside, though, as he had enough to do himself.

In particular, a major opportunity awaited him. For ten years, he'd been going to Adolfs' shop; the butcher had seen Wim grow up as a little boy and had a soft spot for him. He would slip him a slice of sausage or even a bit of meat for home on occasion. Even though he now lived half an hour away, Wim still stopped by just to catch up and tell them how his mother was doing.

This time, Adolfs asked him if he could stick around until he'd finished for the day. Wim patiently waited in a wicker chair for what the butcher had to tell him.

'You enjoying things at the wallpaper factory, Wim?' he asked, his butcher's cap still on his head and the white apron loosely tied around his middle.

Wim talked the butcher's head off about his work, colleagues and adventures. After a while, Adolfs impatiently interrupted him: 'You ever give butchery a thought? I've been dreaming about a second shop, but I can't do it on my own – I'd need help. Right now, you're sixteen. You still need to learn everything, but I know you're a hard worker and smart enough. It can take a few years, but if you become my apprentice, you'll soon be able to open your own branch near Oosterpark. I'll help you do it. And for the time being, you'll earn just as much with me as you do in that wallpaper factory of yours.'

Wim beamed from ear to ear. His own shop, becoming a butcher, Adolfs wanting to help him with everything – it was music to his ears.

'Well, I'll need to talk this over with my mother, Mr Adolfs,' he said. 'But thanks a lot for the offer.'

'All right, you talk to your mother and say I'll be stopping by soon to tell her about my plans – sorry, *our* plans.'

Two months later, on 1 March 1939, Wim became Adolfs' apprentice. It felt like a homecoming. He knew most of the customers personally. His boss was firm, clear and fair. Although he had to work extremely hard, he was soon making a guilder more than he had at the wallpaper factory. Adolfs didn't have any children himself and saw Wim practically as his own son. He took great pleasure in explaining and demonstrating everything for his student.

On a Sunday that summer, Adolfs invited Wim out on his boat to look at the centre of Amsterdam from the water. Wim was utterly mesmerised by the completely different appearance of the city he knew so well. Once back on shore, he asked Adolfs about the old kayaks he saw parked in a row.

'Twenty guilders and one of them can be yours,' the butcher said. 'You'd need to fix it up yourself, though.'

'I could never afford that,' said Wim.

'You know what? Here, I'll lend you the money. No interest. You can pay me back a guilder a week.'

★

At weekends, Wim used every spare moment he had to work on his boat. Where he worked looked onto the back of the Amstel Brewery's stables. The draught horses, with their meaty hind legs, were brushed and readied there for their trips to the cafés. He always chatted with the drivers who came to fetch their horses from the stable. On occasion, when it was a short trip, he was allowed to ride along up front. They were burly men, with their leather aprons, and nearly as sturdy as the animals pulling the carts. The men needed to be, too, since they had to unload the full kegs of beer by hand. The bartender would place a small cushion on the spot where the heavy keg kissed the floor, to avoid it being damaged. Once the keg was tapped, the delivery man and his temporary help were thanked with a small glass. It was how Wim learned to drink his first beer.

After four weeks of spending each Saturday and Sunday sanding, filling holes, painting and sanding again, it was finally ready. The old boat, with its peeling brown paint, had been transformed into a snazzy bright red kayak. Along the bow, in big white print, it read: 'WIM'.

At home, there was more and more talk about a possible war. You couldn't trust that Hitler, his mother said. It wouldn't surprise her if the Netherlands were his next victim. It was April 1940 and the Germans had already taken Austria, Czechoslovakia and Poland.

Over dinner, Wim would repeat what he'd heard at the butcher's back on Kattenburg. Boys who were eighteen years or older were being called up one after another. Before they left, their mothers would fetch a nice piece of a meat for them. That was how Wim knew exactly who had been conscripted. He'd gone to school or got up to mischief with these boys and he knew some of them better than his own brothers. It unsettled him. He would be eighteen in a year. He couldn't bear the thought of trading his life and bright future as a butcher's apprentice for an army uniform.

5

The war

Amsterdam 1940 – 1942

Despite having promised to respect the Netherlands' neu-
trality, the Nazis invaded on 10 May 1940. Hitler's promise
proved to be worth nothing and the Dutch would surrender five days later after Rotterdam, a thriving port city just
sixty kilometres south of Amsterdam, was levelled in a blitz.
Wim hardly noticed the occupation in its first months. The
Wehrmacht, the Nazis' armed forces, had captured Amsterdam without heavy fighting and little changed for him that
summer. He lost himself in his work at the butcher's, while
at home, everything stayed the same. The only thing that
had changed was that his mother now cursed the Germans
to her heart's content. Wim had never known her to be
like this. Occasionally, she mentioned that she'd regularly
dealt with Germans during her childhood in Maastricht
and she could also speak German reasonably well. But
more she wouldn't say. It remained a mystery what exactly
had happened.

The family, though, had enough to eat, as there was always
an extra piece of meat at the butcher's that Wim could take
home. Sugar and peas had already been rationed before the

war and other essential items were added as the occupation carried on. First it was only coffee, tea and bread, but starting in September 1940, all of their customers on Kattenburg had to hand in ration coupons if they wanted to buy meat at the butcher's. Adolfs thoroughly hated it and grumbled as he went around the shop. On principle, he objected to what he called 'those rotten coupons' and loathed the entire administration that came with them, though he could do nothing but go along with the system.

German soldiers, who were barracked at the Marine Etablissement, often came into the shop. They were after extra meat, without wanting to hand in the necessary coupons. Adolfs had them sign a special list for receipt, noting the type of meat and weight. This was easy to tamper with later on. By turning a three into an eight, he could then sell an extra pound of meat to a regular customer, who for one reason or another didn't have enough coupons at their disposal. Wim nicknamed one of the Germans Bismarck, after the old Prussian chancellor from his history books at school. The soldier had the same fat nose and thick, droopy moustache as his illustrious compatriot and walked into the shop with his rotund belly and booming voice at least once a week.

Like his mother and Adolfs, Wim thought the Germans had no business being in the Netherlands but that in the end, they weren't causing so much harm. On the one hand, his mother thoroughly hated them, but on the other, she spoke about their easterly neighbours as a 'master race of high standing with a rich culture and good manners'. Wim would just cling to that, then.

Jo and Joop had married just before the war and settled in the Tweede Oosterparkstraat as well, three houses down. That took some getting used to for both brother and sister, even if they lived so close to each other. He missed Jo and dropped in at even the slightest opportunity. Not only on Sundays, but also during the week, whenever he was in the area delivering meat and had some time to spare.

When his nephew Rinus was born in January 1941, Wim couldn't stay away from his sister. He looked on with fascination as Jo gave the child a bath and then fed him. He would chat for a bit before hopping back onto his courier bike to deliver his next order.

And so the days of wartime passed uneventfully: during the week it was working hard at the butcher's, on Saturday evenings dancing at the Van der Linden dance school and on Sundays taking his kayak out if the weather was nice. Sometimes he was alone, but more often with another girl he'd met the evening before. They were only too happy to join him. He was seventeen and enjoying life. What did he care about those Germans?

By the time Wim's half-brother Henk was thirteen years old, he'd grown from a pest into a petty criminal who spent a lot of his time roaming the streets. Their mother tried to keep him at home after school as much as possible because he was getting into more trouble, but Henk would slip out again with the help of the window and a drainpipe. He robbed and stole to his heart's delight and that went from bad to worse. Their mother often discussed it with Jo, as she didn't know what to do with him. But Jo had her hands full with her own little tot and Henk wasn't taking anything from Wim any more. They'd never been fond of their half-brother and tried not to involve themselves. They had other things to do than worry about a street kid running astray.

In Amsterdam, everyone had Jewish friends or acquaintances: at school, at work or simply in their neighbourhood. That they were Jewish had never played a role for Wim – it was never something he'd thought about. With time, the Germans' sinister intentions grew clearer. It started with the dismissal of all Jewish officials working for the municipality. A few of Wim's friends' fathers were victims. In the space of a day, they were sitting at home and had lost their incomes. He didn't understand any of it. How unjust could the Germans be? But the occupiers soon began taking much stricter measures and there was more unrest in the streets. It started in the first weeks of February, with fights between members of the Weerbaarheidsafdeling (WA; 'Resilience Department') – the paramilitary arm of the National Socialist Movement in the Netherlands (NSB) – and armed Jewish gangs.

Jo regularly visited her friend Emma in the Jodenbreestraat, in the heart of the Jewish Quarter, where she heard how violent things had got. It was a portent of more unrest to come. Already, Jo had once not been allowed to visit Emma, as the Germans had sealed off the neighbourhood. A week later it happened again, this time for the death of an NSB member named Hendrik Koot, who hadn't survived a scuffle with a gang of communists. Jo now had to show her ID card on her way there. Hundreds of Jews were rounded up and hauled off to an undisclosed location. Several days later, on 25 February

1941, a large protest broke out in response to this injustice. Members of the Dutch communist party had disseminated pamphlets headed, in bold letters, with the words 'STRIKE! STRIKE! STRIKE!' – a call that was widely answered outside Amsterdam as well.

A day later, it was already over. Beaten and shot apart by the occupiers. Still, Wim was proud of the people of his city. They'd shown those Germans to keep off their Jewish friends.

But after a few months, the razzias resumed and large numbers of Jews were rounded up again. This didn't pass the brother and sister unnoticed.

'Joop was at our front door watching what was going on,' Jo said, 'when an NSB man just hit him in his face.'

'They're even worse than the Germans,' Wim said. 'Whenever they come into the butcher's, I walk to the back and pretend I don't see them.'

In January 1942, small signs with the words 'No Jews allowed' were hung up throughout the city. A week later, the occupiers made it mandatory that all Jews wore a yellow star. That didn't bode well, their mother thought. It turned out she wasn't far from the truth, since the Jews were being steadily cornered. At the butcher's, Wim heard there were even Jews who had gone 'into hiding'. Initially, he didn't know what that expression meant, but after hearing stories about the razzias, he could imagine all kinds of things.

Over the course of the year, the occupiers issued multiple decrees summoning men to report for work in German manufacturing, the mandatory *Arbeitseinsatz*. At first this was just for specialised workers in the metal industry, but in August it applied to other workers as well. Adolfs was worried about it all.

'Soon they'll want you working over there too.'

'Not a chance,' Wim said. 'I'd never last in a factory. If they put me in front of a machine, guaranteed it'd blow up.'

'I'm not so sure, you never know with those krauts. We'll have to see.'

Henk was arrested after making a grab in the cash register at Wessels' greengrocer on the corner of the Sluisstraat and Schinkelkade across town. Wessels had watched it happen in the mirror at the back of the shop, grabbed him by the collar right away and called the police. As Henk was only fourteen years old, he didn't have to go to prison but was given three months to try to better his life at the National Correctional Facility De Kruisberg in Doetinchem, in the east of the country. Jo had come over to console their mother and she was fuming at the kitchen table when Wim came home from work. 'He just doesn't learn,' she said. 'Let him see for himself that he should keep his hands off other people's things.'

'I already make sure to keep my wallet in my pinafore,' their mother said. 'He can't spot it lying around without taking something from it.'

'And don't you remember, right before my wedding? My expensive linens, the ones I'd spent years saving up for – he just pawned them. And the money was gone. Spent. I couldn't even buy them back and we had to use Joop's parents' old ones.'

'Oh, I'll visit him,' their mother sighed. 'We can't just leave him to fend for himself. Maybe this will finally teach him.'

Starting in June 1942, the occupiers began tightening their grip on ordinary people's freedom of movement. For Adolfs, Wim would sometimes still trade a basket of meat for a load of produce, but he had to be on his guard as they were no longer allowed to transport vegetables. Ger, his brother-in-law's friend, now only came sporadically from Zwaag to Amsterdam with his cargo bike filled with the local harvest. It was simply too dangerous.

That summer the Germans snapped up everything on two wheels. 'They can call it "requisitioning" all they want – those bastards are stealing bikes,' Adolfs cursed behind his chopping block. He had to arrange a special permit for Wim's courier bike. A few days later, he triumphantly walked into the shop with one in his hand. The butcher's bike was safe for the time being, but Wim was worried about his own racing bike. It had been a year already since he'd last ridden it. To be safe, he left it in their small shed, a large blanket draped over it and flowerpots balanced on top.

6

Arbeitseinsatz

Amsterdam, February 1943 –
Brunswick, Germany, January 1944

One afternoon, two older Wehrmacht soldiers entered Adolfs' shop, accompanied by two other men dressed all in black, including their boots. Wim saw the red-and-black insignia of the NSB on their sleeves and knew what awaited him. There was no use trying to hide – they'd already spotted him. The older of the two NSB men spoke first.

'Right then, what's that boy doing here?'

'That's my apprentice,' Adolfs answered. 'Next year he'll be starting his own butcher's shop near Oosterpark.'

'Don't you know that all men between the ages of eighteen and thirty-five are to report to the employment office to work for the Greater German Reich?'

'He presented himself correctly, sir, when the summons was made. It was noted at the time that he's essential to me.'

'Essential? That's for us to decide. What makes him so essential? There's nothing special that he carries out, is there? Does he do anything that you can't yourself?'

'I can't do everything on my own and he helps and supports me in all I do. What's more, he's in the middle of his

apprenticeship to become a butcher. That is going very well.'
Adolfs tried to conceal his rage, but the trembling corners of
his mouth betrayed him.

The younger NSB man now butted in.

'According to my list, he lives with his mother and two
brothers in the Tweede Oosterparkstraat, and his mother
is receiving welfare. It's very simple. He should have been
working in Germany a long time ago. You don't actually
need him – the Greater German Reich needs him all the
more. If his mother would like to keep receiving benefits,
then he'll report immediately upon receipt of a written summons, which will be following shortly at his home.'

'But, sir, I really can't do without him! Running a butcher's
is hard work. Maybe you don't see it, but I just can't manage
on my own.'

'Adolfs, the message is clear: he will report for work!'

The NSB men nodded to the German soldiers who had
been waiting silently at the door. The whole company turned
around and strode out of the shop.

'What now, Mr Adolfs?' Wim whispered. The butcher
shook his head as he didn't know what to say. For a moment,
all was silent.

'I'm afraid,' said Adolfs, 'you don't have much of a choice,
at least if your mother wants to keep her benefits.'

Wim gave a deep sigh. He knew his mother needed them
and realised what the consequences were. That evening, she
was just as taken aback. Wim tried to cheer her up.

'I'll be getting room and board and I can save money and
send some home.'

He knew that his friends who were working in Germany

had sent back reassuring letters, sometimes with money inside them. It all, however, had little effect on his mother.

It took longer than he'd expected, but after about three weeks, the moment came and the letter dropped onto the mat. He had five days to apply for a passport at the office of Public Registry and Elections. After receiving his passport, he was to report to the Atlanta building, across from the Leidsebosje park. Now, there was nothing keeping him from going to Germany. A little while longer and he would be leaving everything behind: his mother, brothers and sister. The butcher's. And Ciska.

He'd only known Ciska for a few weeks but found her extraordinarily charming and attractive. She was a year younger than he was, nineteen years old, and lived on the Nieuwe Leliestraat in the Jordaan neighbourhood, just west of the city's centre. He was usually drawn to young blonde women, but they'd danced so well together when they first met that Wim only realised while having a drink afterwards that Ciska had medium-length dark brown hair, which lightly waved down to her shoulders. And beautiful brown eyes. He might not have had butterflies in his stomach, but he certainly thought she was very nice.

At eight o'clock in the morning on Sunday, 21 February 1943, on the pavement near the tram stop, Wim kissed his mother and Jo on their cheeks and gave Ciska a big hug. She almost didn't let him go. Bertus got a pat on the head. Henk was nowhere to be seen.

With a big swing, Wim tossed a kitbag filled with his meagre belongings over his shoulder and stepped onto the tram to the Leidseplein. He waved to his family and girlfriend while the tram slowly picked up speed. After half a minute, they'd disappeared from view. He looked outside but saw nothing. What his eyes were taking in didn't enter his brain. 'Germany', it echoed in his thoughts. 'Germany'. He'd never been there and now found himself becoming slightly nervous after all.

At the employment office, he'd had to wait for ten minutes before an envelope with documents was pushed into his hands. He signed for receipt and took out a small yellow card. 'Brunswick' and an address were printed on it. He'd never heard of the place. A clerk gave him detailed instructions – the rest would become clear on his way there. First, he needed to go to Central Station. Inside, it was teeming with young men, all of whom were on their way to their own destinations in what he'd always heard German soldiers call, with a touch of melancholy, '*die Heimat.*' 'The homeland.'

After asking around, he discovered that he had to wait another hour before he could step onto the right train. The platform grew more crowded and that put Wim fairly at ease. If they were all headed that way in such a large group, things would have to be well organised there.

At every station where the train stopped, new people boarded, most of them young, but there were also men in their thirties among them. They did all have one thing in common: their faces were visibly tense. It was hard saying goodbye to their families and loved ones and their futures were uncertain. Wim looked for other people who were on their way to Brunswick, without success. He was on his own.

After riding for a few hours, the train stopped in the German city of Hannover. He showed his card to the conductor, who made it clear he could stay seated as one of the few Dutch passengers. A little later, the train started rolling again. Wim wasn't disappointed by what he saw. The landscape was not all that different from what he'd seen outside Amsterdam. Much of it was green, with plenty of fields and small villages, although he did see many bombed-out houses and factories.

Towards the end of the afternoon, the train rolled into Brunswick's Central Station. Wim grabbed his kitbag, stepped out and nervously looked around. Would they be able to help him on his way? Did they even want to help him along in this country, which was at war with his own?

Somewhat hesitantly, he walked along with the stream of people towards the stairs, hoping they would lead to the exit. With about thirty metres to go, he saw a woman who looked about twenty-five years old. She was lightly dressed for the time of year and didn't seem unsympathetic at first glance. He walked over to her with his most charming smile and stopped a metre in front of her. He held up the card. The woman looked up and smiled back.

'Hello, sir, may I help you with something?' she asked in German.

Wim didn't understand a word, but by then she'd already read his letter. '*Ah, Holländer,*' she said and grabbed Wim by his sleeve. They walked underneath the tracks and resurfaced in front of the large station building. Without another word, she walked Wim to the tram stop. She stopped on one of the middle platforms. 'Wait here, OK?' she said. Wim understood that. He pointed to the ground with his right hand.

'Wait here,' he repeated. The woman gave him a friendly look, shook his hand and walked back the way she'd come. 'Thank you very much, little lady,' he yelled after her in Dutch, but she didn't look at him.

For a moment, Wim had forgotten about Ciska and his mood had completely changed. It seemed like a nice country, this Germany. Just those intimidating swastika flags on the station building were a thorn in his side. He spent at least twenty minutes taking everything in. The sun was shining on top of his head so strongly that he fished out a cap from his bag. A tram stopped at the platform. He showed his card to the conductor, who looked from the card to Wim and from Wim back to the card.

'Hop aboard, I'll be with you in a second,' he said in fluent Dutch. Wim looked at him with surprise and scrambled to find a spot. A few moments later, the conductor was standing in front of him again: 'So I don't have a lot of time right now, but just stay in your seat until the final stop and then I'll get you up to speed. Don't worry, I'll help you out.'

Wim thanked the man and sat back in his seat, relaxed. It wasn't long before his eyes shut. In his thoughts he was walking with the young woman from a moment ago, now on his arm, into the fields between some cows, a picnic basket in his other hand instead of a kitbag.

'Are you getting off or were you planning on spending the night here?' a voice roared in his ear. Startled, Wim looked up and shook his head.

'No, no, I'm coming, I'm going with you.' He grabbed his things as fast as he could and walked with the conductor to a bench on a busy street.

'I'm Johan,' the man said. 'About four years ago, I came here to work and it's suited me excellently, I've got to say. I'd been out of a job at home for over a year and I was happy to finally get a shot.'

Wim introduced himself and showed him the card again.

'Yeah, I've seen these before. Everybody coming from the Netherlands has got one. But then you'll end up working in the *Lager* – you don't want to be doing that.'

Wim gave him an uncomprehending look.

'I'll explain later. Just come along with me. I live ten minutes' walk from here in a lady's house in the centre of town. I think she might still have a room free, because it's been a while since I've seen the Frenchman who was living there. And tomorrow you'll need to report to the city tram company – they call it the *Strassenbahn* here – it's quite the job. You'll see it all for yourself soon enough.'

As they walked, he told Wim all about the city. Wim feasted his eyes and was surprised by the many beautiful façades, the tall buildings, the warmth and cosiness of the place. After about ten minutes, the man stopped in front of a tall old house at 6 Stecherstrasse, with a number of small dormer windows along the front. He dug out a key from his trouser pocket and opened the front door. Once inside, he introduced Wim to Frau Bäsling, the landlady, who did in fact have a room spare. Wim beamed: it was all going much smoother than he'd imagined. Johan translated everything and Wim understood he could stay as long as he paid rent. After hearing the rent, five reichsmarks a week, he looked questioningly at Johan, who gestured that it was fine, and Wim received the key.

It was about nine o'clock in the evening and his eyes were burning from fatigue. He didn't mind at all that Frau Bäsling led him to his room. They needed to climb two floors using a spiral staircase; his room was at the end of a small hallway. It wasn't large, but then again, he didn't need much more than a bed, a chair and a closet. It was warm and stuffy, though, and everything was shut tight. He opened the dormer window wide and fell onto his bed, tired but satisfied. Within a few minutes, he was watching the same picnic basket reappear before him and then even more exciting things.

Wim set out the next morning after a good night's sleep and a hearty breakfast, which he hoped was included in the rent. After walking about two kilometres he spotted, on the corner of one of the main streets, a large building that trams were leaving and entering, exactly as the Dutch tram conductor had described. He showed his documents to the doorman and was politely helped further. He was back outside again within an hour. Apparently, he now had a job. '*Arbeit bei der Strassenbahn,*' 'A job at the tram company,' the older man had told him when filling in all sorts of forms. Wim leafed through the contract and could make out a few things from the text: '*7:30 Uhr*' would be the start of his workday; he hoped the amount '*30 Reichsmark*' was his weekly salary.

That evening, he handed the packet of papers to Johan, who went through the most important points with him. He would be trained as a metalworker before being put to work in a factory where tram parts were manufactured and repaired. The '30 Reichsmark' indeed turned out to be his weekly salary and, to Wim's surprise, included lunch. It didn't sound all that bad. He wasn't part of the war effort and could take his time mastering a trade. And if he was a bit careful with his salary, he'd be able to regularly send his mother a little something as well.

For Johan, the unexpected arrival of his young country-man was a welcome distraction. He was completely on his own and didn't have much to do outside work. He bent over backwards to get Wim settled in. After a few weeks, Wim already knew enough German to make himself understood. When he lost his way, he would simply approach someone and so always make it back home and learn something new about daily life in Germany.

The *Strassenbahn* office was located on the same site as the depot. An open area twenty metres wide separated the two buildings. In another building made of red bricks were a number of large workbenches on a concrete floor; a small window had been inserted every few metres. In the mornings, when the lights still had to be turned on before work, you saw very little. Wim was to get the hang of the metalworker's trade by doing little jobs under the guidance of an experienced supervisor. There were run sheets on his bench and whenever Wim finished a task he had to check it off the list. That was how he learned how to file, drill and work metal.

His boss was a German man, about forty years old, who looked rather unhealthy. He was far too heavy and had an ashen face. He had trouble breathing and coughed all day long, but he wasn't unfriendly and let Wim go about his work. Wim called him 'Boss' and never found out his real name.

Wim's boss told him that he was worried about the course of the war. More and more German workers were being called up for military service and he just hoped his poor health would keep him safe.

Wim felt sorry for the dear man. The work he'd been doing for the last twelve years wasn't especially healthy and yet he was proud of the company. In those first months, he'd told Wim that there were no fewer than thirty-six kilometres of rails in Brunswick and that they had ninety-five tram engines and seventy-eight tramcars — all of which needed to be maintained for the transportation of eighteen million passengers a year. His boss rattled off the figures and Wim remembered them. Whenever he walked through the city and saw the light-yellow trams riding past, decked out with green stripes and a large, protruding headlight, he would be overcome with pride. After all, it was partly thanks to him that they ran so well.

So far, this wasn't too bad compared to the poverty on Kattenburg.

After a couple of weeks, Wim was well on his way to mastering the basic techniques. He decided to make a copy of the key to his room. Taking a steel plate, he routed and filed until he had something that resembled it in shape. This easily took a few weeks, which was fine with his boss, as long as he knew where Wim was hanging out.

He was assigned his own workbench as well as his first real job: overlooking and, where necessary, repairing the restraint system on the metal bow that pushed against the tram's electrical overhead lines. A kind of pulley, made from metal, was supposed to press the bow back down as soon as contact with the overhead line was lost. Most of them went straight through to the pile of approved pulleys before testing the next one. He could work at his own pace and made sure there were never too many in the wooden crate awaiting his inspection.

Nearly every day, he popped into the large depot, where people of all nationalities were at work. Young Polish and Russian women walked around the whole day with heavy buckets, mops and sponges. They had to clean the trams inside and out. There was also a group of ten French soldiers, whose job it was to apply black paint to the underside of the trams. They worked as slowly as they could and, whenever they had the chance, would slip out for a few hours. Wim understood they were prisoners of war, but they had the freedom to move around, not just inside but also outside the depot. They wore their own uniforms, which now bore a large coloured stripe across their backs. A Belgian overseer was supposed to keep an eye on them. The man was a Nazi sympathiser and had volunteered to work in the country of his dreams. His two daughters worked there too, in the cleaning crew. They didn't look all that bad, but given their background, Wim preferred to keep his distance.

He wrote, in handwriting that was as neat as possible, to his mother and Jo that he was doing well and that they didn't need to worry about him. His mother wrote back that his money had made it and that he needed to make sure to eat enough and dress warmly as soon as autumn arrived. It had made Wim laugh; it was so typical of her.

He also wrote to Ciska that he'd been given other work, a bit heavier than he'd done during the first months. He now had to cast metal caps that were meant to seal off the tram's steel wheels and so prevent passers-by from getting caught between these and its underside. His boss taught him autogenous welding and how to cast metal for making sliding bearings. He poured glowing hot metal into a bronze basin, then into a mould. He first needed to tin the metal before he could form a seam – a process that released vapours Wim couldn't imagine were very healthy. He delivered the half-finished product to the metal fabrication shop, where oil grooves were cut and the bearings further made to order.

While Wim was a hard worker, at the slightest opportunity he shirked – it was still the Germans he was working for. By now, he'd got to know many of his colleagues and knew exactly where he could chat and yap away a morning or an afternoon without attracting too much attention.

Autumn arrived. Wim had been living and working in Brunswick for six months and was getting the feeling he wouldn't be staying for the second half of the year. He saw that in little things. People were becoming moodier and more nervous and they reacted differently. It was becoming harder to buy extra meat from his butcher. When he strolled through his workshop and the depot, Wim could feel the eyes of his German colleagues boring into his back.

He wrote a letter to his mother to wish her, Jo and Ciska a merry Christmas. He didn't want to make her unnecessarily worried and didn't mention the changing mood. 'I'm getting money for doing nothing,' he let her know, 'and enough to eat and drink.' It was not really a lie in itself – but his instincts didn't let him down.

Midway through December 1943, the authorities in Brunswick introduced a drastic measure: all foreigners were to move into the *Lager*, the camp of huts set up on an empty field not far from the station that Johan had warned him about. Wim said goodbye to his landlady, but Johan wanted to see how things unfolded first. He'd been living in Germany for so long already; he didn't think things would get that bad.

Together with three other Dutchmen, Wim was assigned to one of the wooden barracks at the back of the field. It reminded him of a small wooden cabin like the ones they had in Amsterdam, the boy scouts' permanent base. Five reichsmarks were deducted from his salary for accommodation. Certainly, when compared with the comfortable room at his landlady's, this wasn't even worth one.

Each evening, he could be found in the city centre, in order to spend as little time as possible with four people in that cramped space. After only a few weeks, he was completely sick of the barracks, but his hands were tied. He was forced to celebrate Christmas in his green-stained hut with boys from every corner of the Netherlands. They tried to make the best of it.

In January 1944, the Allies started intensifying their bombings of German cities, their intention being to wear down the German civilian population. Even Brunswick wouldn't escape several waves of air attacks and Wim's employer was scared to death the depot might be a target. To avoid all of the trams being destroyed in one fell swoop, at the sound of an air raid alarm, they had to ride the trams out of the depot and spread them over the premises as quickly as possible.

Wim had to complete a short training course to become a tram driver.

His employer introduced a special shift for night watch, which was mandatory for everyone alongside their regular work, on a rotational basis. They had to sleep with about six people in a concrete bunker with the most minimal comforts, no more than a few mattresses on the floor. If you were lucky, you were able to sleep through the whole night, but more frequently you had to risk your life getting the trams to safety. If they'd been out multiple times in a single night, they were sometimes given a day off to recover from the shock and to catch up on sleep.

Despite the increased tension, Wim almost found himself enjoying the work. Whenever an air raid alarm sounded, he would jump onto a tram and ride it at high speed through the darkness to the edge of the premises. The sparks would jump from the overhead lines, as if the cables had been on fire. His boss gave him an earful every time about how he was making the Allies' jobs extremely easy by riding like that.

In the boys' hut, the course of the war had turned into a frequent topic of discussion. At times they didn't know what to believe, since the Germans kept coming up with different stories. The boys would then hear something else on the radio. If anything, the atmosphere wasn't improving because of it. Wim felt he could allow himself fewer and fewer freedoms. Occasionally, he discussed it with one of his friends in the barracks, Klaas van Doorn. Klaas had grown up near Rotterdam and was also in his early twenties. He was the only person with whom Wim spoke openly about his worries and plans.

Klaas sometimes gave him a sort of secretive look. 'I won't be here for much longer,' he'd said a few times already. Initially, Wim had dismissed it as hot air, but after hearing the latest news about the war, he intended to take Klaas aside sometime.

Wim's boss sat across from him, his hands trembling. Since Wim had known him, the man had always had an ashen face, deeply grooved, but now he looked like a whitewashed zombie. The vapours from the molten tin had had their destructive effect, certainly, but something else was the matter. He'd been informed that, with immediate effect, he would be going to the feared Eastern Front. First some refresher training and then off to fight the Russians.

Wim felt sorry for him. In his current state, the dear man seemed to be more of a danger to his own platoon than to any well-trained Russian soldier – an imminent nervous breakdown wouldn't improve his situation, either.

'While I'm gone . . .' he started.

His voice broke, but he pulled himself together.

'While I'm gone, Wim, you'll replace me.'

Wim felt the blood drain from his face. He hadn't exactly been hoping for this. It meant that he'd now have to actually be part of production and that his head would be hovering among those poisonous vapours the whole day.

Wim looked at his manager and couldn't help himself: '*Das ist grosse Scheisse.*' 'That's some real bullshit.'

His boss nodded: '*Dieser ganze Krieg ist ja grosse Scheisse.*' 'This whole war is a load of bullshit.'

7

On the run

'You know something, Klaas? They're keeping an eye on me,' Wim said.

'How do you mean? Who's keeping an eye on you?' Klaas asked.

'Well, the company management. They've been doing it for a while now, but ever since my boss was called up a week ago, I'm sure of it. There are people at work tracking exactly where I go. I can't go anywhere unnoticed and when I want to poke my head into the depot, the doorman asks me where I think I'm going.'

The two young men were sitting in a corner of their dimly lit barracks, on a couple of old chairs at a table they'd made themselves. They'd nailed it together from raw planks and two trestles. The chairs had been sneaked out of the depot so that they could at least relax in the evenings. Wim didn't usually spend much time sitting there as he preferred to be out and about, but he now wanted to speak to Klaas in private.

He didn't have a good feeling about his boss's bad news and, on top of that, he had been tipped off by Willy, the old man who had helped him to fill in forms when he'd first showed up at the *Strassenbahn*. He had a soft spot for Wim. At least once a week, they drank a cup of tea in his little office. Willy had told Wim that his name was on a list of people who were being followed everywhere they went, both inside and outside the workplace. Wim had been speechless; his feeling had been correct, then. Willy couldn't tell him why he was being monitored. Or perhaps he didn't want to.

'Klaas,' Wim said. 'You mentioned you wouldn't be here for long. Do you mean you want to leave this place?'

Klaas nodded and said nothing.

'I want to go back to the Netherlands,' Wim said. 'I can't hold out here much longer. The whole situation is weighing down on me. It doesn't feel right.'

Klaas was still silent and looked Wim right in the eyes. Then he walked over to his bed and dug out a small booklet from among his things, which he showed Wim. On the grey cover was an eagle and beneath its talons a swastika. At the top it read 'DEUTSCHES REICH' and under the swastika: 'REISEPASS'. Wim looked at Klaas, startled.

'You a German or something?'

Klaas gave a quiet laugh.

'No, but my mother's German. She and her parents moved to the Netherlands thirty years ago and later, she married my father, a born-and-bred Rotterdammer. But I could still apply for a German travel pass because of her background. And so at the start of the war, I did – you know, just in case. Nobody knows about it – you're the first person I've shown it to. I can travel to the Netherlands with this. And you'll just have to take your chances.'

'We're getting out of here as fast as we can,' said Wim, who understood he was running an enormous risk. 'And I've also an idea for when. In two days we'll be on night shift again. Big chance we'll have the next day off to catch up on sleep. Then we'll have the whole day to get away. By the time they notice we're missing at the start of the next night shift, we'll already be in the Netherlands.'

That sounded good to Klaas.

Three days later, Wim and Klaas were sitting across from each other in a third-class compartment on a train to Hannover. They'd bought tickets without any issue. Wim had let Klaas do the talking at the counter, though he hadn't even needed to show his pass. Aboard the 8:11 train, they were travelling in a westerly direction, towards home. The boys had agreed to exchange as few words as possible, so as not to reveal that they were Dutch. Their plan was to travel via Dortmund and Essen to Duisburg and to change trains there to go to Emmerich, near the border. Wim didn't want to travel via Bentheim, ninety kilometres to the north, though it was the quickest route. If the alarm sounded, the Germans would be waiting for them there.

As for crossing the border itself, their plans were still vague. The security would probably be very tight, which was why they intended to try to get onto a freighter near the Dutch village of Lobith, to sail in on the Rhine.

Soldiers were spread throughout the train, but Wim and Klaas acted like perfectly normal passengers and weren't stopped by anyone. Along the way, Wim again saw the traces of Allied bombings, especially in the cities. In Dortmund, there were more houses in ruins than there were standing. That must have been a real inferno.

Their train pulled into Emmerich by early afternoon. They alighted and asked an older woman in which direction the Rhine lay. According to their calculations, it was supposed to be about five kilometres to the harbour. They just followed the main road, which was the least likely way to catch someone's eye. On their way, they passed cyclists, walkers and cars. Klaas and Wim stuck up a hand to the occasional greeting.

After an hour, they walked onto a small rise and finally saw the river, which stretched out before them like a long ribbon gently winding its way to the horizon. They were five hundred metres from the Rhine when they spotted an approaching patrol and darted into the bushes. To their great relief, the soldiers marched past them in tight formation. Wim and Klaas now continued along the screen of trees and thickets. It was close to freezing and there was a stiff easterly wind, but Wim didn't feel the slightest cold because of the adrenaline. They trudged across the semi-frozen ground for about ten minutes, sometimes sinking without warning up to their ankles in the mud, until they ran into a fence two metres high and topped with barbed wire, separating them from the paved dockyard behind it.

They stopped and assessed the situation. A few hundred metres further to their right were four Rhine barges. They needed to somehow try and get onto one of them, but they were guarded by at least three soldiers. A fence ran straight through the field that stood between them and the barges. They looked at each other silently and knew the score. 'It might be less heavily guarded on the other side,' Wim whispered. They fought their way for another half an hour through empty fields, jumped over at least seven ditches and reached the fence a second time. They had circled around it. The boats were now moored to their left, but the situation wasn't any better for it. On the contrary: from this position they could see that a large dog kennel had been built behind the shed where two soldiers were smoking. They hadn't been able to see it from the other side and the infeasibility of their mission was obvious at a glance. They didn't say a word to each other but slunk away in disappointment.

When they'd reached the road again, they went and sat on a couple of boulders hidden from sight near the thickets. It was the afternoon. The Netherlands felt so close, but at the same time it was still so far away. As they ate their last sandwiches, they discussed what they would do. They agreed that they had no other choice but to give Bentheim a shot, with all the risks involved. They wouldn't be missed at work in Brunswick until later that evening, so they still had some time – though they really did need to get going.

Once again, Klaas took it upon himself to buy the train tickets and once again, there were no issues, only he did have to show his pass this time. The clerk at the station in Emmerich gave him a friendly smile as he took the Reichsmarks. With two tickets in hand, Klaas gave his friend a wink and together they walked to the small station's platform. They were on their way to Duisburg again in less than half an hour. There, they changed trains to head north-east to Münster, where they would have to change again to reach Bentheim.

They ran into trouble in Münster. The train had been standing still for a suspiciously long time. Just as Wim was beginning to ask himself what the matter was, the sliding door was thrown open and two German soldiers were standing right in front of them. They didn't even get a chance to feel afraid and scrambled to pull out their papers. Ten seconds later, they were led by their arms outside and stood on the platform with a small group of about twelve men, all of them foreigners. Wim heard English, French and Dutch being spoken. A soldier, judging by his stripes one of a higher rank, was in charge and asked the men one by one where they were coming from and what the purpose of their journey was. Eight of them were hauled off after answering, their destination undisclosed.

Then it was their turn. They repeated the story that they'd memorised: they'd been bombed in Brunswick and lost all of their belongings. They were now on their way to meet family, who were waiting for them at the border. They would receive new clothes and essentials and then travel straight back to Brunswick. The pair told it so convincingly that even they started to believe it. The German hesitated visibly. Klaas gave him his passport, which the man leafed through with a serious look, and then he signalled to a pair of subordinates. '*Nach Bentheim.*' 'To Bentheim,' he said to the soldiers and pointed to Klaas and Wim. They rushed to grab their kitbags.

They sat down again in the same compartment from where they'd been plucked, giving a friendly nod to the other passengers. Despite the cold, Wim could feel sweat droplets running down his neck. After a few minutes, the train started moving and an hour later, they were stepping out in Bentheim. They walked over the platform as if it were the most normal thing in the world, searching in vain for a train headed to Arnhem in the Netherlands. The sun was now starting to set and they left the station among a stream of people.

'We'll wait until it's completely dark,' Wim said. 'Then we'll climb onto one of those freight trains over there.' He pointed to the wagons that were lined up in the classification yard on the other side of the station.

Klaas nodded: 'All right, but let's stand a little further away, so we can climb on when the train's still rolling slow. They won't be able to see us from the station then.'

They let the first freight train pass, observing closely.

'When the next one comes, we're jumping on it,' said Klaas.

'OK, you first. I'll follow right behind you.'

In the distance, a heavy locomotive was pulling out. They could hear as much and it wasn't long before they saw the dim headlight boring through the night air. It was tugging about thirty wagons. When half of the train had passed, they came out of their hiding place and started running over the gravel along the tracks. With three wagons to go, Klaas grabbed hold of a rung. He managed to get a shoe onto the footboard and, using all of his strength, pulled himself up and pressed his chest against the wood of the freight wagon. That would be the last Wim saw of his friend. He was running as fast as he could and was about even with the final wagon. Just as he went to grab the rung, he slipped on a few frozen stones and fell, crashing his face into the ground.

For a moment he was dazed. Lying on his stomach, he lifted his head, only to see the train disappearing into the darkness. He could still hear the locomotive's chugging and the rhythmic pounding on the tracks, which lay a mere fifty centimetres from his head. He realised how lucky he was that he'd tried grabbing the last wagon.

Wim walked back to the station. He was alone again and had no one else to rely on. Klaas was now probably hidden between two wagons, like they'd agreed. Maybe he was already in the Netherlands. He had to follow him as soon as possible before something went wrong and the alarms were sounded after all. Jumping onto a moving train hadn't gone well for him, so he tried climbing on top of a stationary carriage. He waited for half an hour before a passenger train with a sign on the first carriage reading 'ARNHEIM' pulled into the station. That was the one he needed. He crawled under another freight train nearby to wait. When the coast was clear, he raced to the back of the stationary train, where there was a small balcony. Using a narrow ladder, Wim climbed onto the curved roof of the carriage. He belly crawled ten metres and lay behind an air vent, flat on his stomach.

The train slowly picked up speed, but after about fifty metres, it came to a stop again. All of a sudden, there was light all around him. He looked up and saw to his horror that he'd stopped directly underneath a station lamp. It had been dimmed but it still gave off so much light that Wim quickly crawled a few metres further to a darker spot. A quarter of an hour later, he heard the conductor yell '*Abfahrt Arnheim,*' 'Departing for Arnhem,' and he breathed a sigh of relief. The train gradually eased into motion and Wim felt the wind in his hair. It felt as if freedom was caressing him, but he wasn't going to cheer too soon. He didn't dare to turn around but slowly crawled backwards again, past the air vent, until he was out of the wind and could clasp the vent with two arms. He soon lost his bearings and then his sense of time completely. It was only when he saw the sign 'HENGELO' at one of their stops that he was finally sure he was back in the Netherlands.

Just past Hengelo, as the train was still gaining speed, he clambered down using the same ladder and walked along the footboard to the compartment door. He went inside and greeted the four passengers who were sitting there.

'It's so cold in that other compartment,' he said, 'and I was all on my own. I thought I'd join you.'

They looked at him with surprise. Wim hadn't realised until then that his grubby outfit and bleeding head might make an unusual impression. He kept his mouth shut and calmly took a seat on a bench.

In Arnhem, he changed trains to go to Utrecht. Everything was going smoothly. No checks – it was almost too good to be true. He would have to change one final time in Utrecht for the train to Amsterdam, to home.

Nevertheless, things almost derailed there. Inside the station, he just managed to see that German soldiers were waiting to inspect travellers. He didn't hesitate and opened the door on the other side of the carriage. Wim looked left and right and, seeing no one, lowered himself onto the tracks and walked to the far platform. It wasn't long before a service with the destination he so desperately longed for pulled in, though he had to crawl under another stationary train to reach it. He slipped into a compartment and sat in a corner. Wim's heart was still in his mouth, but no one came to check their papers. The train soon started moving and he rode out of Utrecht.

★

Not half an hour later, he saw the sign he'd so looked forward to seeing: 'AMSTERDAM CENTRAAL STATION'.
It was far past the curfew and now pitch-dark, so it was
good that he knew the area like the back of his hand. He
was so overjoyed at leaving Central Station that he almost
barged into a young woman. Apologising, he asked where
she needed to go. 'East Amsterdam,' she said. Wim offered to
walk with her, since there were no trams at this hour and he
was heading in the same direction. In that way, they walked
together for a while, by way of the Prins Hendrikkade and
the Plantage Middenlaan.

From out of nowhere, two German soldiers suddenly appeared in front of them.

'Are you guys together?' they asked.

'No, we don't know each other,' was Wim's honest
answer. It came out of his mouth before he'd even realised.
He had just one thought: that's it, I'm screwed.

'Then you get out of here,' said one of the soldiers harshly
and let Wim pass. The men were more interested in the
woman's appearance than Wim's papers. He couldn't get
away from there quickly enough.

It was around midnight when he finally reached the
Tweede Oosterparkstraat. He didn't want to wake up his
mother and so he knocked at his sister's. She opened the
door a crack and looked at her brother in astonishment. He
was a mess with his soiled clothes and shoes, but she didn't
care. She jumped into his arms and muffled her tears with her
right hand before quickly pulling Wim inside. That night,
Wim slept on the couch in the living room.

8

Buried alive

Zwaag and Baarsdorpermeer, the Netherlands,
January – July 1944

Early the next morning, Wim and their mother joined Jo and
her husband, Joop, at the kitchen table for breakfast. Little
two-year-old Rinus was sitting on Jo's lap and kept giving
Wim mischievous looks. Their mother had been completely
surprised when Jo had woken her up that morning. She'd
already hugged Wim three times. He was astonished by so
much affection; after all, she'd never cuddled him this much
during his childhood.

Joop pestered Wim with questions. He wanted to know
everything about his time in Brunswick. How it had gone
in Germany and how the people there were experiencing
the war. And whether Wim knew any more about the war's
course. Patiently, Wim told him all he knew, meanwhile enjoying the bacon sandwich and coffee substitute that Jo had
made specially for him.

The happiness lasted just a short while; he knew only too
well that he couldn't stay at his sister's for long. The Germans
would come looking for him, maybe first at his mother's, but
if they couldn't find him there then certainly at his sister's

house as well. Joop said he could very discreetly ask a few good friends for an address, of course without immediately mentioning that it was for Wim. At the table, they looked at one another; in the end, no one had a better idea.

They left it at that for the time being. They spoke about other things – about trams, about sauerkraut and about his old boss with the face of a gravedigger.

Two days later, Joop's best friend, Ger Jong, came by after dinner. His parents lived near Hoorn, in an area of farmers and market gardeners, where his father earned a living as a farmhand on various nearby properties. They also had a small patch of land next to their house, but it yielded too little to make ends meet. Ger often helped out on his neighbours' farms, even though he was more of a businessman. Before the war, he'd driven a large cart filled with the latest harvest to the surrounding towns and villages, where he had many regular customers. But now that just about everything was rationed, it had become too dangerous. Now and then he still brought some fruit or beans in a small hessian sack. Jo was always happy to receive the gift as a welcome supplement to their ever more minimal daily meal.

This time Ger had left his sack at home. After half an hour of cracking jokes in the kitchen, he asked Joop if they could have a seat in the front room, just the three of them. They shoved three chairs together, so that no one would be able to hear what they had to discuss.

'So I told my pa about Wim and asked what he thought was wise,' he said. 'He mulled it over for a while and got back to me this afternoon with some great news. You can stay with my parents, as a farmhand. During the day you'd work on the land and at night you'd sleep in a little room in the attic. It's empty anyway. You'll just act like they hired you as a paid worker. My pa's got arthritis in his hands and it's getting worse. He can use the help. We don't have any money to pay you, but you'd be getting room and board, and you'd be safe.'

'And what about your neighbours?' asked Wim. 'Can they all be trusted, and won't they rat me out?'

'Oh, you don't have to worry about that,' said Ger. 'There are plenty more farmers hiding people among us in Zwaag and Blokker. So far, the handful of NSB members have kept nice and quiet.'

Joop gave Ger a clap on his shoulder and thanked him warmly for the generous gesture, while Wim rose and gave Ger a firm hand.

'Your parents are risking everything for me,' he said. 'That's really something. I can't thank you enough.'

Ger just nodded and told Wim he was expected the next day at 10 Unjerpad in the village of Zwaag. They only told Jo that Wim was going into hiding.

She wasn't happy about it and impressed on him that he needed to be extra careful: 'You just never know with the Germans. When you were gone, something terrible happened to me. I wasn't actually going to tell you. You'd only get worried, but now that you're going into hiding, I want you to know. I was walking through a park, the Weteringplantsoen, when two German officers from the *Ordnungspolizei* stopped me. Together with a bunch of other people they'd just picked from the street, I had to watch as they shot a handful of Dutch people from that detention centre on the Weteringschans. One by one. Not criminals but resistance people – people who were caught in hiding, ones who were difficult for the Germans and had been picked up. They'd found a German soldier in a canal – he was dead. So they hauled those people out of their cells, just like that, and shot them dead as revenge. When I tried to look away, they shoved a gun barrel in my back.'

Wim put a comforting arm around her shoulders. Ger knew the story already, so he grabbed his jacket, waved goodbye to everyone and said to Wim: 'See you tomorrow.'

Wim reluctantly took leave of his family again. This time Ciska wasn't there to see him off. After a few months of waiting, she'd found a new boyfriend and Wim hadn't heard from her since. But Wim was fine with it. He looked forward to the freedom that awaited him. A freedom polar opposite to working in a factory for the Germans. A freedom to do what he pleased, to breathe in fresh air and enjoy nature.

Wim got a warm reception from the Jong family and he soon felt completely at home. In the first weeks he had to help with jobs in the neighbour's barn, tending to farm implements. One morning he was walking around with an oil can greasing parts, at other moments he was painting metal sections. Jong senior couldn't believe his eyes when he saw Wim's work after a few metal parts from a plough had needed to be welded together.

'Your welding is as neat as a blacksmith's,' he said, amazed.

A few months passed and in the spring of 1944, work moved outside, to the West Frisian countryside and its vast pastures. The Unjerpad connected the row of houses on Zwaag's main street to the next village along, Blokker. The country lane emerged onto a main road that ran between the two villages. According to Jong, that was where you needed to watch out for German patrols. Whenever Wim spotted them, he made good use of the plum trees and berry bushes on either side to keep out of sight. These were some of the few moments when he realised that a war was still going on. Occasionally he did hear, via Jong's illegal radio, reports about advancing Russian troops in Ukraine, among other countries. However, there was still no news about the long-awaited Allied invasion on the Western Front that Jong had mentioned.

His work on the property and in the greenhouses was a welcome distraction. There was always enough to eat and Ger's mother was a wonderful cook. In Wim she had a thankful guest who always finished his plate.

After a month or two, Ger said that for a time they'd be working at a neighbour's: his boss, a member of the NSB. 'But a good one.'

The man had asked Ger if that boy at their place didn't want to earn something extra. He had a few large green-houses, which they called 'warehouses'. Wim had to dig over the soil around the grapevines and tomato plants. Weeks of work, but he didn't mind. This way, he had something to keep him busy and he could earn some pocket money too.

The boss's daughter was about the same age as Wim and displayed an excessive interest in the new farmhand. She asked her father who the boy was and where he came from.

Ger heard him say to his daughter: 'Oh, he's from the big city and here to recover.'

Ger helped out as much as possible but would sometimes disappear for a few days without warning. 'On a job,' his parents would say. Wim never asked what the job entailed.

Wim kept in contact with his family through short letters, never including a return address or any allusions to where he was hiding, in case Ger was arrested. Ger played courier and delivered the letters to Joop and Jo, who made sure that Wim's mother also got to read them. The other way around, things went the same.

There wasn't much news to report, as life seemed to pass uneventfully. Until the night of 31 May 1944.

Wim was fast asleep after a hard day's work at the neighbour's, where he'd helped to dredge a few ditches. He'd gone to bed before ten o'clock, tired but content and with blisters on his hands. It was warm and muggy in his room and he was lying in a shirt and underwear on top of his sheets.

He had no idea what the time was or how long he'd slept, when he was awoken by a series of muffled blasts. He sat up straight in bed and heard them again. The noises came from further away, but they echoed in through the bedroom's open window. They sounded like gunshots and came from the direction of Blokker. After a few minutes, it was quiet again and he fell back asleep.

The next day, all of Zwaag and Blokker was in uproar and there was a lot of excitement at breakfast. Not a kilometre from where he slept, a gunfight had taken place, said Jong. In Westerblokker, near the old auction house, members of the West Frisian resistance had run into a group of NSB police officers called *Landwachters* and shot two of them dead. A resistance man had died as well. The story went that he was from nearby Berkhout, but Jong wasn't sure. Wim immediately understood that this was bad news for him, but his mind was put at ease: 'We'll first figure out what happened. For now, you'd better stay inside. Go on and clean the barn, that should keep you busy for a while.'

A few days later, one of the NSB men was buried. He'd been from Zwaag. As a matter of precaution, Wim stayed in his room. He peeked outside through the roof window of his hiding spot, one eye between the curtain rail and the wooden frame. He looked south along the Unjerpad towards the main road. In the distance he could see the funeral procession approaching. Wim did feel some sympathy for the man's wife and children walking in front.

That afternoon, Wim was busy with some small tasks in the barn, when Jong came in.

'Bad news,' he said. 'I was called in by the mayor of Blokker. Koeman, an NSB member, but not the worst one. There will be German reprisals. He couldn't say when. The only other thing he said was: that boy at yours – he needs to leave right away.'

Wim felt the ground fall out from underneath his feet and didn't know what to say. Old, experienced Jong, however, was bold and assured.

'I'll know more by the end of the afternoon,' he said. 'It's already being worked out. Nothing's going to happen to you, but you go and grab your things, then we can leave as soon as we know where you're off to.'

By that night, Wim was already sleeping in a new bed, a haystack somewhere eight kilometres away. Ger had ridden him there on the back of his bike. Zwaag had been a tiny village where little ever happened, but where he'd landed now was no more than a hamlet, a few farms lumped together in an open landscape.

Wim awoke at the crack of dawn. The straw poked at him through his coveralls from all sides and he instantly remembered where he was. He crawled out of the haystack, beat the stalks from his clothes and peered outside through the slit in the peeling wooden door. He could see for kilometres without spotting even a farm or a house.

Dirk Jong had told him he'd be going to a farmer friend in Baarsdorpermeer, not far from Zuidermeer and Wognum. The name didn't ring any bells. Zuidermeer and Wognum didn't sound unfamiliar to his ears, but he'd never heard of Baarsdorpermeer. Then again, if he didn't know it, perhaps the Germans wouldn't either. The thought reassured him.

Once again, he was lucky with his address. The Van Diepen family were incredibly welcoming. Van Diepen senior was firmly anti-German and wanted nothing to do with 'those traitors', as he invariably called NSB members. Ger knew him well; they sometimes set off together at night. No one knew where, not even their families.

Wim was allowed to eat in the kitchen, but sleeping in the farmhouse was too dangerous. For now, the hay shed would be his domain until they'd found a better spot for him. That would take just a few days, said Van Diepen when he came to tell Wim food was ready and give him a worn pair of clogs. At Jong's farm, Wim had had a pair of sturdy work boots, but now he'd have to make do with these wooden blocks. They were just about his size, though he felt every step.

He clumsily walked with the farmer from the haystack to the kitchen, the brim of the beige cap he'd been given pulled low over his forehead. At the table, a surprise awaited him. It turned out that Wim was not the only one in hiding. Next to the farmer's wife sat two other boys of his age. They introduced themselves as Cor and Bernd. Cor was apparently hiding at the neighbour's but regularly joined the Van Diepen family for a meal.

Somewhat awkwardly, Wim began spooning his soup. The mother handed out a few hefty chunks of bread to all of the guests. Not much was said. The couple's children, about ten of them, spanning the ages of one to twelve, curiously eyed Wim up. It even made him a little uncomfortable.

After the meal, the farmer sat with his guests. He told them that Bernd would be moving to another address in Baarsdorpermeer at the end of the afternoon. He thought it was better to 'spread the load'. Wim could then take his place and help out Cor a bit with the work. Cor was from Hoorn, a baker by trade, and seemed to come from a well-to-do family. He wore his blond hair with a tight parting and spoke without the typical West Frisian accent. Cor said his father was also in hiding. He mentioned something about forged property deeds used to deceive the Germans. That's why he and his father had been lying low for a while now. By chance, Wim later heard that Cor's last name was Sombeek, but he'd rather have forgotten it straight away. It was too dangerous.

They hadn't been overly cautious by switching addresses. Wim could gather as much from the last updates Van Diepen shared with the young men. Members of Nazi intelligence, the Sicherheitsdienst, had murdered Doctor Wytema in reprisal for the two dead NSB members. Wytema had lived in the neighbouring village and had apparently been shot in front of his house. Van Diepen didn't know the finer details, but those would follow in the coming days.

Wim was shocked. He knew the doctor had three young children. It was at these moments that the German occupiers showed their true colours. He shook his head. What would it all achieve? He didn't understand the war at all. In Brunswick, he'd met so many nice, decent Germans, all of them ordinary and good people, just like the ones around the table. And then this news – he didn't understand what came over them. And what to make of those NSB members? Were they good or bad? He couldn't figure it out and was lost in thought. Van Diepen roused him with a firm clap on his shoulder: 'You all right, boy?'

Wim looked up and could just stammer a yes. He silently helped to take the plates to the kitchen sink.

'You'll be staying in the hay shed for one or two nights more,' said Van Diepen. 'Until we're sure the coast is clear and the Krauts have got their pound of flesh. Then we'll take you to a new hiding spot that we're getting ready. You won't believe your eyes when you see it.'

For two days, Wim hid himself in the barn and slept in the hay. He practised walking in clogs and chatted with Cor, who regularly popped in. Cor slept in a small boarded-up cubbyhole at the top of the neighbour's house, similar to what Wim had done at his previous address. But this farmhouse had a thatched roof. Cor told him that at night all kinds of animals crept out from underneath it. He heard their paws on the wooden planks above his head but didn't know what they were. 'Bigger than mice,' Cor said, 'since I can hear them, too, and that's a very different noise.'

'Rats or martens,' Wim tried. 'Or maybe just a cat looking for those mice.' They laughed a little.

Wim got on well with Cor. Cor had been on the farm for six months already and hadn't heard anything about his father in all that time. No news was usually good news, but he couldn't be sure. In any case, the food was good, he said. He'd had to adjust in the first weeks, since at home he'd never eaten fat and here they weren't as fussy about it. Wim talked nineteen to the dozen about his time in Brunswick, which couldn't hurt, though he wisely kept silent about his previous address.

Two days later, Van Diepen took him into the field: 'Everyone's calmed back down, so it seems like we're out of the woods now, Wim. But you can't stay in the hay barn – they'll probably look there during a razzia, just like in the house. So I've made you a new hiding spot. Come along.'

They jumped over two ditches, which were nearly dry this late in spring. At a grove roughly eighty metres from the farmhouse, the farmer halted. He pointed to the ground between two shrubs. Wim looked and saw nothing unusual. 'Take a good look,' said Van Diepen. Wim saw a large ditch with wire posts marking the property's edge, grass, shrubs and a small rise. Van Diepen pulled him by his coveralls towards the ditch.

'Here,' he said. 'This is your front door.'

Wim crouched down and had to bend far over to see it, it was so well hidden in the embankment. The top was fully decked with turf and he needed to crawl part way into the ditch to reach the little door, which was about half a metre wide and forty centimetres tall. As it was painted green, it barely stood out from the vegetation along the ditch.

'Go ahead and crawl inside,' said Van Diepen.

Wim wriggled through the opening with his lithe figure. He was inside two seconds later. The bottom was a stretch deeper than the doorway and the straw on the floor ensured a soft landing. It cost the farmer more work, but within half a minute, he'd squeezed himself inside too. Wim curiously took in his new hiding spot. It seemed like a big chest, at least two and a half metres long and a metre wide. He could just about sit in a kneeling position. Van Diepen shut the door. Wim now saw the air holes between the planks in the ceiling, one at the head end and another at the foot end of his new home.

'Well, if it rains a lot, you're out of luck,' Van Diepen said. 'You'll probably get a bit wet. But no German will come looking for you here. After the summer, we'll see whether they've chased the Krauts out of the country or if we'll have to find somewhere warmer for you. For now, you'll be safe here.'

Wim just hoped they had a nice summer and autumn ahead of them, since the prospect of having to sleep in a chest underground while it was cold out was already giving him goosebumps.

From the beginning of June 1944, Wim helped Van Diepen on the land every day, often together with Cor and sometimes with other boys from the area. He could immediately tell from their accents whether they were local or young men in hiding trying to make themselves useful. Usually they had a hot afternoon meal in the farmhouse kitchen, where Van Diepen's wife surprised them every time with a plate piled high with wholesome food. There were home-grown fruits and vegetables in abundance. They were only careful about their meat, as the local food distribution organisation was struggling with that the most.

One day, Cor signalled to Wim from afar; he'd been turning over freshly mown grass with a pitchfork. Cor was standing behind the shed and he pointed at Wim and then at the farmhouse. Wim had no idea what the matter was, but he understood that he had to head inside. When, a moment later, he opened the small door, he heard his mother's voice. He kicked off his clogs and, his eyes wide, walked to the front room, where she was chatting with the farmer's wife.

'Boy, I just had to see you,' she said. 'I know it's dangerous – that'll be my maternal instinct – but nobody else knows I'm here. Ger dropped me off a second ago and he'll pick me back up in a bit, so I don't have to ask anybody for directions.'

At first, Wim was concerned, though he still had to laugh at so much practicality. She'd thought it through. He calmly took in his mother's face. Despite all the war's difficulties, she still appeared charming and well-looked-after. Had she put a little blusher on her cheeks, or would that just be the healthy fresh air? Apparently, his mother was also happy with what she saw, since she kept looking at Wim with a satisfied smile.

The farmer's wife prepared a pot of tea in the kitchen and then left mother and son alone. In the half an hour before

Ger came to the door, she spoke about the whole family and the latest news. The farmer's wife had, in the meantime, laid out a big chunk of bacon and a large ham for Wim's mother to take back to Amsterdam. After their goodbyes, Wim had already forgotten half of what she'd said. The most important thing was that his mother, Jo and Joop were doing well. Wim was happy to hear that Mr Adolfs hadn't forgotten about him. The butcher regularly stopped by and was never empty-handed. After the war, Wim would be able to start again right away, he'd told Wim's mother.

But when would the war be over? In the past weeks, the conversations around the kitchen table were mainly about the progress the Allies had made after the successful landing in Normandy. Van Diepen was always up to date with the latest news. Somewhere on the farm, not even Wim could say where, a radio was hidden away.

More and more details trickled in about the cruelties committed by the German army and its collaborators. They now knew why Doctor Wytema had been murdered. The Sicherheitsdienst had asked Koeman, the NSB mayor, for the names and addresses of notable residents. Koeman had mentioned Wytema's name and three men had gone to the doctor's house. They rang the doorbell and pretended that one of them was heavily wounded. When Wytema opened to the door to rush to their aid, they shot him dead in cold blood, right in front of his wife. Ger said that even a Dutchman had been involved, Wouter Mollis. He was not only a member of the Sicherheitsdienst, but also the Germanic SS. The bastards, Wim thought, listening without a word.

Afterwards, he spent a restless night in his chest. Snippets of the conversation kept flashing through his head. It had all happened at such a short distance from his previous hiding place. The war seemed to be coming closer.

A week later, he got the fright of his life. The advantage of his cave was that it stayed fairly cool, while it had been at least thirty degrees outside that day. He'd even wrapped himself in a thin blanket and was fast asleep, when in the middle of the night he was jolted awake by footsteps next to his hiding spot. He was wide awake and held his breath. They came steadily closer. He instinctively felt for the stick that he always kept within arm's reach, mostly for vermin; but this was a lot more threatening. Softly, his door opened and he heard a familiar voice whisper his name: 'Wim, it's me, Cor.'

'Cor?'

'Yeah, easy now, I'm coming inside. There's a razzia.'

Wim scooted to the left to make space.

'The old man woke me up and pushed me out into the fields through a back door,' said Cor. 'I'm supposed to hide with you. There are *Landwachters* a few doors further on and they're scouring the farms one by one. Any minute now, they'll be at our door. I got away just in time.'

The next morning, they didn't dare to go outside, as they were afraid someone would be waiting for them. It had been light for several hours, when someone banged on the door with a stick.

'Hey, you couple of moles, don't you need to eat?'

Van Diepen roared with laughter. The boys crawled out through the narrow door on their hands and knees and sat next to the farmer in the dried-up ditch. They squinted their eyes against the bright light. In front of them was a basket with cheese sandwiches and a pitcher of milk.

'Those fuckers combed through half of Baarsdorpermeer last night,' Van Diepen snorted. 'They caught four people. From now on we'll need to be even more careful, boys.'

9

The wrong decision

Baarsdorpermeer, July 1944 –
Amsterdam, August 1944

In the weeks after the razzia, the soldiers and *Landwach-ters* stayed out of Baarsdorpermeer. Peace seemed to have returned. The summer was kind to the farmers: warm, beautiful days alternated with the occasional heavy thunderstorm. Only once did the ditch fill up with any real water and Wim had to be careful not to get his feet wet while crawling into his underground home. Luckily, it stayed practically dry inside. The air holes let in little if any moisture and the high threshold held the water in the ditch at bay. After a few days, the ditch was bone dry again.

Cor and Wim often talked about what they would do once the war was over. Cor really wanted to start his own bakery. When they were finally liberated, Wim said, he'd turn up that very day at Adolfs' shop, so as to pick up where he'd left off, and would hopefully be able to open his own butcher's shop soon afterwards. But the Allies would have to speed things up. Van Diepen said the German resistance in France was considerably stiffer than everyone had been expecting, including the Allies themselves. They needed to be patient, very patient.

Now that it was the beginning of August, there wasn't all that much to do on the land. It was still too early to harvest. The boys spent most of their time flipping mowed grass, spreading manure and dredging dried-up ditches. One afternoon, when work had finished, they were talking with Kees Bos, who lived on a farm nearby. He was about thirty-five, had tremendous protruding ears and wore small metal-framed spectacles. His scrawny appearance led you to expect that he couldn't handle much work, but it turned out to be an illusion. With his sinewy body, he spread just as much manure in one forkful as Cor and Wim combined.

They were busy talking to a few people in front of a house further on in the village and paid no attention to the surrounding area.

Kees was the first to hear them. He looked up and hissed at the two boys: '*Landwachters* – I recognise the sound of their motorcycles. Two of them.'

He pointed with his head in the direction of his father's farm and then to the road that ran behind the property where they'd been working.

'They've already seen us and split up. You guys need to get out of here.'

The officers were trying to trap them. One approached from the front and kept watch at the entrance to Van Diepen's farm. The other blocked them in by riding slowly towards them along the road on the far side of the field. Their only escape was through the back of the Van Diepen farm. They left their pitchforks in the ditch and ran as fast as they could in their clogs through the fields to the house. They could hear the sound of an engine approaching.

Cor was the first to reach the barn. He swung the door open and climbed on top of the haystack. Wim shut the door behind him and for a moment looked at the mountain of hay and straw. He squeezed his way between a few bales and found the spot where he'd hidden during his first nights. He shoved the bales together behind him, creating a kind of cave around him. Carefully, he sat down on a bale. Between the hay and the straw, he could just make out the far wall of the barn. As he tried to get his breathing under control again, he wondered where Kees was. He must have run around the back of the farmhouse. He wasn't in the barn, in any event.

His eyes slowly started adjusting to the semi-darkness, but he didn't get much time. The barn door abruptly swung open and a beam of sunlight fell in. He could discern the outlines of two officers. These guys didn't sit around.

'We saw you run in here! Come on out!' they shouted.

No way in hell, Wim thought. You'll never find me here. He pinched his nose shut to suppress an itch. The *Landwachters* walked through the barn, jabbing a stick here and there in the hay, without any luck.

'If you don't come out, we'll start shooting and burn this place to the ground.'

Silence for a few seconds. Wim couldn't imagine that they'd actually shoot their own countrymen, but all of a sudden, there was a deafening bang. He peered between the straw bales and saw that the taller of the two officers had a pistol in his hand. He'd shot into the air, though that was enough for Cor to come out: 'Don't shoot, don't shoot – I'm coming down.'

'Where are the other two?' the smaller of the two officers barked.

'I don't know,' Cor squeaked. 'I was the first one in here and didn't pay attention to the others. Maybe they ran off into the fields.'

The *Landwachters* looked at each other. Wim's thoughts were racing. Could he abandon his friend? And what if these traitors searched the surrounding farms? Or torched Van Diepen's farm? It couldn't be that bad. In the worst-case scenario, he'd be sent back to Brunswick. But he also remembered what Jo had said about the ruthless way the *Ordnungspolizei* had acted. In the end, it was not being able to leave Cor on his own that was the deciding factor.

He got up and pushed his way between the straw bales. The officers were already walking Cor to the door. They heard the rustling, turned around and watched, to their amazement, as Wim walked towards them, his hands raised. He knew at that moment that he'd made the wrong decision.

Cor and Wim were put on the backs of the officers' motor-cycles, which had been parked next to the farmhouse. Their wrists were bound to the chrome luggage racks, the thick rope allowing them just enough room to steady themselves with their hands. Both motorcyclists had slung their guns over their shoulders, so that the weapons were hanging across their chests. Just as they were about to start their engines, Van Diepen came striding out of his farmhouse, his face red with rage.

'Hey! You keep your hands off my boys,' he snorted.

'Your boys? *Your* boys? You must mean illegal persons in hiding. They're coming to the station for questioning.'

'But I need them on my farm,' Van Diepen said. 'They're paid workers that I've hired.'

'If you don't shut up we'll arrest you too. Sheltering people in hiding can cost you dearly.'

Van Diepen was speechless and realised he was playing a dangerous game. The officers didn't even wait for a reaction. The motorcycles slowly started moving. Within a few minutes, Van Diepen and the farm had disappeared from sight.

They rode south to nearby Hoorn. A quarter of an hour later, they stopped in front of the police station, right in the centre of town. It was late in the afternoon and the sun beat mercilessly on the top of Wim's head. The tightly wound hand ties were loosened and he was instructed to remain standing next to the motorcycle.

Wim stood with his back to the city's central square while one of the officers went looking for a colleague with keys to the holding cells. Sweat gushed from his forehead – he didn't know whether from the heat or his nerves. The magnificent monumental buildings on either side of the square were wasted on him.

The other officer was struggling to undo the rope wound around Cor's wrists and paid no attention to Wim. He could have easily made a break for it. Clogs off and hooked it. But he didn't dare – he had no idea what was in store for him. He still thought they'd just be sending him back to Brunswick and didn't want to take the risk. These *Landwachters* had no scruples about shooting you in the back, he knew that only too well.

Ten minutes later, Wim was sitting in a cold cell all by himself. As he was being locked up, Wim had asked about

Cor but got no answer. The officer had only said that Wim would be taken to Amsterdam before slamming the thick steel door shut with an echoing clap and turning the grinding lock. Their freight delivered, the *Landwachters* were long gone now, off searching for new prey.

After a restless, cold night spent on a hard bunk and underneath a horsehair blanket, Wim woke up early the next morning completely stiff. It was dark in his cell and for a moment he thought he was still lying safely in his wooden chest until a pale light came on and, with a lot of jangling of keys, the door was opened. The officer who brought him a plate with a few meagre sandwiches was strikingly nice, but when Wim asked what awaited him, he was met with silence.

He started to wonder whether they even knew themselves. They would probably have to go through the German authorities to reach the *Strassenbahn*, which was still his employer. Had they actually missed him there? Had Klaas made it? And where was Cor?

That afternoon, two middle-aged *Landwachters* abruptly appeared in his cell's doorway.

'You're coming with us to Amsterdam, sonny,' said the bigger of the two, a man with a poorly shaven face, coarse hair and deep-set, watery blue eyes. Not too gently, they grabbed him under his arms and dragged him out of the building. On their way to the train station, Wim saw bitter powerlessness in the eyes of his countrymen as they watched him pass. The officers paid them no attention. At an unrelenting pace, they stepped onto the platform, where the train was already waiting. In Amsterdam, they took the tram, this time not one of the usual lines that had so often brought him to the

Oosterparkstraat, but going in a southerly direction, through streets and neighbourhoods that were less familiar.

Wim became more worried. It was as if he'd left everything he knew behind him, without knowing what lay ahead. He only had to glance at the guards' faces to know it couldn't be very good. They didn't even deign to look at him and when he so much as cleared his throat, they blew up at him. 'Shut up!'

They rode over a bridge and Wim's breath caught in his throat. He knew exactly where they were – this was the Noorder Amstelkanaal, which flowed into the Amstel river. He'd paddled along here in his kayak so many times before. He now started to suspect where they were headed. A street that, as the occupation wore on, had acquired a sinister reputation: the Euterpestraat. Where the headquarters of the Gestapo and the Sicherheitsdienst were found.

The Euterpestraat. He'd only heard its name whispered as people told one another about family members, neighbours or colleagues who had disappeared. One of Ger's friends had been inside for two weeks and come out unrecognisable. In a building that had once been an all-girls' high school, people were now tormented, tortured and murdered. A great many resistance members had been put to the rack there, some to the point where they could no longer endure it and had gone insane. The stories Wim had heard from Ger had given him a few nights of bad sleep.

'Move it!' the smaller of the officers barked when they ground to a halt at the nearby tram stop. The other passengers didn't dare to watch as he was shoved out of the tram and almost fell forwards onto the pavement. They walked the last stretch and through the entrance; a black flag with lightning bolts waved overhead. After the paperwork was arranged, a Dutchman wearing a uniform from the Sicherheitsdienst (SD) took him deeper into the building. The place was crawling with members of the SD and the SS, most of whom were speaking in German. He'd occasionally seen the uniforms on Kattenburg, but never so many together at once. In a long row of doors, the Dutch SD man opened Wim's cell, shoved him in on his back and locked the door behind him. Wim was locked up for the second time in two days.

Sitting on a bunk was a man of about forty years old, who said that he was from Utrecht and that his name was Frederik: 'Just call me Fred.' He shook Wim's hand and gestured invitingly: 'Have a seat, my boy.'

Fred had a black eye and his face was swollen and covered in blood, bumps and bruises. 'They worked on me for two hours,' said Fred, 'but I didn't say anything.'

'What did you do?' Wim asked.

'It's better you didn't know, then it can't be beaten out of you either. That Aus der Fünten, he's the worst. Fucking Kraut. My comrades had warned me about him. A sadist through and through and then at the highest SS rank too. Shows you how the Germans operate. And they call them the Master Race. That man enjoys seeing you in pain, lets his subordinates do his dirty work and keeps his hands clean.'

'All I did was escape from Germany,' Wim said. 'The *Arbeitseinsatz*. I didn't do anything else.'

'They don't give a shit. They'll want to know how you escaped, who helped you, who gave you shelter and how you got enough to eat. They'll torture you until you're even saying things you don't know.'

That night, Wim barely slept. Fred's words kept echoing in his head: 'What you don't know can't be beaten out of you.'

The next morning, the cell door opened with an enormous yank. 'Aloserij! *Mitkommen!' 'Come along!*' bellowed an SD man, baton in hand. It was about seven o'clock and the first morning light was already shining through the cell window. Fred was still asleep, or pretended to be.

Wim complied, walked with the guard up a flight of stairs, turned left a few times and then right. The overwhelming stench of alcohol that hung around his escort made him slightly nauseous and he was happy when the man pushed him into a room and left him.

The walls were bare. On a table in a corner were gleaming metal objects he couldn't place. He had to remain standing in front of a desk with a black Bakelite telephone. An SS officer was sitting behind it.

'Wilhelmus Johannes Aloserij?' he asked in a surprisingly high voice.

'Yes, sir,' he said. 'That's me.'

Wim couldn't keep his nerves under control. He was sweating and his voice trembled. The telephone rang.

The man looked at him for a few moments in silence and grabbed the telephone from the hook. He listened for twenty seconds and then slammed it back onto the base. He stood up, opened the door and, addressing an SD man in the hall-way, he said: '*Sofort abführen!' 'Remove him, immediately!*'

Wim experienced the meaning of '*sofort*' at first-hand and before he knew what had happened, he was already back in his cell. He looked around in surprise. Fred was gone. Wim spent another two nights there, expecting at any minute that his name would be called and that he would be tortured after all. These thoughts were a torment in themselves and it reached the point where he just hoped they would fetch him quickly, but all the guards did was bring him food and water. His name was never called and he never saw Fred again.

It was early in the morning on day three when a guard peered into his cell for a few minutes. Wim felt uncomfortable but didn't budge.

'You're leaving in half an hour,' the guard said. 'Make sure you're ready.'

Wim wondered what he even had that needed readying. His only possessions had been taken from him at the police station in Hoorn. All he could do was wait. The half an hour felt like half a day. What were they going to do with him now? Was he going to be interrogated after all? Maybe at another location? Or perhaps something much worse? He pulled himself together and tried to switch off his thoughts.

The footsteps in the hall grew louder. Two SD officers opened his cell door and, without a word, led him by his arms out of the building. Outside, Wim breathed in the fresh summer air but wasn't given much time to enjoy it. He was sitting on a tram again five minutes later, travelling north-wards towards the city centre.

When they passed the Mauritskade, he realised where they were taking him: the detention centre on the Weteringschans. He knew the building but had never been inside, as he'd often cycled past while delivering orders for the butcher's shop. There, he was handed over to the next SD man, who took him to a dismal whitewashed room. One of the walls was covered in reddish-brown smudges. Three members of the Sicherheitsdienst were sitting behind a desk and they asked him for his name and address. After Wim answered truthfully, the middle one, by the look of his insignias the highest in rank, said: 'Now, we're going to take your picture.'

The way the other two chuckled sent shivers down Wim's spine. He was supposed to stand thirty centimetres from the smudged wall, with his nose to it. The officer then belted him in his lower back. As his torso lurched forwards, his head crashed against the wall. The blow was so hard that he fell to his knees. He could just hear the men bursting into laughter as he lost consciousness.

The entire cell block reeked and when Wim came to, he nearly retched. The stuffy air that hung throughout the rest of the building was a fresh breeze compared to this. Five pairs of eyes were staring at him. Wim mumbled his name and sat up straighter in a corner on the floor, where there was just enough space for him. The cell was built for one or a maximum of two people. A wooden bunk stood against the concrete wall and there were a couple of mattresses on the floor. In a corner to his right he saw a metal bucket, the toilet. The stench it gave off mingled with the smell of people who hadn't washed themselves in weeks.

Wim trembled. He raised his hands to his face and first checked his nose. It was covered in blood and it hurt like hell. When he touched his forehead, he got a fright and his entire body tingled with pain. It felt twice the normal size.

He had a huge bump right in the middle of his forehead, which was completely swollen and bruised. His top lip was also split, but his teeth seemed to have survived their encounter with the portrait wall. His neighbour held out a bowl of water to him. 'Here, rinse off that face of yours. It can't get any uglier.' With that kind of humour, he must have been from Amsterdam.

Not until the next day did Wim feel truly wretched. He had an awful headache and his injuries had swollen up further and hurt even more. The previous night he'd slept on the concrete floor in a cell that, despite it being summer outside, was cold and damp. They had at most forty centimetres apiece on the pair of thin mattresses and he'd rolled off without noticing. He itched constantly from the lice and just couldn't stop scratching himself. What little food they got had no taste. A bit of potato with some vegetables mashed in that he ate with a spoon on a metal plate. No meat. One time, the guards did toss in white paper bags showing a red cross for each person. These contained a tomato and half a handful of sugar.

Now and then someone was plucked from their cell and roughly brought back after questioning, usually out cold and their head covered in blood. After about three or four days, Wim felt so unbelievably grimy that he would have skipped eating just for a chance to wash himself. His head felt like an overripe melon.

They were allowed half an hour each day to air out. All of the doors in their hallway were then opened at the same time and they were driven with loud shouts to a kind of cage in the courtyard. This cage, in turn, was split into compartments, so there were never too many prisoners together in the open air. There were bars everywhere – escape was impossible.

One afternoon a group of about eight guards walked down the corridor of the wing where his cell was located. The door of the cell opposite was opened and the prisoners were dragged out. Not five minutes later, the scene repeated itself in another cell diagonally across from them. Hours passed. Wim wondered in what state they'd be brought back. The next morning, when he saw that the cells were still empty, his blood ran cold. It seemed to be only a matter of time before it would be his turn again.

During the course of the morning, prisoners from the floor above were rolled down the stairs with a lot of shouting and cursing. Wim paid close attention to their faces as they walked past his cell. They'd evidently had their pictures taken too, but these were not the same men who had been hauled off the day before. His thoughts drifted back to Jo's story, about the prisoners who had been snatched from their cells and shot dead.

In the week that followed, another two batches of prisoners were taken away, never to return. Time and again Wim lay motionless on the floor, hoping the guards would pass over his cell. And twice it happened too. The mere thought that a drunken German soldier lurching into one of the canals could lead to the execution of an entire cell block nearly drove Wim insane. After two weeks in the detention centre, he was at his wits' end. He couldn't imagine there being a worse place on earth than that lice nest in the middle of Amsterdam.

IO

Transit camp Amersfoort

Amsterdam, August 1944 – Amersfoort, the
Netherlands, September 1944

Slowly but surely, the summer came to an end, as did Wim's time at the detention centre and his excruciating uncertainty. On 28 August 1944, the guard who fetched Wim from his cell told him that he was going to Polizeiliches Durchgangslager Amersfoort. Wim asked what that meant and was informed he was going to a work camp. He let out a deep sigh of relief. In Brunswick, he'd also had to work – he didn't give it a second thought. Plus, Amersfoort wasn't far from home, fifty kilometres away at most. Maybe his mother and sister would be allowed to visit.

That same morning, he left Amsterdam on a train, again with a guard on either side of him. This time there were no hand ties or other constraints to prevent him from fleeing. But the loaded holsters at his escorts' waists nipped every thought of escape in the bud.

From the station in Amersfoort, it was a walk to his new residence. The streets were busy, but no one paid him any attention; they were used to seeing the SD bringing someone to the camp.

They marched on. After a quarter of an hour, the densely packed buildings of the city gradually gave way to a rural wooded area. To his left and right, Wim saw impressive mansions pushed up against the forest's edge. He could smell the scent of pine and enjoyed seeing the sun again.

His guards turned left near a majestic beech tree and soon halted before a barrier, where a soldier stood stiffly at attention right outside a guard post. He greeted them, looked over the documents that Wim's guards handed to him and raised the barrier. A small sandy path led the rest of the way into the forest. Wim thought they'd entered the camp, but they had at least ten minutes more to walk.

Slowly, the camp loomed up in front of them. They passed through a gate and the first thing he noticed was the excessive use of barbed wire. The barracks were painted black and he counted eight of them. There were curtains hanging behind the windows and, to his surprise, even flowerpots on the sills. The camp was teeming with black uniforms and he instinctively made himself as small as possible, his head dropping between his shoulders.

After twenty metres, the guards pulled him by his arms to the right. They walked along an elongated building and entered through a wooden door. An SS man received the officers' documents and they left without a word to Wim. The man looked him up and down for a minute, without saying anything either. Some friendly bunch here, Wim thought, though he wisely kept silent.

An older man stood up from behind a desk in a dark part of the room, nearly at the back wall. His head had been shaved and he wore an old uniform from the Dutch army.

He shuffled forwards with a friendly expression on his face.

'Welcome to paradise,' he mumbled as he handed Wim a small stack of clothes and a buttoned-up sack of jangling items. On top of the clothes was a pair of old clogs containing thin strips of cotton with numbers on them.

'Your kit while you're here,' he said. 'Just a little further on, you'll take off your clothes and put these on. The numbers you'll sew onto your left chest and thigh. They'll help you do it. Good luck.'

Behind him came a loud call: '*Häftling, mitkommen!*'

His German was good enough to understand they were now addressing him as 'prisoner' and that he was supposed to follow. Wim turned around and walked along with the SS man, who had been waiting for him. The actual prison camp appeared before him, at least as vast as the SS camp he was leaving. A large stone arch above two wooden doors served as a welcome sign. A soldier was standing guard. One of the doors opened for him and he followed the SS man into the closest barracks, where yet another prisoner was sitting behind a table. The man made it clear to Wim that he needed to strip down to his underwear and sit on a chair in the corner. Five minutes later, Wim was as bald as the barber who had divested him of his fine blond curls.

'You're covered in vermin, young man,' he said. 'Lice and other pests. We'll quickly take care of that for you.'

Now, his underwear had to come off, too, and he stood under the shower. The cold water did him good and not only freshened up his body, but also freshened up his mind. A rag that doubled as a towel held together the bundle the reception committee had given him. Wim untied it and laid its contents on the

97

concrete floor. When he'd dried himself off a little, he put on the camp clothing. The underwear was slightly clean, but the seat of his trousers was covered in the previous owner's blood and the army jacket had dark oil stains. On top of that, the trousers were far too large and the jacket too small. It looked like an old uniform of German origin. Only the cap fit.

'You'll just have to trade what doesn't fit,' the barber said, looking on from a short distance.

Wim spread the damp towel on the ground and one by one, picked up the things it had contained: two thin blankets, a mess tin with a cup and spoon inside and a piece of soap. He threw the blankets over his shoulder and tied up the rest in the towel. There remained a pair of socks, the old clogs and the two strips of cloth. He now had a closer look at them and saw they'd been stamped with the number 6178 in black ink.

The guard reappeared behind him and Wim had to follow. He put on the socks and clogs and walked across a large, dusty courtyard to a wooden barracks, where 'BLOCK III' was chalked on the front.

Once inside, a prisoner took Wim over from the SS guard and introduced himself as the *Blockälteste*. Wim had no idea what that meant, but he soon found out that this was a man with some authority within the camp.

'Come along,' he said. They walked down a hallway with sleeping areas on either side. 'This one on the right is your *Stube*, three-C.' The man pointed to a triple bunkbed up against the partition. 'The middle one is yours and that's your locker.' He pointed to the space between two rows of beds where there were six lockers. 'Go ahead and wait here until the *Stubenälteste* finishes up with his job,' he said. 'He'll show you the rest.'

Wim took in his new accommodation. On the other side of the barracks were rows of wooden bunkbeds; only two high, because the ceiling was lower. In the middle, extending for all of about twenty metres, were tables with benches. It didn't smell the freshest, but compared to the cell block on the Weteringschans, this wasn't bad at all.

After waiting for half an hour, he had yet to see the *Stuben-älteste* or any other prisoners. He urgently needed to pee. He stood on his tiptoes, looked over the partition and saw a set-up identical to the one in his room. But no toilet. It was urgent and so he had a look around. In the middle of the barracks he found a door with two toilets behind it.

Just as he was about to walk back to his room, he heard a mass of people gathering in front of the building. Through a window in Stube IIIc, he saw that a hundred prisoners were standing in the courtyard, in neat rows of five and with their caps in their right hands, arms pressed to their sides. Everyone's heads were shaved and no one wore clothes that fit them. They were in old, worn-out uniforms from the Dutch army, the national postal service and various logistics companies, none of it actually matching. Everything was torn and filthy, jackets were held together with baling wire and string, there were large holes in their trousers.

'*Mützen auf!*' resounded across the sandy yard. In a single motion, a hundred men donned their caps at the same time. Not ten seconds later, the command was followed by a loud '*Mützen ab!*' The entire group slapped their caps to their right thighs. Wim tried to see who was giving the commands.

'Kotälla,' a voice suddenly said behind him. Wim jumped out of his skin and spun around. A tall man with an almost girlish face was standing less than a metre from him. The *Stubenälteste* burst into laughter at his reaction.

'You wanted to see who was giving the commands, right?' he asked. 'That's *SS-Oberscharführer* Joseph Kotälla. He calls roll. Steer clear of him, you don't want anything to do with him.'

He stood next to the *Stubenälteste* and followed his out-stretched finger with his gaze. A small man in an SS uniform, with a hat that looked far too big for his head, was roaring in front of a group of prisoners who had just come back into the camp from their work detail.

'*Augen links!*' he yelled and, like trained circus animals, every head moved to the left in unison. '*Augen rechts!*' he bellowed, and the heads snapped to the right.

'What an idiot,' Wim said.

The *Stubenälteste* gave him an angry look: 'If you plan on surviving this place, don't say those kinds of things. At most, you're only allowed to think them.'

'*Wegtreten! Marsch! Marsch!*' 'Dismissed! March! March!' Kotälla shouted.

The men scattered over the yard and walked back to their barracks. Wim watched them in the hope of picking out Cor, but didn't see him anywhere, not even after the barracks had slowly filled with inmates.

The camp held a mishmash of prisoners. People who, like Wim, had dodged work, but also contrabandists, small-time criminals, Jews and political prisoners – altogether a few

thousand men. He didn't see any women. The most important lesson he'd learned was that if you didn't want to be hit,
you above all had to make sure not to stand out. To blend
in with the crowd, that was the name of the game. At roll
call he tried to position himself somewhere in the middle of
the group, so that others had to stand not only in the guards'
line of sight, but also within range of their truncheons. He
developed a sense for everything that went on around him
and needed to have eyes in the back of his head.

He learned that a whole system of ranks and positions
existed among the prisoners. At the very top was the
Lagerälteste, the camp's head inmate. The prisoners slept in a
barracks, which was called a Block. Each Block was run by
its own *Blockälteste*, while a Block's two sections, the *Stuben*,
were each overseen by a *Stubenälteste*, who in turn was helped
by prisoners from the *Stubendienst*. Some had already been in
the camp for years and had worked their way up the ranks.
The higher your rank, the more of a say you had and the
more privileges you enjoyed.

Every day in the camp was the same. In the mornings, at half
past six, a guard sounded the first bell. Wim then had over
an hour to wash and dress himself. Behind his barracks was a
separate building that was called the *Abort*. Inside it, a row of
taps emptied into a zinc basin and there was a row of toilets,
separated only by thin partitions and not hidden by doors
or anything else that might obstruct a view of their users.
The beds had to be neatly made, the blankets tightly folded
and the straw mattress sacks fluffed before the bell sounded a
second time at around eight o'clock.

Roll call followed. As they had work to do, this never took long. The *Blockälteste* made sure that everyone stood in neat lines. The men who were standing at the front yelled out their row numbers in German in consecutive order: *Eins, Zwei, Drei, Vier* and so on. After the counting was completed, they were immediately commanded to march out: '*Abmarschieren!*'

Wim was assigned to the Soesterberg *Kommando*, a work detail sent out each day to the airfield in the nearby town of the same name. After roll call, this detachment marched down the long forest path, past the guards at the front gate, to a tram stop. The boy who slept in the bunk below Wim, Drees – who was from Driebergen, not far from Amersfoort – would walk next to Wim on their way to Soesterberg. Every morning his fiancée threw him a packet of sandwiches, which he hid underneath his jacket. Wim often got a slice of bread too.

After a short tram ride, they got off at the stop for Soesterberg and marched on to the *Fliegerhorst*, the military airbase now used by the occupiers and where the real work began: filling in bomb craters and removing unexploded duds. Being on the go with a shovel all day long, repairing the damage the Allies had caused, was heavy and, above all, incredibly dangerous work. He shovelled as carefully as possible, unless a Kapo, a foreman or, worse still, an SS guard was keeping a close watch on him. Then he worked with just a little more enthusiasm. The SS had very cunningly enlisted prisoners to do their dirty work. When working beyond the gates, the Kapos were in charge and supported by numerous foremen, all recognisable by their armbands. The surveillance was left to young German SS members in training. They were fanatical and were hounded in turn by the older officers, who drove these hungry wolves completely crazy. As a result, they were dangerously worked up around the prisoners.

Kapo stood for *Kameradschaftpolizei*, comrade police. They were prisoners with a privileged position. They got better food, warmer clothing, had their own places to sleep and weren't beaten or psychologically tormented. In exchange, they helped to keep their fellow inmates under the thumb of the SS and made them work hard. They drove them like dogs. Absolutely everything was permitted: beating, kicking, torture and even murder. The Kapos knew that if they weren't ruthless enough, they would lose their spots and be returned among the ordinary prisoners – who, of course, hadn't forgotten how they'd been treated. In that way, the system maintained itself and the SS could make do with fewer guards. And they didn't have to pay the Kapos, meaning it was cheap as well. *Reichsführer-SS* Heinrich Himmler had thought up this diabolical structure for all of his concentration camps and prided himself on it.

In Wim's first week at Soesterberg there was an escape. At the end of the morning, when work would stop for the midday meal, roll call was always taken so that the guards could be certain that no one was missing. It turned out they were a man short. The Kapo counted the men up to three times. They were, and remained, one too few. He flew into a rage and asked whether anyone had seen anything. Naturally, no one had. To punish them, he had all of the food collected and personally set it alight. As the prisoners didn't get breakfast in the mornings, the sight of this burning food made their stomachs ache. But no one said anything.

Work stopped promptly at five o'clock. After roll call, it was back to the tram stop and from there to the camp, where they arrived towards six o'clock for yet another roll call. If they were lucky, they finally got something to eat at around half past six, but if the mood struck one of the head SS officers, that could also take until eight o'clock in the evening.

The camp cook, Frans, also a prisoner, did his best to make something different every time from the limited means with which he was supposed to work. Built from red brick, the cookhouse stood in the middle of the camp, next to the roll-call square. It had a tiled roof and looked well kept. They called the cart that brought food from the kitchen to the different barracks the '*lagerexpress*'. First to be served were the nearby wooden Blocks, so Wim was lucky. He didn't have to wait as long as the prisoners at the back of the camp, housed in newly built stone barracks.

The food was dished out under very strict rules. Wim was only allowed to come forwards, his mug and tin at the ready, when the number of his bunk was called out. In order to avoid arguments and fights, everyone got exactly the same amount of soup or porridge, bread and boiled cabbage with potatoes.

It wasn't much and Wim could see that from the prisoners who had been in Amersfoort for some time already. They had clearly lost weight and had a dulled expression in their eyes, as if resigned to their situation. Some bore visible traces of Kotälla's work.

At seventy kilos, Wim still looked pretty healthy. He'd lost a few kilos to the detention centre and certainly wouldn't be gaining them back here. As he was part of a heavy work detail, after seven o'clock he could pick up an extra ration of bread, half of a normal portion, with some kind of topping – a slice of sausage, for example. He then shared that with the prisoners in his *Stube*, who needed it more than he did.

During roll call, deputy camp commandant Kotälla screamed like crazy and furiously stamped his boots whenever a prisoner didn't follow a command fast enough. 'Fix it!' he'd bellow straight into the unlucky inmate's ear. On the fifth day of Wim's stay in Amersfoort, out of exhaustion or maybe fear of the short devil, a prisoner accidentally dropped his headwear at the moment Kotälla shouted '*Mützen ab!*' While he quickly picked it up off the ground, his fate had already been sealed. Kotälla, his eyes bloodshot, stood right in front of him and mercilessly smashed the butt of his gun between the poor man's legs. Groaning and gasping for air, he fell to the ground. His neighbour went to say something, was promptly given a huge kick to his crotch and crashed down as well. No one said anything, but the prisoners' eyes flared fiercely. The other SS officers were laughing at the scene. Drunk as always, Kotälla swaggered back to his position in front of the group.

A day later, Wim learned the meaning of the camp's 'rose garden'. A young guy, eighteen years old at most, had stolen a potato from his *Stube*. Together with Dutch SS officer Westerveld, Kotälla got his hands on him. They thrashed him with a riding crop and their boots and dragged him, half unconscious, to the strip of ground roughly fifty metres in length and three metres in width that separated the roll-call square from the SS camp and lay between double wire fencing. In this 'rose garden', he then had to sit on his heels with a potato in his mouth, his arms raised in front of him. Kotälla stood beside him and every time he let his arms sink or he fell over or backwards, he was beaten. Wim and the other prisoners were forced to watch for more than an hour before they could head in for food. They never saw the poor boy again. Nearly every day a prisoner was punished in the rose garden. Usually, they had to stand there for a whole day, without food or water. As soon as they went to sit down, the SS would smack them back upright.

By paying close attention and talking a lot with the more experienced prisoners, Wim got a clearer picture of camp Amersfoort. He learned that you couldn't paint all SS members with the same brush: there were bad ones among them, sure, but also decent ones. The key was to get a job in the camp, so that you no longer had to work in a *Kommando* and could stop running the daily risk that an unexploded bomb might blow you to pieces.

All of these jobs had German names. For example, in the bed above Wim slept a *Schreiber*, a clerk. He said a team of seven men did the camp administration and the work there was bearable enough. They worked inside, there were hardly any SS who meddled with them and sometimes they could even 'organise' – the camp term for stealing or procuring goods for one's own survival – a little something extra to eat. Wim would have to try to become a *Lagerläufer*, a delivery boy, the *Schreiber* said, or a *Maler* with the other painters, or try his luck as a blacksmith, carpenter or tailor.

★

By Tuesday, 5 September, Wim had been in the camp for a week. That morning, for the first time since his arrival, there was no roll call. The work details didn't march out. The wildest rumours went around. Prisoners who had a small radio in the mechanics' garage said the Germans, soldiers, SS and even NSB members throughout the Netherlands had fled to Germany in a blind panic. The camp leadership was in uproar. A number of prisoners were given their civilian clothing and released. Wim couldn't work out the logic of who was being released and who wasn't. Impatiently, he waited for his name to be called and to be allowed to go back home.

For the first time, he even saw the camp commandant, *SS-Untersturmführer* Karl Peter Berg. Where he'd been keeping himself this entire time was by no means clear, but now that danger was closing in, he nervously roamed through the camp. Wim watched him giving instructions as multiple cars were packed with suitcases. The euphoria among the prisoners was widespread. Was their liberation at hand?

Their joy was tempered late that afternoon. The worst of the panic had passed and a calm seemed to slowly be returning. Wim's name hadn't been called.

He was sitting with a couple of friends at the tables in the middle of his Block. The *Stubenälteste* walked in, looking down in the mouth.

'False alarm,' he said. 'No Allies in Breda. Not in Amsterdam. Not in Rotterdam. Nowhere.'

Wim's heart sank into his boots. No liberation, no going back to Amsterdam, but back tomorrow to filling bomb craters in Soesterberg.

★

Nevertheless, just a few days later, he had to ready himself to leave. Not for home but for Germany. Half of the camp was to be evacuated and rumour had it they were headed to Hamburg, nearly 400 kilometres to the east in northern Germany.

On the morning of 8 September, a procession of more than a thousand prisoners marched through camp Amersfoort's gate to the train station. Wim was walking somewhere in the middle of the group, dressed like the rest of them in his civilian get-up, which the *Häftlingsbekleidungskammer*, the prisoner clothing storehouse, had washed for him. It was the only positive thing he could see in all of this.

On the way over, they drew a fair amount of attention. The SS guards made sure the prisoners couldn't receive anything from onlookers. Still, they had fruit and bread thrown at them from different directions; the SS couldn't prevent it from happening. The inmates along the edge of the group quickly shoved the food into their pockets or into their mouths.

The trip took about an hour, alternating between a jog and a march. With each step, Wim was getting further from home and closer to Germany. An old passenger train awaited them at the station. The long string of carriages stretched from one end of the platform to the other. A hundred men were supposed to fit into a single carriage, armed guards included. A number of guards would be staying behind at the station. In passing, one of them pushed a packet of sandwiches into Wim's hands.

'Do you actually know where you're going?' he asked.

'I don't know anything,' Wim said.

'You're off to an extermination camp.'

II

Concentration camp Neuengamme

Neuengamme, Germany, August 1944

After the last prisoners were crammed aboard, the guards locked the doors and the train pulled out of the station. The older, more experienced prisoners carefully took in the new situation. It was only when you paid close attention that you saw them probing everything with their eyes. Two men, about thirty years old, who were sitting against a side wall across from Wim, reached over their shoulders to gently tug on the window. It shifted a centimetre at most, after which they immediately pushed it back into place. They knew enough.

While boarding, Wim had seen that guards were posted at the ends of each carriage, their guns loaded and ready to shoot. To attempt an escape was to risk your life. Nevertheless, a handful of inmates took the plunge. In the first half-hour, he heard bursts of gunfire multiple times, most often when they'd dropped their speed. In any event, the train didn't stop for them.

As they approached the bridge over the Ijssel river near Deventer, the train slowed. The two men opposite Wim yanked down the window with all of their strength and dived out. A big commotion in the carriage followed and before the next prisoner could so much as move to take the same path to freedom, gunshots rang out all around. The guards in the passenger carriage shot into the air and shouted they would put a bullet in anyone who got within a metre of the window. Pointing their guns at a prisoner, they ordered him to close it.

The train continued its journey unperturbed, not stopping until Almelo. Wim hoped in vain they would now get something to drink. He wrote a short letter, addressed to his mother: 'Dear Mother, I'm on my way to Germany. Love, Wim.' He threw it onto the platform in the weak hope that a passer-by would mail it for him. The train started moving again and was shunted onto a side track. After an hour, it continued on and passed the station at Hengelo, though they wouldn't be riding much further. At both Oldenzaal and Bentheim, the train stood still for hours again; exactly why remained unclear to Wim. He'd passed this border checkpoint before, but in a very different position. Once the train started moving again, it travelled deeper and deeper into enemy territory, without the prisoners having any idea as to their destination.

It was dark outside and the carriage's lights were left switched off. The Germans wanted to avoid being an easy target for Allied planes. Usually they bombed large German cities, but if they could also squeeze in a train, they did. Wim was packed between his fellow prisoners and dozed off. He'd lost all sense of time and his thoughts wandered back to Kattenburg – to his days spent roaming the islands and to Adolfs. How would he be faring?

Just as he was about to picture taking a glorious shower in the bathhouse by the Kippebrug, he shot forwards and slammed his head against the shoulder of the prisoner opposite. Brakes squealing, the train came to a stop. Within a few minutes, all of the guards had jumped out and locked the doors behind them.

They hadn't yet left the train, when Wim heard the roar of heavy aircraft engines. Now, he could see the beams of light thrown up by German anti-aircraft batteries as they searched for enemy planes – the same ones the prisoners had secretly cheered on while in camp Amersfoort.

There was no escape. Jumping out of the windows was pure suicide; the Germans were sitting outside with their guns pointed at the train. They could do nothing but lie on the floor and just pray things would end well. To their left and right, they heard bombs going off, but the train was spared a direct hit. After a short while, the sound of aircraft engines faded into the distance. It didn't take long for the heroes in German uniforms to board the train again, their guns at the ready. They were back on their way, as if nothing had happened.

It was a scene that would repeat itself several more times, without their being bombed again. Progress was slow. They stopped often and when the train did move, it was at a crawl. In Hannover, they stood still for half a day. The little food they'd managed to smuggle in with them had run out long ago. The thirst was becoming unbearable, as was the stench. There were toilet buckets on board, but it was a whole job just to reach them and they were soon full.

Twilight was setting in, when in the distance the silhou-
ettes of the large cranes of Hamburg's port appeared against
the horizon. The city lay in ruins, having been devastated
the year before during Operation Gomorrah. The RAF had
spent more than a week carpet-bombing the place with thousands of tonnes of firebombs. Tens of thousands of residents
had died in a terrifying sea of flames. The combination of
firebombs and extremely dry summer air had meant that
temperatures had risen to more than eight hundred degrees
Celsius. Civilians who had thought it was safe in their bomb
shelters suffocated from a lack of oxygen and the poisonous
fumes. The aftermath of that inferno now seared itself into
the prisoners' memories.

They wouldn't have much time to dwell on it. The air
raid alarms sounded and the guards raced out of the train
again. Like the other prisoners, Wim could do little more
than ball himself up in fear. He was following a searchlight as
it scanned the sky, when an enormous bang shook the train.
Chunks of debris landed on the roof and they could hear
shouting outside. The prisoners instinctively threw their arms
over their heads. Miraculously, the train emerged unscathed
from the attack yet again. Hours later, they continued on.

It was night when the train crawled into *Konzentrationslager*
Neuengamme. The glare of floodlights filled every carriage
and the prisoners came back to life. Finally, they would be
able to get off this reeking shit train. At the prospect of fresh
air, an invigorating shower and hopefully a nice bed, Wim
enthusiastically tried standing up, but his legs had become
rigid from sitting for more than forty-eight hours in the
same position.

Everyone suffered when they were driven out of the train. There was neither a platform nor stairs, so they had to jump quickly or else be pushed out, but when they landed, the prisoners fell to their knees or stumbled over the men already lying on the ground. They squinted in the floodlights the watchtowers threw onto them.

The guards were shouting at the top of their voices: '*Aussteigen! Raus! Raus! Schneller! Schneller!*' 'Stand up! Get out! Get out! Faster! Faster!'

Wim rolled on the ground between the tracks next to the train and caught a baton in his neck: '*Los! Los! Schneller! Schneller!*' 'Move! Move! Faster! Faster!'

Within seconds, another blow.

He got up and ran with the stream of prisoners. Heavy rain only completed the dismal scene. With truncheons and rifle butts, dozens of SS guards pounded the inmates. The latter were totally surprised. They were defenceless victims, exhausted and weak from hunger and thirst. Twenty metres further on, still other SS men did little to keep their German shepherd dogs at bay. They formed a funnel, into which the guards drove the new arrivals with the butts of their guns. Those who strayed too close to the edge painfully made acquaintance with the aggressive dogs' teeth. Wim just barely avoided being bitten on his calves.

'*Weiter! Weiter! Zu Fünft!*' 'Forward! Forward! Ranks of five!'

As not everyone immediately understood that they now had to walk in rows of five, the SS guards ruthlessly pitched into the group again.

★

With each step in the direction of the camp, a sickly smell grew more intense. *'Mützen ab!'* 'Caps off!' echoed through the night. After about five hundred metres, they were herded, drenched to the bone, into a basement underneath a stone building. Wim took a seat on a stone ledge in the stuffy space, shocked and confused. He felt as if he'd landed in a bad dream. They slaked the worst of their thirst there with water from a few cauldrons.

Every ten minutes, fifty men were supposed to go outside and if they took too long, the guards beat them out of the basement. These weren't SS guards now but fellow prisoners wearing a large green triangle on their clothes. If at all possible, they screamed and hit even harder than the SS, ranting and raving at the prisoners as savagely as they could so as to get in their masters' good books.

The green triangle was the camp symbol for criminals. They were scum, vermin of the lowest order, often having come from German prisons. Murderers, rapists, swindlers and psychopaths – he was now at the mercy of these men.

When it was Wim's turn to go outside, he made sure to stay somewhat in the middle of the group. Outside, they had to take off all of their clothes and throw them into large bins. Some of the men still had something to eat with them and had no choice but to get it down quickly. The group was driven into a large Block called the *Effektenkammer*, a storeroom for their personal belongings. Not only valuable things like watches, wedding rings, jewellery and money, but also family photographs, all had to go into brown paper bags. Wim had nothing that was worth the trouble and gave back his bag empty. The names of those who did hand something in were written on their bags and noted in a large book.

Still naked, they continued into the next room, where SS guards looked into their mouths with flashlights. One by one, they then had to bend over and have their rectums inspected with the help of a light and a stick with a sharp tip. Wim had nothing to hide, but the man behind him had thought to save his wedding ring in this way. It was violently fished out. Afterwards, two fellow prisoners wearing green triangles mercilessly thrashed him. He lay on the floor bleeding and moaning. The SS men looked on with sadistic amusement.

In the next Block, their heads were shaved first. For Wim, whose hair had been buzzed in Amersfoort, this was quick work, but then they were divested of all of their body hair while lying on top of a kind of butcher's chopping block – their arms and legs spread wide.

From what he could hear, the bloody task had fallen to Russian prisoners. Their old-fashioned razors were dull and worn-out, meaning it felt more like chopping than shaving. The newcomers screamed and groaned from the pain. Whoever hesitated caught the guards' truncheons again.

SS guards made sure they kept up the pace: '*Schneller! Schneller!*' 'Faster! Faster!'

Wim was bleeding all over his body. When another prisoner then rubbed him with Lysol disinfectant, he could have screamed. He bit his lip and dodged a blow from a guard who thought it was all taking too long. Quickly on to the next room.

'*Zu Fünft!*' 'Ranks of five!' the SS shouted. Twenty-five at a time, they were driven into a cold room. The windows on its opposite sides were open. Several of the older prisoners couldn't take the torture any more and collapsed onto the concrete floor. With boots, truncheons and an awful lot of shouting, they were helped back onto their feet. When that didn't work, the guards dragged them by their arms and legs across the floor to a corner.

Wim stood like a statue under the showerhead. There was a rumbling through the pipes along the ceiling, after which a boiling hot stream racked his body and open wounds. He felt as if he were on fire but didn't budge an inch for fear of being beaten.

The boiling stream suddenly turned ice-cold and he gasped for breath again. He barely heard the guards bursting into laughter.

'*Los! Los! Schnell! Schnell!*' 'Move! Move! Quick! Quick!'

On to the next Block, the *Bekleidungskammer*, the clothing storehouse. Wim walked through a wide corridor; to his left and right, partitions separated the different areas from one another. In the first he was thrown an old towel. He hastily dried himself off in the semi-darkness before they could take it away from him again. He looked over his shoulder to be sure he was out of reach of the shouting guards. In the next area, he was thrown underwear and, a little further on, a striped pair of trousers, a jacket and a hat. Everything was dirty, everything stank. At the last station, he was outfitted with wooden sandals and bits of cloth that were supposed to be socks.

Wim scrambled to put everything on – and it fit him too. Before he could go back outside through the final door, he had to stop at a table where a few prisoners were sitting, their pens at the ready, while behind them SS officers were keeping an eye on everything. They asked him his name, birth date, place of birth and current residence. When mentioning his mother's address, he felt a sharp pang go through his heart and a wave of memories engulfed him. He stated metalworker as his profession.

A prisoner gave him a small metal number plate on a cord and the next one gave him two pieces of cloth measuring ten by three centimetres, bearing the same number and beside it a black capital H for Holland. He was no longer Wim Aloserij but the number 49019. It meant that almost fifty thousand prisoners had come before him.

On the next table were large needles and thread, but Wim couldn't pick up a needle as his fingers were so cramped. Two older prisoners helped him to sew the adornments onto the left breast of his jacket and his left trouser leg.

Once outside again, he watched as prisoners traded their clothes in an attempt to get something on that actually fit. They also tried wrapping the strips around their feet and ankles, so as to actually be able to walk in the wooden soles and straps. Wim had learned to do that in Amersfoort and fashioned something he could just about walk on. He looked like a zebra in his striped pyjamas. His whole body was shivering. Autumn hadn't even started, but the cold nights and hardships had done their work.

They stood there for at least half an hour, arranged in rows of five, twenty of these lined up behind one another, until the next group of a hundred prisoners was completed. Finally, the guards drove them into a barracks, fenced off with so much barbed wire that for a moment Wim thought he'd landed in the rose garden. Their Block was completely cut off from the other barracks, which he could discern some distance away in the dark. But he had other issues to deal with first – the fight for a sleeping spot was now fully under way.

In the barracks were wooden bunkbeds two metres tall and just sixty-five centimetres wide, built three tiers high. At the back of the barracks, Wim found an empty stack and lay on the top bunk. Within no time, another young man was lying next him. They managed to keep the berth for themselves, while many others had to share a bed with three. In that way, they fitted up to nine men into a single wooden bunkbed.

They were only allowed to keep their shirts and underwear on and the thin blankets didn't offer much warmth. In any case, Wim didn't notice a difference. Utterly overwhelmed by exhaustion, he immediately fell into a deep sleep. He didn't even feel the wooden planks under the meagre straw mattress just a few centimetres thick.

The night's rest was short-lived. After a few hours, a guard was already shouting: '*Raus! Raus! Schnell! Schnell!*' 'Get out! Get out! Quick! Quick!'

In less than a minute, he'd jumped into his clothes. Men and boys who took too long getting up were thumped out of their bunks by the *Stubendienst*, the same scum wearing the green triangles he'd already encountered. But these men were much worse than the ones in Amersfoort. The *Blockälteste* was in charge of the barracks and these were his criminal helpers. They made it clear to everyone that the beds were to be neatly made.

This is absurd, Wim thought. His grubby blanket had to be folded over the even filthier straw mattress as straight as an arrow. And if it wasn't tidy enough, then the truncheons made sure the whole affair was tightly made up in the end. The prisoners also had to sweep the floor with a besom broom. The pieces of straw that had spontaneously fallen out during the night then flew around and never failed to pop up somewhere else.

The *Stubendienst* kept an eye on everything and if you weren't working neatly enough or were working too slowly you caught a baton in your neck. After this task, too, was done, Wim was allowed to join the line and received a piece of dry bread next to the Block's entrance door. With his breakfast in hand, he could go straight outside. It was six o'clock in the morning.

A curtain of barbed wire cut off the quarantine barracks from the main camp. Next to their Block, number ten, there was an identical barracks, on which the number eleven was painted large. A strip of open ground about twenty metres wide surrounded both barracks. It was the only place they could stand outside in peace. Fortunately it was now dry, but again he smelled a persistent sickly stench. All of the new prisoners from the previous night were standing outside together and looking for acquaintances or family who had come on the same transport. Their efforts were soon interrupted.

'*Antreten!*' 'Fall in!' the *Blockälteste* shouted.

Most of them knew what roll call was from camp Amersfoort. But while their lives had been terrorised by a small group of guards there, it now seemed as if everyone here was doing their best to lay into them. Wim raced back into

formation, in the middle of the third row. He resigned
himself to the *Blockälteste* and his henchmen's drilling. They
made sure the prisoners lined up in twenty rows of five again.
The SS guards walked among the prisoners with their noses
in the air and if they didn't like a prisoner's face, they belted
him in his back or stomach. Counting was apparently not
one of their strong suits, since the prisoners were counted,
recounted and then counted again. It didn't seem that hard
to Wim, those blocks of a hundred, but it was all a game for
the camp leadership. The prisoners' bodies and minds had to
be broken as quickly as possible, in order to get the greatest
benefit out of their forced labour and have the least trouble
from them as people. They practised the commands outside
for hours. It was never right. Some of the exercises were
repeated twenty or even thirty times.

'*Richten!*' 'Eyes front!'

'*Augen links!*' 'Eyes left!'

'*Mützen ab!*' 'Caps off!'

An SS officer pointed to a prisoner and a Kapo dealt the
man a few kicks and worked him over with his truncheon
for good measure.

'*Mützen auf!*' 'Caps on!'

Wim stood with his cap on until the command '*Abmarschieren!*' 'Fall out!' sounded.

By ten o'clock in the morning, the first roll call of the day
was done and they had a few hours for themselves. No one
was allowed inside. Acquaintances sought one another out
again and Wim got to know the group of men he'd sat with
in the train wagon. Through the wall of barbed wire rolls,

they tried to see what was happening in the main camp. Their view was partly blocked by a row of barracks, each at least forty metres deep, built along the barrier.

From a distance came the sound of marching music, slowly approaching them. Within no time, dozens of men had thronged in front of the barbed wire in the quarantine Block. They tried to catch a glimpse of what was being celebrated. The mood was initially almost merry, but it soon turned. Between two barracks, they watched a group of fifteen emaciated musicians pass. Behind them walked about ten living skeletons dressed in camp clothing. They were straining to pull a horse cart.

The men behind the barbed wire were suddenly silent. The wooden cart carried mounds of corpses, stacked head to toe, skin stretched over bone, their expressionless faces gaunt, eye sockets hollow. The cadavers bore a strong resemblance to the men pulling the cart. These prisoners were working at the threshold of their final destination; they could see it with a glance over their shoulders. They struggled hard to keep tempo with the marching music. But where was this macabre procession heading?

Wim peered past the barracks. Then he saw the stone building. From a chimney came an oily yellow smoke and the sickening smell was stronger than ever. Wim felt a wave of nausea as it dawned on him – he wanted to escape this nightmare, which only seemed to be getting worse. He turned around, but didn't make it further than twenty metres, back to his own barracks. Someone from the *Stubendienst* was standing in front of the door. Off limits. Wim took a deep breath and forced himself to calm down. He promised himself one thing: to never become like one of those emaciated skeletons. Never. They wouldn't break him.

The *Blockälteste* shouted that all prisoners were to go inside and the *Stubendienst* took over. Just swinging their batons was enough to get the whole procession moving. Inside, Wim had to join the line and was given a damaged brown enamel bowl and a spoon. The man from the *Stubendienst* who was stirring a rusty cauldron with a big soup ladle looked at him. There was a capital P in his green triangle. Wim gave him a friendly nod and got a gush of liquid of indefinite colour that was supposed to be soup from the bottom of the cauldron. Afterwards, he could take a seat at a row of tables and benches in the middle of the Block. He fished around his bowl with his spoon and tried to discover what was drifting at the bottom of this so-called soup.

'You're lucky,' said the young man next to him. 'You at least got some potato and swede. That guy beat me this morning. I think he still remembered, because he scooped from the top of the pot. Look, nothing but water.'

He let the thin soup run off his spoon into his bowl. Wim lifted a few bits of vegetable into his neighbour's bowl. He really didn't want to eat this slime that was called swede soup, but after remembering the scene he'd just witnessed, he forced himself to start getting it down nonetheless. Eating could be the difference between life and death. New prisoners were sometimes stupid enough to leave their bowls and spoons on their bunks. They immediately lost them – a mistake that could end up being fatal.

Wim wasn't even half finished when the *Stubendienst* started shouting again: '*Raus! Raus! Schnell! Schnell!*' 'Get out!

Get out! Quick! Quick!' He tipped the rest into his throat and ran outside.

The roll call took hours and then they were let free again. The sun even broke through the grey cloud cover. He discovered new details about the main camp. There were small beds of red and yellow flowers around the barracks, the watering cans beside them. In the distance, a row of barracks with the same double wall of barbed wire around it. He wondered who was there and what the functions of those barracks were.

He even had some time to get to know his bunkmate Johan and his neighbour at the table from that afternoon, Siep. Their sob stories didn't especially raise his spirits; that wasn't what he needed to survive here. He said it flat out to Siep, who turned out to be just nineteen years old, two years younger than himself: 'Chin up, you need to try and stay strong, otherwise they'll have you right where they want.'

The boy nodded, but Wim wondered whether or not his words had sunk in. They walked together to a corner of the enclosure where prisoners from the main camp had gathered. There were several Dutchmen among them and well-meant pieces of advice flew over the barbed wire. Wim absorbed everything. There were men among them who had been in the camp for years already. So it could be done – surviving in this inhuman environment. But they also told stories about many deaths, dozens a day. In particular, what they called 'outside *Kommandos*' were extremely deadly.

'You need to get yourself a job in the camp itself quickly,' they said. 'And make sure you don't end up in the *Revier*.'

'The *Revier*?'

Wim realised he still had a lot to learn.

'The *Revier*. The camp hospital. Your chances of leaving that place alive are zero. If they run out of space, you'll get a nice little jab.'

He asked about the prisoners who wore an armband with 'TORSPERRE' in big letters.

'They've been sentenced to death: "not allowed to leave" is what it means. You see that guy there with a red circle on his back? That's a bull's eye – if he ever gets too close to the fence, the guards in the watchtowers have an easy target. Their fates are sealed anyway, just nobody's carried out their sentences. Could be tomorrow, or take a year.'

Of those prisoners with a *Torsperre*, a portion had had a strip shaved into their hair. This was the 'Thumann Free-way', named after *SS-Obersturmführer* Thumann. He'd cut his teeth in other concentration camps, including Dachau, and was one of the most feared SS officers in the camp. With such a conspicuous haircut, the men who had been sentenced were immediately recognisable and escape became even harder.

Many of the *Torsperre* prisoners couldn't take the mental pressure. Particularly during the dark winter months, they sometimes opted for a quick way out. At night, the outer-most barbed wire fence carried a charge of 15,000 volts. To throw yourself against it was to end all of the misery at one fell swoop – a temptation not everyone could resist.

Many of the Polish, Russian and Hungarian prisoners in Wim's barracks had been in quarantine for some time already and no longer washed themselves. They had filthy hands and feet and untended wounds. Their compatriots who didn't have bowls passed a rusty dish from mouth to mouth. In a panic, Siep told Wim he'd lost his bowl and spoon. Wim handed him his.

'Go and stand at the front of the line and quickly eat your food,' he said, 'then give these back to me fast and I'll hop in.'

Siep did as he was told and Wim was one of the last people to receive his portion. A Russian member of the *Stubendienst* was ladling out and even if Wim had had a magnifying glass, he wouldn't have been able to discover a solid element in his soup. He looked at the man, who pretended not to see him. Wim could see that the ladle kept almost vertical in the nourishing goo at the bottom of the cauldron. He didn't say anything so as to avoid the risk of being beaten, but he knew enough. Especially when the *Blockälteste* and five members of the *Stubendienst* disappeared with the cooking pot behind a wooden partition on the other side of the barracks.

After food came the evening roll call. It took two hours this time. Seven men were thrashed, three of whom didn't stand up again. When it was over, towards nine o'clock, everyone had to go inside while the three poor wretches were left for dead. Wim knew one of the men from the train ride.

12

Satellite camp Husum–Schwesing

Husum, Germany, September 1944

On 28 August 1944, Hitler issued an executive order for the construction of the Frisian Wall. The Nazi high command feared that the Allies had plans to open a second front along Germany's northern coast, or that they perhaps wanted to force a breakthrough from the north towards the Ruhr Valley by way of Denmark.

Under the leadership of *Chef des Oberkommandos der Wehrmacht, Generalfeldmarschall* Wilhelm Keitel, the defences along the entire German North Sea coast were to be expanded with strongholds, anti-tank trenches and bunkers into a fortress, modelled after the Atlantic Wall. Additionally, six defence lines were to be constructed through Denmark and the German state of Schleswig-Holstein, straight through the countryside, from the west to the east coast.

As everyone remotely capable of fighting had been called up and the German army was part of the final effort to hold out, the work fell to volunteers, retired soldiers, Hitler Youth, farmers with agricultural tools, and wounded and unfit soldiers. Essentially, anyone who could hold a shovel. Nevertheless Keitel needed more hands. On account of the construction's great haste and extensiveness, they deployed concentration camp prisoners as well.

The line was so important that Hitler personally drew out the design for the *Panzergräben*, the anti-tank trenches or tank traps that were supposed to hold back enemy military vehicles. One of these lines ran northwards from the East Frisian town of Husum to Bredstedt and continued to the Danish coast, forty kilometres further to the north.

Husum was well-disposed towards the Nazis. In the previous election an overwhelming majority of the population had voted for the National Socialist German Workers' Party (NSDAP). It was home to a naval base, an airport and an SS base. In total, more than seven thousand military personnel of various stripes were stationed in the town of a mere ten thousand people.

For the construction at Husum, prisoners were sourced from the nearest concentration camp, Neuengamme, close to Hamburg. The camp's commandant, *SS-Standartenführer* Max Pauly, initially set aside eleven hundred prisoners. A portion of these came straight from the *Revier*.

Near Husum and right along the railway line to the city of Flensburg to the north-east was an old camp of huts, where a 300-man construction battalion had camped in the years just before the war while building the airport for the Husum-Schesing region. The airport itself was never actually used by the Nazis but was instead converted into a fake one, intended to throw the Allied bombers onto the wrong track. During the first years of the war, *Ausbildungsstammkompanie* Schwesing, a naval training cadre, had used the wooden huts for gathering sailors and ship personnel before going on board. Since January 1944, the neglected camp had been empty.

In order to house the prisoners, it was fenced off with double barbed wire and watchtowers were posted at the four corners. The 42-year-old *SS-Untersturmführer* Hans Hermann Griem became commandant of this satellite camp of Neuengamme. He had served in various other satellite camps and was notorious for his barbaric treatment of prisoners and his thirst for alcohol. Griem had bluffed to the Nazi leadership that he'd finish his section of anti-tank trenches within six weeks. The *Arbeitsamt*, the labour office, at Neuengamme concentration camp had also selected the Kapos for the new camp, most of them sentenced criminals from a psychiatric institution near Lüneburg.

But these green triangles were in the minority. The largest part of the camp internees wore a red triangle on their clothes – the political prisoners, communists and opponents of the system. There was another category for hostages, citizens and men picked up in reprisal for not wanting to work for the Germans. They weren't given a coloured triangle. Wim only had an H next to his number. He'd also seen men with black triangles walking around the camp. These were apparently people deemed antisocial – Roma, drunks, the work-shy and other people whom the Nazis felt didn't have a place in the society they envisioned. Rather than a red, black or green triangle, yet other prisoners wore a pink or yellow one with the number 175 on their jackets. It referred to the German article of law that forbade homosexuality. He didn't see anyone with the yellow stars that Jews in Amsterdam had been forced to wear every day.

★

After a week or two in the demarcated quarantine section at Neuengamme, Wim understood that surviving in a German concentration camp was an art in itself. Because they hadn't yet been assigned to *Kommandos*, enough time remained during the day to observe the movements in the main camp. In the meantime, the SS instilled the newcomers with discipline, aided by a whole army of helpers who were every bit as awful as them and took care of their dirty work.

Wim found it strange that they were being isolated for so long, just to prevent them from transferring diseases to the camp. Whenever he saw the ragged, worn-out figures walk past, it seemed to him that there were more diseases in the camp than outside. He didn't see anyone inside who still had any kind of fat.

While in hiding, he'd easily weighed more than seventy kilos, minus a few when in Amersfoort, but in Neuengamme, he lost weight quickly. The food here was of poor quality and totally inadequate for robust guys like himself. Without a weighing scale, he reckoned he now weighed sixty kilos.

One afternoon at the end of September, roll call was taking especially long. The green triangles were laying into them more fanatically and bellowing more loudly than usual. Never had the prisoners stood in such orderly lines. An entire SS platoon came marching in from their left. Then came loud shouts: '*Mützen ab!*' and then '*Augen richten links!*'

Staring straight ahead, the SS men passed the first group of a hundred prisoners and halted. Like marionettes, they made a half-turn and clicked their boots. The platoon commander stared down the prisoners for several minutes without so much as a blink. The men were afraid a command would follow for the guards to pick out a victim for a thrashing, but this was about something else. The commandant started speaking, kept speaking and didn't seem like he was going to stop. A Dutchman, one of the *Stubendienst*, translated parts of the speech. It was about the Greater German Reich, the coming victory and the noble work of the SS. The prisoners, too, could do their bit and be part of the new Germany. After the war, they would be able to count on good positions in the new civil society. However, they first needed to deal their enemies a final blow and this was where they could help, by joining the ranks of the SS. Whoever did so would be allowed to leave the camp immediately and could expect a great future.

Wim listened impassively and couldn't imagine that anyone would heed this call. Becoming a member of the SS not only meant collaborating with the enemy, but was also a one-way ticket to the front. Nevertheless he watched, to his astonishment, as a few prisoners came forwards, hesitantly at first. Three men stepped up in the end. The commander greeted them with a nod and an outstretched arm accompanied by a '*Heil Hitler*', and an SS officer took them to the main camp. The platoon then marched another fifty metres to the next section of prisoners, where the scene repeated itself. Each time, a few prisoners let themselves be persuaded, but the majority didn't take the SS up on their offer.

That same afternoon, Wim heard from the *Blockälteste* that his barracks had been assigned to an outside *Kommando* and that they would be leaving immediately after the evening meal. He didn't mention where they were going or how, but Wim knew very well that there were just two ways to leave the camp – on a train or through the chimney.

The train was ready that evening: that's to say, a freight train with fifteen open coal wagons awaited them on the improvised track. The guards lined up the prisoners in sections of a hundred men. For some unknown reason, they were made to stand there for hours until the SS guards enthusiastically bludgeoned them aboard. Wim managed to avoid the blows and found a spot at the outer edge, where he could lean with his back against the iron wall. Fifty men were pressed together on opposite sides and an armed SS guard planted himself in the middle. It took several hours before the other wagons were loaded in the same way. The special *Funktionshäftlinge*, prisoner functionaries who were higher in rank than the ordinary prisoners, got their own wagon.

It was close to midnight when the colossus finally started rolling. Everyone had been given a hunk of bread for the journey, but the lack of space meant it was a genuine challenge to actually take a bite out of it. They rode through the night and Wim didn't shut an eye. Everyone was so pressed together that it was impossible for him to stretch his legs. As there was no water on board, the thirst became torture as well.

They took nearly a day to ride a stretch that, at a normal speed, would have taken a few hours at most. It was early in the evening when they arrived at their destination, hungry, cold and with only two wishes: a toilet and a plate of decent food.

The train stopped right outside the improvised Husum-Schwesing concentration camp. Here, too, they had to step out under floodlights. Wim remembered all too well how they'd been smacked out of the carriages upon arrival at Neuengamme and, after waiting an hour, he warily let himself down from the wagon. His feet hadn't even touched the ground, when the first blow landed on his neck, just above his collarbone.

'*Schnell! Schnell! Los! Los!*' 'Quick! Quick! Move! Move!'

With a loud scream, he let go of the wagon and fell onto the ground. Out of reflex, he continued rolling, tucking his chin to his chest and his head between his arms. Most of the prisoners didn't come off as lightly and were beaten black and blue by the arrival committee. Then they had to stand in rows of five, twenty metres further on. All this was combined with the overpowering shouts of their new guards, who indulged their every whim with the camp's first supply of prisoners. A young Russian thought he was clever and tried taking advantage of the chaos. He ran for the forest's edge, but didn't get further than about twenty metres before a bullet in his back cut him down. Two guards dragged him by his legs back to the train. They left him there, bleeding heavily and moaning loudly.

Wagonload after wagonload was unloaded and set to roll call. When everyone was standing in orderly lines, Griem came forwards, his face red, his nose purple from too much drink, his eyes bloodshot. He'd observed the welcome ceremony with a grin and took the floor: '*Husum ist ein Vernichtungslager. Hier gibt's nur Lebendige und Tote. Es ist hier keine Versorgungsanstalt.*' 'Husum is an extermination camp. There are only the living and the dead here. This is not a care home.'

Wim understood these words only too well.

Then his group was marched into the camp and shouted into the third barracks. In the semi-darkness, everyone had to search for a bunk. Little fights broke out over sleeping spots because the prisoners had to spread all eleven hundred of themselves over a camp that had been built for just three hundred. The bunkbeds were three high and had been stowed together with almost no room between them. Wim ended up with two other men in a wooden berth seventy centimetres wide. Shivering from cold and hunger, he pulled a dirty blanket over himself, with two strangers' feet on either side of his face and a mattress under him that was half as thin as the straw sack in Neuengamme. He hadn't had anything to eat on that first day in Husum and his stomach rumbled. He fell asleep, dead-tired, but it wasn't to last.

Bang!

A baton smashed against his left neighbour's head and clipped Wim's foot.

'*Raus! Raus! Schnell! Schnell!*' 'Out! Out! Quick! Quick!'

His neighbour's ear was bleeding like a pig. The *Stubendienst* got all of the prisoners up. It was four in the morning. They had an hour to wash, dress themselves and make up their beds. The floor needed to be swept, too – and forgetting a single bit of straw was punishable by baton or riding crop. As for getting down their hunk of bread and the black muck that was supposed to be tea or coffee, they were given less than ten minutes.

'*Schnell! Schnell! Los! Los!*' 'Quick! Quick! Move! Move!'

The roll call on the wide camp street lasted from five until nearly seven o'clock. Apparently, they couldn't count in

133

Husum either. Shivering from cold, Wim stood in his thin striped uniform among the men from his Block, as always as near to the middle of the group as possible. The Russian who had tried to escape the day before lay dead on the ground beside the roll-call square, a potato stuffed into his mouth. The guards said he'd stolen potatoes.

After two hours, the SS officers were finally satisfied and they drove the group down the street that cut through the camp, to the main road connecting Husum and Flensburg. The day was starting and it was only now that Wim saw the appalling state of the barracks. Inside, he'd felt the wind blowing and now saw why. All the walls were jauntily fitted together and full of cracks, gaps and holes. Here and there, windows were missing. The camp wasn't large – two hundred metres long and a hundred and fifty metres wide, at most. There was a row of nine barracks and they had four latrines at their disposal. These were located on the other side of the camp street, where there were also two ponds, a large L-shaped barracks and sheds for tools. That's where they were heading. Everyone was given a shovel, a spade or a pickaxe and, if it took too long for the foreman's liking, a few knocks as well.

A platoon of about two hundred guards joined the group, mostly old soldiers from the Husum naval barracks. At their age, they should have been playing with their grandchildren or sitting with a fishing rod at the waterfront, but they'd been mobilised to save the German Reich.

Towards seven o'clock, the command '*Abmarschieren!*' 'March out!' sounded and the group marched in quick time onto the main road, towards the town of Husum.

13

First day at work

Husum, September 1944

The men weren't even a kilometre under way, when the first stragglers were beaten back into the group. Wim, too, was having trouble keeping up the marching pace. He was in good enough shape, but his feet hurt. The prisoners still wore their same old sandals, but no one had two that fit. They were too big or too small and the straps that were meant to keep the wooden soles in place chafed and rubbed the top of their feet, while their toes were jammed crooked against the outer ridge or stuck out over the sole. Wim grit his teeth and walked on as fast as possible so as not to fall to the back of the group. To their left and right, spaced every few metres, armed marines walked alongside them.

After a quarter of an hour, everyone was soaked to the skin and the prisoners were cursing and swearing to themselves just as much as the guards were at them. The flat, bare landscape stretched to the distant horizon. The wind was blowing hard and the few trees and bushes offered not the slightest protection. Occasionally, they passed a desolate farm with a modest farmhouse.

After half an hour of walking, at least a quarter of the group had been beaten because they were going too slowly for the guards. Nor had the weather improved. The drizzling rain had turned into steady sheets.

Walking next to Wim, Jan Kok, about thirty years old and from Amsterdam, addressed the prisoners around him: 'When I start singing, you've all got say I'm a famous Dutch singer, all right?'

Another few hundred metres further, the young man suddenly started. Softly and carefully at first, but when he saw that the guards didn't intervene, he began raising his voice. Dutch and Italian songs floated over Husum's fields. After a while, a Kapo asked who the man was. The men mumbled something about a famous singer from Amsterdam and one after another they confirmed his reputation. After hearing that, the Kapo ordered him to keep his mouth shut and to report to the SS lounge at eight o'clock that evening. No one knew whether that was good or bad news.

When they marched into the pleasant-looking town of Husum, its residents opened their curtains. From their warm living rooms, they observed the work detail drag itself past. Several passers-by stopped. No one said a word and the guards kept up a good pace with their shouting. For a change, they were using their truncheons less.

After a bridge, just beyond the inhabited world, at a spot where the road curved away to the east, the head Kapo finally stopped. The prisoners at the back had just caught up with the group, when he shouted '*Los geht's*' 'Let's go', making it clear they were to jump over the ditch and into the fields. Two foremen took up positions in front of the water, one on either side, and would let fly whenever a prisoner took too long to move. The ditch was a metre wide at most and Wim jumped over it with ease. On the other side, his feet immediately sank about ten centimetres into the marshy ground. The older inmates clearly had a harder time with this obstacle and the screaming foremen didn't make it any easier for them. Not everyone had enough strength for a fair jump, the consequence being that a number of prisoners landed in the ditch with a splash. It meant wet clothes for the rest of the day. The guards enjoyed the game. The men who didn't reach the other side were loudly jeered and caught a few whips from one of the guards' riding crops.

In this way, the group advanced through the fields from ditch to ditch, where the humiliating spectacle repeated itself time and again. A group of a hundred men stayed behind at each worksite. The journey through the soft, wet subsoil was torture.

Wim sank up to his ankles in the swampy, soggy surface. The water spurted with every step, so his thin trousers not only got wet, but also filthy with mud. Because ripping their feet free again from the sucking clay mass put full strain on the sandals' straps and ties, every step hurt and the wounds on their feet only grew worse.

After half a kilometre, Wim reached the spot where he and his group were supposed to work. He saw only a flat, vast expanse. No houses, no trees, nothing but fields and ditches. They'd trudged for an hour and a half to dig holes in the middle of nowhere.

Sixty prisoners had lost their foremen as a result of the brutal journey. As a punishment, they had to run from one side of the field to the other while Kapos stood at either end to beat them back the other way again. They ran back and forth like that for hours, their tormentors roaring with laughter. In the meantime, the rest of the group were put to work. Hundreds of men on stretches of roughly fifty metres each. The foremen had marked out a line where they were to dig a trench nearly six metres wide and four and half metres deep.

The prisoners set their spades to the marshland, all except for two men, who both wore a purple triangle on their jackets. They remained standing and didn't move. The Kapo nearest to them, a small, fat man with scars on his face, took exasperatingly slow steps in their direction. Wim saw the two men talk to each other softly, after which they stood up as straight as possible. The fat Kapo approached to within a metre of them and snarled: 'And what do you think you're doing? You will work!'

The blows rained down on them. The men were protecting their heads and wanted to explain: 'We're not allowed to work – we can't do this.'

'Not allowed to work! Just see what happens when you don't!'

Beneath a new rain of blows, one of the men cried: 'Our religion won't let us carry out military acts.'

The Kapo didn't hear him or wasn't listening. His face now red, he was completely out of his mind and hacked away at them. They were left lying motionless on the marsh.

After just several shovels into the swampy soil, the cold water started to pool and Wim was standing up to his ankles within no time. The mud landed on a pile next to the trench, which after several hours had progressed to a depth of about two metres. They had to dig. This was nothing like dredging ditches at his own pace and with a full stomach, under a pleasant summer sun in Holland's fields. Just lifting his head was enough to get himself hit. Whenever a Kapo was nearby, Wim would shovel strongly, but as soon as the tormentor had walked off far enough, he went back to pretending and shovelling air.

Around midday, the SS showed up with large cauldrons. The prisoners were allowed to drop their tools for a moment and stand in line for something that was supposed to be coffee. Two appointed prisoners did the pouring into old, rusty bowls. A German Kapo with a face like a clothes iron was standing next to them, lying in wait for a mistake.

About half of Wim's group had got the lukewarm brown liquid. A French prisoner was too slow in understanding the order to keep walking and that was all the Kapo needed. He lashed out with his truncheon against the man's knees. When the man balled up in pain, he caught a series of blows on his head and shoulders until he lay in the grass bleeding. Rather than be left alone, he then got a series of kicks to his head. The dull sound cut straight through Wim.

The Kapo still hadn't satisfied his appetite and looked with shifting eyes at the other prisoners. They were now standing at a safe distance, meaning his swinging baton only beat the air. The veins in his neck had swollen to abnormal proportions and ran up to a sharp corner around his chin, where his flat face ended. He was still completely out of his mind and now the half-cauldron of coffee had to know it. The Kapo kicked it over and its contents mixed with the groundwater.

'*An die Arbeit! Schnell! Schnell!*' 'Get to work! Quick! Quick!'

The break hadn't lasted ten minutes and Wim hadn't seen any coffee. The clothes iron Kapo lit a cigarette and caught his breath after so much effort.

That afternoon felt excruciatingly long. Wim was miserable, cold and numb. Towards the end of the day, there wasn't a muscle in his body that didn't hurt. Nevertheless, he kept shovelling, or at least convincingly pretending that he was.

The way they worked didn't at all resemble the kind of well-oiled machine Wim had seen in Brunswick and Amersfoort. It was an unorganised mess that came to an end only at five o'clock with a whistle and the command to gather together. His hands had been clamped on the shovel's shaft for all those hours and were now stuck in the same position, even after he'd jammed it under his right arm.

They lined up with a hundred men in the field and after being counted, they set off. While most of them had been reasonably fresh on the way out, the prisoners were now exhausted, dehydrated and famished. Only the Kapos were still as fanatical as that morning. One consequence was that at least half of the inmates ended up in one of the many ditches, having been beaten in or been too weak to reach the other side. But it didn't matter to most of them: they'd been soaking wet and dirty anyway.

Once back on the public road, they were forced to continue at a high march. This was problematic for many, and prisoners from the same country or region looked to one another for help. At least half of the group was Dutch and then there were many Danish, French and Belgians, and some Polish and Russians. Sometimes a wounded inmate was carried between two fellow prisoners. Others looked for a supporting shoulder or just an encouraging word. The company dragged itself like this towards the camp. However, they first had to march straight through Husum, where the number of curious townspeople watching them was now substantially larger. It was getting towards seven and the sun had just set. The sight of the houses, with their lights glowing inside and fireplaces heating their living rooms, made the prisoners wistful and they thought of home until their harsh reality loomed before them.

At the camp entrance they had to hand in their tools and roll call inevitably followed. Wim's hope for a quick counting and then finally a warm meal was quickly dashed. The guards made another circus of it. Whoever didn't stand neatly in position with their cap in their right hand and their head high could count on the familiar truncheons and riding crops. And whoever had thought the guards might also be longing for food and a warm place was totally disappointed.

'*Mützen ab! Mützen auf! Augen richten links! Augen richten rechts!*' 'Caps off! Caps on! Eyes left! Eyes right!'

It didn't stop. Counting, beating, recounting and even harder beating, while the cold and fatigue mercilessly ravaged their bodies. After an hour and a half, the torture finally came to an end. Some of the prisoners crumpled where they stood and had to be dragged by their friends to their barracks. The others staggered in on their own, relieved they had survived the first day.

Inside, a cauldron of watery and now lukewarm swede soup awaited them. The hunk of bread they got with it, as well as a slice of some unidentifiable sausage, was meant for breakfast the next morning. Within a few minutes, everybody had eaten that too.

They went to their bunks still soaking wet, where they stretched out on the hard planks and had to lie against two other wet, dirty and smelly bodies. In the distance, they could hear the Amsterdam singer's Italian songs. Each night, he was made to sing for the SS until he dropped. In exchange, he got enough to eat and no longer had to dig tank traps.

Wim fell dead asleep from exhaustion, only to be beaten out of bed again at four o'clock the next morning and begin a new day in clothes that were still damp.

14

Broken shovels

Husum, September – October 1944

The situation in Husum worsened with each passing day. It was still wet, everywhere and all the time. Barely a day went by without rain and in the first half of October, temperatures started dropping as well. The prisoners' conditions deteriorated rapidly. Dozens of men were lying in the infirmary, where two Danish doctors had got permission from the camp commandant to set up a consulting room and ward. The cold, the wet, the bad food and the murderously hard labour were taking their toll. On top of it all, there was also the SS, Kapos and foremen's criminal and often psychopathic behaviour. It was little wonder the doctors soon had their hands full.

One morning, a week and half after Wim's arrival, it didn't rain for a change and the local population had come out of their houses in droves to watch the procession of emaciated and stinking prisoners pass through town. They were cursed, jeered at and laughed at. Dragging themselves along, the wretches resigned themselves to suffering the shower of filthy comments. Fortunately, they didn't understand everything, but a comment from a woman farmer was unmistakable: '*Was sind das für Schweine?*' 'What kind of pigs are they?'

Now and then they caught a glimpse of the bustling fishing port – a reminder that a real world existed as well, alongside their own ghostly existence in the camp. At the back of the column, three men were struggling to drag themselves through Husum's narrow streets. Suddenly, they had all kinds of things thrown at them: from the upper floors, chamber pots and rubbish bins were emptied over them. When the men realised what had happened, they threw themselves on the potato skins, gnawed apples, bread crusts and other leftovers, until the Kapos beat them back into the parade. For the local people, brainwashed by Nazi propaganda, this only confirmed they were dealing with a group of antisocial and beast-like criminals. The motley crew that passed through their town twice a day – those were felons, saboteurs and rapists. In their eyes, most of the prisoners fully deserved their death sentence and could be glad it hadn't been carried out yet. The guards, in turn, were self-sacrificing volunteers who had declared themselves prepared to manage this scum, in full service of the Greater German Reich. They were heroes who, through wind and rain, kept the riff-raff of Europe in line. And that riff-raff? They deserved the rubbish bin.

That first week in the marshland had been glorious compared with what took place in the days and weeks afterwards. They had to go further and further into the soggy fields. When, after a torturous march, they finally arrived at the place they'd left the day before, they found the trenches now half collapsed and filled with water up to knee or even waist height.

With the appointment of extra foremen, the work was now better organised. The prisoners spaced themselves out every few metres in groups of three. Naturally, no one wanted to go down and stand up to their waist in freezing-cold water. On some mornings, it was even covered by a thin layer of ice. Whenever things dragged on too long for the Kapos, they came by and invariably clubbed the tallest of the three prisoners down into the trench. The wretch was then drenched before his work had even started. Standing in the ice-cold water, he lifted the muddy mass with an extra-long shovel a level higher, where a bay along the edge of the trench had been dug and where a colleague shovelled the mud a level higher again. At the top, the third inmate shovelled it a metre to the side. The pile of earth then had to be covered with turf, so that enemy tanks couldn't see what lay behind and, according to the Nazi leadership's theory, would drive straight into the trap.

Wim wasn't very tall and usually managed to stay above; however, this didn't always work out. On the same day that a group of prisoners had had rubbish tipped over them, a notorious and feared Dutch Kapo, nicknamed Red Jan, slowly walked towards him. Wim always had a pile of mud ready for these moments. Whenever a guard became suspicious, he would start shovelling furiously.

It was a game of cat and mouse. Red Jan came progressively closer. From out of the corner of his eye, Wim observed him and waited for the right moment; until a Russian prisoner suddenly threw himself on Wim's pile and frantically began shovelling. Flabbergasted by the man's nerve, Wim looked the Kapo in the eyes – for a second too long. In an instant he'd caught a tremendous whack and a few moments later, the next one.

'Prisoners who refuse to work do not belong up here!' Red Jan roared, and before Wim could say anything, he was lying sprawled in the trench with a black eye and a wet suit. He clambered up to the middle section to keep out of his tormentor's sight and to avoid having to stand up to his knees in water. He got off easy that day. As long as the Kapos and the SS were observing him, he visibly worked full-out. When the coast was clear, he shovelled air again.

By staying sharp and alert, he was regularly an inadvertent witness to the arbitrary thrashings that took place every day, while evading the brutal violence himself. He now knew the Kapos and SS guards well enough to know who could transform, from one moment to the next, into a wanton murder machine.

A Kapo with the nickname 'The Extractor' was one of these unpredictable brutes. He was called that because he could twirl his baton as fast as a fan, while those who came into contact with it usually never lived to tell the tale. Most of the time he would walk, his arms folded, past the toiling prisoners and at the slightest cause, or just because he was bored, grab one of them and let loose on him until he'd had his fill, or simply because the prisoner was as dead as a doornail.

One of the wretches working in the icy wind a few metres from Wim was mentally broken. Only that morning they'd helped him through roll call and, with several friends, supported him during the long journey, but he was finished and collapsed during work. The Extractor had a good nose for these situations and it wasn't long before he was standing next to him, kicking him back upright. A little later, the poor man threw away his shovel and let himself fall into the trench, pushing his face underwater. His friends fished him back out while the man, with his final ounces of strength, shouted: 'I want to die! I want to die! I can't keep going!'

The prisoners explained what was going on, hoping for some sympathy. The Extractor laughed in their faces but didn't immediately use his bludgeon. The desperate man threw himself into the water again and his friends pulled him out a second time, risking their own lives, since they were supposed to keep digging. Not a quarter of an hour later, the poor wretch made an attempt to escape. A guard spotted him and shot into the air. The man turned around, raised a hand above his head, put his other over his heart and awaited the delivering shot. It never came. The Extractor kicked him to the ground and pounded away at him with his dreaded truncheon like a man possessed. Blood spurted out of his victim's ears and nose, which only seemed to encourage even more violence from his tormentor. An SS guard looked on with a wide grin as The Extractor delivered kick after kick into a body beaten lifeless. The SS guard barked that he was wasting his time and energy as the man was dead anyway. Satisfied, The Extractor resumed his patrol along the trench, in search of a new victim. The corpse lay there for the rest of the day, just a few metres from where Wim was working.

After the evening meal, Wim crawled into his bunk, exhausted and upset, and tried to let the day's misery roll off his back. Things couldn't go on like this for much longer if he planned on leaving the camp alive. The straw mattress had shrunk to the thickness of a centimetre or two. He barely noticed the fleas, lice and bedbugs any more. They'd become a natural part of his residence, wedged between his bunkmates' stinking bodies.

Tomorrow was Sunday. He hoped the marines would be milder. They were the only guards with whom he could occasionally strike up a conversation, though only when the SS guards were far enough away.

Sunday might have been the day of the Lord, but their murderous work on the desolate plain, in a landscape forsaken by God and everyone, carried on as usual. Four o'clock in the morning was and stayed the time at which they were rammed out of their beds with the usual violence, to appear in rows of five at roll call an hour later. As best they could, everyone lined up. Those who were too slow at standing to attention or taking their caps off or putting them on knew what awaited them.

After the *Blockälteste* and the *Stubendienst* had done their destructive preparatory work, the SS inspected the sections of a hundred men. A few inmates were mercilessly thrashed, as on other days. When everyone had been counted to the satisfaction of the SS, camp commandant Griem honoured the prisoners with a drunken visit. His face now purple, he stood among the first few sections of a hundred men and started orating incoherently. It was a disgrace that the prisoners needed so much time to stand decently at roll call. Did they have any idea of how much of the German *Ubermenschen*'s valuable time they wasted? His anger kept growing – until he grabbed his pistol and began shooting at random. A number of men fell to the ground. Griem didn't so much as glance at them and staggered back to his accommodation to sleep off the alcohol. The remaining SS men kicked the wounded prisoners back onto their feet. Those who were so wounded they could no longer stand got a few extra boots in their faces before being hauled off to the infirmary.

The other prisoners were ordered to the latrines. There, they had to strip fully and wash their clothes with ice-cold water in the metal sinks outside. Without soap, without towels and the temperature three degrees above freezing, while a blistering-cold easterly wind rushed over their numb bodies.

Many of the prisoners suffered from diarrhoea and had to clean their trousers as well. The Kapos saw to it with loud shouts. They had to put their wet clothes back on straight-away. Shivering, they walked to their barracks, where at least they were protected from the screeching wind.

Wim forced himself to stay strong, but he'd got a fright that morning when washing himself. His eyes had roamed over his own body and to his horror, he had seen how effective the Nazis' methods were. '*Vernichtung durch Arbeit.*' 'Extermination through labour.' That was truly what was happening. He couldn't have weighed more than fifty kilos. He was working himself into the ground, quickly burning through all of his reserves. Something had to happen, but what? Escape was impossible. Shirking, maybe. Only the most serious cases were allowed to stay in the infirmary and there were more of them every day, though he was also thankful he wasn't part of that group. Not yet. Every day, a few prisoners from the *Revier* were thrown onto the large pile of cadavers. He thought for hours, weighed up the risks against one another and gauged the consequences of everything going through his head. He just couldn't figure it out.

The next day, the prisoners' daily lives were unexpectedly given a substantial improvement. Apparently, the sick count was too high and they weren't making headway quickly enough. Neuengamme's camp commandant had paid Husum a visit. Wim could only guess at the reason, but from then on they no longer had to march to the worksite. Early each morning, a freight train would stop right outside the camp. Sixty prisoners were driven into each wagon. As there were no running boards on these wagons, it took a lot of clambering to get on board. Wim was still reasonably fit. He made sure to stay out of the jostling and climbed quickly over the edge, but the wounded and older prisoners weren't as lucky. They became prey for the Kapos, who then got an extra opportunity to lay into them.

The train stopped in the middle of the fields, after which it was still between one and two kilometres of jumping ditches and dodging blows.

Back in camp, they were also given other clothes. They could get rid of their striped pyjamas; in their stead came slightly thicker civilian clothes, old and worn-out, with coloured patches on the sleeves and trouser legs and a large yellow cross on the back, so that if anyone escaped, everyone could immediately see it was a prisoner. These were still totally inadequate when it came to protecting them from the cold and rain but were a bit warmer than their old get-up. They did take longer to dry though, when Wim came back to camp soaking wet.

The prisoners soon figured out that some of the wagons were covered. These were the most popular. Every day, fights broke out because everyone wanted to climb into them.

Wim and his friends from his bunk helped one another when they had the chance by folding their hands and crouching to serve as a step up. Often, they didn't get the opportunity to do so, since time and space were extremely limited. Once you'd found a spot, so many people were crammed aboard that you couldn't move any more. You were just out of luck if someone with diarrhoea or dysentery sat next to you.

Still, the train journeys were a welcome relief. It was only in these moments that the men could sit safely without toiling away or being beaten. Whenever the train, for one reason or another, stopped for a time, everyone just hoped it would last for as long as possible.

The camp leadership used some of the time saved by these train trips to extend the morning roll calls. During the dark mornings, it took the SS longer to get the counting right and the prisoners had to be counted again and again and again. If it turned out that prisoners were genuinely missing, the SS guards and the Kapos dived into the barracks. Sometimes they found them dead there, in bed or in the aisles. Or men were so sick and weak that they hadn't been able to climb out of their bunks. For that there was no excuse. They were driven with many kicks and blows to roll call regardless. Often, they were still barely able to walk or stand. Meanwhile, the prisoners who had been standing at roll call for hours in their wet clothes were by now completely numb and this was before their workday even began.

Wim was at the end of his rope and he felt his strength dwindling away until the day came when he decided not to dig. Exactly how he was supposed to do so, he didn't know yet, but to continue digging in his condition would mean digging himself to death.

After arriving in the fields the prisoners lined up, as usual, in groups of three, spaced every few metres. The previous day they'd reached a depth of about three and half metres in the trench, but at least half a metre of this was now water and they still had more than a metre to dig. Wim looked at the men around him. He was certainly not the shortest among them and of course it would be just his luck, out of everyone, to be knocked into the trench by a Kapo and condemned to doing the heaviest work.

While shovelling, it sometimes happened that a spade's shaft snapped in half without warning. A little further on lay one such shovel's blade, with a short snapped-off stump of wood still attached. Wim picked it up, stuck it underneath his arm and looked around. Nobody paid him any attention. He started walking along the trench, his head raised and the broken shovel demonstratively in his hand. He walked past the first Kapo and a moment later past the two foremen. No one said anything to him. A little further on lay another broken spade. He put that one underneath his arm too. After a few hundred metres he stumbled on a third snapped shovel and took it with him as well. In that way, on his first round he collected five shovels that needed repairing.

A marine was standing guard just beyond the digging work. He was approaching seventy and looked less surly than the rest. Wim took his chances and threw three broken shovels onto the ground in front of him. He arranged them neatly next to one another and slowly walked back with the remaining two under his arm.

The trench was about a kilometre long. When, on his way, toiling prisoners looked up at him, he sometimes stopped to check their shovels, at one time exchanging theirs for a slightly better one. The guards assumed another Kapo or an SS guard had given him the task of sorting out the equipment.

Wim kept this up for two days, avoiding physical labour, so that he could have a brief opportunity to regain some strength. The old marine even sneaked him an extra slice of bread at lunchtime. After those two days, the risk of being unmasked became too high for him and he decided to disappear again among the stream of the prisoners forced to work on the tank trap. Although the short break had certainly done him good, it was the moral victory against the system that really gave him new energy.

15

New arrivals

Husum, 19 October 1944

The barracks, latrines and storage depots, the compost pile behind the ponds – within three weeks absolutely everything had transformed into a chaotic, stinking and rotting rubbish dump. Not that things had ever been neat and ordered, but during the first week the camp had at least stayed reasonably clean. The lack of everything, most notably soap and disinfectants, was leaving its mark. Hygiene was virtually non-existent and the infirmary was overcrowded. Of the two doctors, one was on the verge of death and the other didn't have medications or other means to help the torrent of patients.

As a result of the gruelling marches and the work in the fields, many of the prisoners had wounds on their hands and legs and as there was no care to speak of, these were left to fester away happily. Instead of being given time to heal with a sterile bandage, the men were forced to stand with their open wounds, the cold, dirty water up to their hips, for ten hours again.

The number of cases of dysentery had skyrocketed. The camp management saw no reason why these men couldn't go back to work. So dozens of men could do nothing but relieve themselves where they were, be it on the train, on the land or in the trench. A blend of phlegm, excrement and blood mixed in with the groundwater in the anti-tank trenches, with disastrous consequences.

Three weeks of toiling away in the icy wind while wearing thin, wet clothing had also caused a surge of lung infections and other sicknesses along with their accompanying symptoms. Wim had miraculously remained standing; the farming life in West Friesland had given him more reserves than he could have imagined. But he knew it was a question of time before he'd be stricken too.

The morning of 19 October started like any other. It just took longer than usual before the SS showed their sadistic side. During the roll call they were busy talking to one another. Griem was nowhere to be seen, to Wim's relief. His right-hand man, *SS-Oberscharführer* Dörge, gave instructions to one of the worst camp tormentors walking around Husum: *SS-Rottenführer* Klinger. He in turn instructed the Kapos, who ordered the prisoners back to their barracks. Inside, the *Blockälteste* told them to shove the wooden bunkbeds closer together and that all lucky prisoners no longer sharing a bunk with more than one person were to make room for a third. After a lot of pushing and pulling, a number of empty spots were freed up, though this didn't create much extra space, since the barracks was already overcrowded.

Red Jan, the Dutch Kapo, stormed into Wim's barracks and into every bunk where there were only two prisoners, he rammed a third. This work finished, Klinger came to inspect everything. The men held their breath, but it went better than expected. Whereas he usually raged liked a beast and thrashed innocent prisoners, he now quickly returned to the door after making a round. He nodded to Red Jan and without a word, walked to the next barracks.

That whole day was abuzz with rumours as they dug, but no one dared to ask a Kapo or a foreman what was going on. The question was whether they'd even get an answer and the risk of being beaten to death was too high.

The day was excruciatingly slow. Two men were missing at roll call. The prisoners were counted again and again, but they were gone and stayed gone. Just as Wim was wondering whether they might have actually succeeded in escaping, Klinger yelled and pointed to the trench.

'Over here! And take prisoners with you!'

Foremen grabbed five or six prisoners standing at the front and dragged them to the beckoning *SS-Rottenführer*. The two missing men were floating face down in the water. The inmates in the work gang had been able to muster neither the courage nor the strength to carry the corpses back to camp and had left them there. Now, all of the prisoners were being made to suffer. They'd stood at roll call for half an hour longer in the rain and cold while everyone longed for a bowl of lukewarm swede soup and a chunk of mouldy bread.

Klinger was furious and asked the foreman which prisoners had worked in the group with the two dead men that day. He held the poor man responsible and personally thrashed him on the spot but, remarkably enough, left him alive. The foreman was dragged to the train among the prisoners. The two corpses were thrown into a corner of a wagon and the unfortunate man was forced to sit on top of them.

The roll call after their return lasted only an hour and was taken by fewer *Blockältesten* and SS members than normal. Everyone then hurried to their barracks, where they were in for a terrible fright. That afternoon, a new group of prisoners had arrived. The hundred and fifty fresh faces in Wim's barracks had, without suspecting anything, spread themselves over various beds. Many of them turned out to be Dutch, which at least made communication easier.

The *Stubendienst* didn't involve themselves, as the food had to be dished out. The newcomers were taught the ropes as well as possible. They still found it hard to believe that they were to sleep three men to a bunk, or on the ground, but once everyone was inside, they understood it was serious.

They couldn't avoid converting some beds into four-person bunks. In Wim's barracks, the prisoners in the work gang were too exhausted and the newcomers too astonished for any fights to break out. From the din in the camp, they could hear that things weren't going as peacefully everywhere.

How did they come up with it? Wim asked himself. With the original eleven hundred men, they'd already been packed in like sardines and now there were another thousand who were supposed to spread themselves over the seven remaining barracks. It made sense that the camp leadership had been busy that day ensuring everything went according to plan. At any rate, the kitchen didn't seem to have been expecting them; there was far too little food and the cauldrons were already empty while there were still dozens of men standing in line. This led to cursing and ranting but no actual fights, simply because the starving men had wolfed down their food right away, leaving nothing to even fight for.

When things finally settled back down a bit, the questions started. Everyone was curious. The newcomers wanted to know what life in the camp was like and what working on the land exactly entailed. The answers, however, seemed to be falling on deaf ears. They just couldn't believe them – and it all was barely comprehendible too. Three weeks earlier, these men had been at home just doing their daily work and now they were here, like pigs crammed into a shed, listening to stories that went beyond their imaginations.

Many of the new Dutchmen came from Putten, a village in the Veluwe region. They'd been rounded up in a razzia about three weeks before in reprisal for a resistance group's partly failed attack around there. More than six hundred men had been arrested on 1 October 1944 and a day later transported to camp Amersfoort. Most of them were sent on to Husum via Neuengamme, to get the Frisian Wall's construction back on schedule as quickly as possible.

Wim noticed that the new group was dressed considerably warmer than they'd been in their early days at Husum. The arrivals weren't wearing thin striped pyjamas but instead, like them, mostly tattered civilian clothing and in some cases even old coats. The same yellow cross had been painted on their backs. Pieces had been cut out of their sleeves and trouser legs, and then filled again with old kitchen curtains. A droll sight, but warmer than the striped suits. Only later would they learn that a large portion of these clothes had been sourced from the clothing depots at Auschwitz.

For the first time since leaving camp Amersfoort, Wim heard news about the course of the war. In Husum, they were cut off from the rest of the world and could only guess at the Allies' progress. What he heard didn't cheer him up. A large part of the southern Netherlands had been liberated, but the march north by way of Arnhem had failed. The German army was far from admitting defeat. It was unlikely that the Allies would be liberating their camp in the near future. Much less was known about the Eastern Front, though nothing indicated that the Russians would be descending on the work camp like guardian angels any time soon either. It sank in that they had a long winter ahead of them.

The next morning, the *Stubendienst* got them up in the customary fashion. Immediately after Wim awoke, he heard a strange noise coming from outside – it sounded like someone imitating a rooster. Early in the mornings, every sound travelled for kilometres over the vast plain, but this seemed to be coming from nearby, from between the latrines. He put the thought aside until, a little while later, he clearly heard Klinger's roaring and shouting, followed again by a man's strained clucking. On his way to the toilet, he saw that groups of prisoners were trying to catch a glimpse of the dismal spectacle.

The toilet buildings were on the other side of the camp street, thirty metres from the barracks. The guards were making sure prisoners couldn't watch for long. A single look while passing was enough for Wim anyway.

The unlucky prisoner from the previous day who had neglected to take pity on his workmates' corpses had been forced by Klinger to sit on top of the *Wasserhahn*, the camp's fire hydrant, which directly translated from the German to 'water rooster'. Wim's face went pale as he realised what was happening. Next to the prisoner, a Kapo held his truncheon ready. The metal hydrant, measuring a metre and a half in height, stood between the four latrines. At the top there was a small iron cover plate, several centimetres thick, screwed on with two iron bolts, which stuck out sharply. If the victim didn't mimic a rooster every few seconds, the Kapo slammed the truncheon into his neck. He also got a bash whenever he fell from the hydrant, which happened constantly because of the device's shape and because he was completely exhausted.

During the hour and a half that Klinger took to call roll, in the background they heard the alternating sounds of a rooster, the dull thud of a baton and the Kapo's shouts – to the *Rottenführer*'s great delight. It was only after they'd marched out of the camp that the rooster had stopped crowing for good.

Wim had been in camp Husum for a month when, on a day late in October, he was happy to hear the whistle for the short midday break. He'd been shovelling as the middle person in his team and clambered out of the trench to stretch his back on the embankment. In a flash, he spotted someone walking towards him who had something familiar about him. It couldn't be true. He looked again and shook his head, as though he wanted to be sure he wasn't dreaming. The skeletal figure emerging from the mist was Cor. His old friend in hiding was almost unrecognisable, ruined by life in the camp, broken. His eyes were hollow, his mouth sunken and covered in scabs. He slowly shuffled, a blanket wrapped around him, towards Wim.

'Cor . . .' was all Wim could manage.

Cor was apathetic and didn't seem to recognise him.

'Do we still have long to go?' he asked.

Wim recognised the voice of a dying man, but was unsure as to what he meant.

'The Americans, they're close, aren't they?' Cor said.

'Yeah,' Wim answered. 'The Americans are close.'

Cor nodded almost imperceptibly and with an empty gaze, stumbled on along the trench, the mist swallowing him, leaving Wim petrified behind. It was the last time Wim would see him.

One evening, not long after this incident, Wim was devouring his meagre meal at the long table in his barracks. Sitting next to him was Jean, a French prisoner about forty years old, with whom he got on well. Jean had also been sent to work in Germany and spoke some German. Over the last few weeks, they'd told each other about their experiences and adventures in the *Arbeitseinsatz*, to try to pass time in the evenings and not slip into complaining.

Jean told him that Doctor Paul Thygesen, who was in charge of the *Revier*, had got permission from the camp leadership to take on an extra nurse in the hours before and after the normal work outside. He simply couldn't handle the workload any more, given the enormous influx of sick prisoners. In the camp were two qualified French doctors who went out with the work details and helped out in the infirmary in the early mornings and late evenings.

'They asked if I wanted to help too,' Jean said. 'But I said no. I couldn't do it. I'm exhausted from the digging.'

Wim thanked him for the tip, stood up and walked straight to Thygesen's consultation room, Jean staring after him with surprise. He waited for a patient to come out, slipped inside and introduced himself as the new *Sanitäter*. Thygesen looked at him, didn't ask any questions and stressed that he could only come before and after the regular work: 'Be here tomorrow morning at five.'

Thygesen, arrested in Denmark as the editor of a resistance publication, had been trained as a psychiatrist and was the last lifeline for hundreds of prisoners in the camp. He couldn't even go to the toilet without being clutched at by prisoners who wanted medication or gauze, though he only had calming words for them. When he finally took his seat above the hole, prisoners to his right and left invariably gestured wildly, complaining to him in Dutch, German, French, Polish, Russian, Spanish or Italian about their stool: '*Très, très, très liquide, docteur, nix dobra, kamerad, diarrhoaea, scheisserei, acquosi, avec sang, mit schleim.*'

After answering nature's call, he still had to wrestle his way back through all of these desperate people to reach his post.

Thygesen had carefully brought the inhuman conditions to the SS's attention on several occasions. He got the same answer each time: '*Hier gibt es nur Lebendige und Tote.*' 'There are only the living and the dead here.'

Wim showed up right on time at the *Revier* door, where a long line of impatiently waiting men had already formed. He was assigned tasks: cleaning the consultation room and letting in the next patient were the most important. Thygesen only cared about his patients and didn't pay him any further attention.

When, at seven o'clock, the signal to march out was given, Wim said goodbye to the doctor and joined the work gang. He presented himself punctually at seven o'clock that evening again. Now, he at least had something to pass the time and he saw and heard a lot more than when he stayed in his own barracks. There wasn't much to the work itself.

On the second day, he had to work in the infirmary too and keep everything clean, count patients and fill in lists. The doctor slogged away until twelve o'clock at night but still hadn't got through the entire waiting line. New men kept lining up.

On the corner of his table was a large pot of cod-liver oil ointment, which he rubbed on most wounds. He would then bind them with strips of cloth torn from old shirts, as the little gauze he'd been given had run out a long time ago. Wim helped to hold the piece of fabric in place while the doctor tried fastening it.

So as to somewhat regulate the permanent stream of patients and avoid fights, Thygesen had posted a burly nurse at the entrance door, a Dutchman who answered to the confusing name of Albartus Dokter. The prisoners first had to report their symptoms to him and he determined whether someone was allowed inside or not. By doing so, Dokter often decided who lived and who died.

Now and then, they got something extra to eat in the sickroom, but more important still was that a wood burner heated the consultation room and office. Wim could at least climb into his bunk wearing dry clothes.

★

In the fields one day three prisoners had died, killed by disease and exhaustion, or the guards' doing. Now, their bunkmates, or men originally from the same region, faced a truly hellish march at the end of the workday. The corpses had to come back to the camp, otherwise the count at roll call would be off. It sometimes happened that they buckled underneath the load they were forced to bear during the long journey and fell down exhausted. Other prisoners helped them back up and took the cadaver over from them. In camp, the dead bodies were laid next to the roll-call area and, after the count, were taken to the morgue, next to the entrance gate.

After the daily agony of roll call, the dead-tired prisoners who could still walk headed to their barracks, where in their rusty bowls they received the hot tinted water and could only hope that a bit of old potato or swede was drifting around somewhere in it. The bread delivered by the baker from Husum grew worse while Wim was at the camp. Instead of flour, he started using sawdust and ground fish scraps, so that he could save hundreds of Reichsmarks per delivery and pocket them himself. It didn't matter: the prisoners all ravenously gobbled the bread down as quickly as they could.

Wim was still intent on finding a way to get out of the gruelling work on the tank traps. For that, he needed the strictly organised roll calls to be disrupted by an unusual event. Something chaotic or confusing that would create the tiny gap he was after. The opportunity arose sooner than he'd expected. Griem and his camp leadership were making preparations for a transport to a new camp that needed to be manned. That a large group of prisoners would be leaving worked out well, since the situation in the overpopulated camp had become completely unsustainable. The infirmary was overflowing and the SS guards and Kapos could barely keep the chaos in the barracks under control.

The Germans wanted to build defences, dozens of kilometres further north, near the Danish border. The prisoners' work was reallocated and the three blocks at the back of the camp were fully vacated. In the end, a thousand men were put on the train to concentration camp Ladelund. Griem went too, in order to lead the camp's organisation on site. He did, however, maintain final responsibility for Husum-Schwesing. *SS-Oberscharführer* Eichler became deputy camp commandant, while Griem would only occasionally visit Husum. The *Revier*'s severest cases went on another train to Neuengamme. The chaos this caused upset the camp's organisation even further. Wim saw his chance. The next morning, he didn't report for roll call and didn't march out through the gate. Instead, after hearing the command to assemble, he darted into the infirmary, where he hid. After the trains and work details had left, he reported to the doctor, who got the fright of his life: 'But you can't do this – you had to leave the camp with them. I only have permission for one *Sanitäter* – if the SS see you here, I'll be responsible.'

He was in a total panic, but Wim stayed calm and said it would be fine. He went back into the *Revier* and entertained himself with small tasks. In that way, he kept himself hidden for the whole day until the work detail returned from the clay and roll call was done with. He then reported to Thygesen again. He'd done it – they hadn't missed him. Neither at the morning roll call nor at the evening one. As an illegal camp resident, the trick was to stay unnoticed for as long as possible. However, he could now work inside during the day and was no longer exposed to the Kapos' cruel tempers and the murderous conditions in the East Frisian fields.

16

The *Revier*

Husum, October – November 1944

During the first month, Wim had left through the gate in the dark and come back in the dark. After roll call and dinner he had sometimes wandered for an hour along the barracks, but the camp was so small and the supervision so sharp that there was little to 'organise'.

Now that he didn't have to leave, he slowly but steadily got a more complete picture of what took place in the camp. In the mornings he worked with the doctor up until the march out. The *Blockälteste* counted him and thought he officially belonged to the infirmary staff. He stayed inside until, according to the rules, he could go back to work for Doctor Thygesen. He lived as a shadow. There was always something extra to eat, he stayed warm and dry, he wasn't beaten and he didn't have to toil away. He helped the patients in the *Revier* and passed their questions on to the doctor, who as a result only went into the infirmary when strictly needed. After that first time, Thygesen never mentioned the matter again and increasingly allowed Wim to carry out small medical procedures as well, such as cleaning and wrapping wounds.

Behind the office was a broom closet, about a metre and

a half square. He'd organised a clean straw mattress, which he pushed up against the wall during the day. He leaned a handmade broom and basin against it, so that it wouldn't immediately draw any attention during a check. After the doctor's consultation hours in the evenings, when the doctor would lie down on his mattress in his office, exhausted, Wim grabbed his things in the closet, lay the straw mattress on the floor and pulled the door shut behind him. He could then sleep diagonally on the closet floor, his knees slightly pulled up. He hadn't lost his touch; it felt just like before. The only difference from the draughty house of his childhood was that instead of just one stepfather prowling around, here he had as many as thirty – every one of them so ruthless that his stepfather looked like a softy.

In the beginning, he was still awoken by the prisoners who lined up outside in order to be the first ones seen by the doctor. Sometimes that started at three o'clock. Wim then caught some snippets of their heated discussions with Albartus Dokter, but soon he slept through even this. His hiding place came in handy during daytime checks as well. Whenever a Kapo showed up, he crawled between the straw sack and the wooden wall, keeping out of sight in the dim closet.

During Wim's first week, the barracks that bordered onto the *Revier* had been added to the infirmary. It was the first of a whole series. They'd now been in the concentration camp for six weeks and every week a barracks was converted. The number of sick cases rose alarmingly and prisoners would sometimes simply fall dead during roll call or at work, withered and emptied. It was hard work for Thygesen. The strain on the benevolent doctor's mental resilience was immense.

The conditions in the infirmary worsened even further. Patients lay two or three to a bunk, three bunks on top of one another. Because virtually all of their fat and muscles had disappeared from their bones, these almost poked through their skin. In order to fit themselves in with three in a bunk, they had no choice but to sleep on their sides, which in no time led to sores and open wounds that in turn became infected, kept festering and only grew bigger. A large portion of the prisoners suffered from a severe form of diarrhoea. At the front of the infirmary barracks near the entrance door were large oil drums that served as toilets, because the distance to the latrines was too great for these human wrecks. Patients were so weak that they couldn't leave their bunks more than about ten times in a day and as a result, they just let everything run, sometimes without even realising it themselves. The wounds of the men next to and below them became infected in no time, with deadly blood poisoning or cellulitis as a consequence.

In these difficult conditions, Wim handed out the food and tried to keep everything a little clean with a besom. Now and then, he pretended not to see when someone took a portion of food that was actually intended for their neighbour, who hadn't moved for some time. The stench was soon so unbearable that the corpse was pushed out into the aisle. This happened, on average, three or four times a night. The next morning, prisoners from the corpse *Kommando* would carry them to the morgue or to the pile by one of the latrines, right next to the spot where everyone was supposed to wash themselves and use the toilet.

Through the infirmary window, Wim watched multiple times a week as a farm boy would ride along the camp street on a flat cart and stop his horse twice, once in front of the toilets and then the morgue. In the absence of coffins, the corpses were sheathed in paper sacks and laid head to toe on the cart. If it then rained, the sacks would rip and often body parts hung over the cart's edges. The farm boy sat huddled in his seat and had the horse set off at a walk. Six prisoners carrying shovels on their shoulders and a guard would follow out of the gate and only come back hours later. Wim heard from the doctor that the corpses ended up in a mass grave in Husum's public cemetery.

Every morning, before the work details set out, the camp leadership addressed the Kapos and foremen. Usually, it was about the disappointing number of metres of tank traps that had been dug the previous day and they demanded a higher output. The Kapos were held responsible. The prisoners would need to dig even quicker. If this couldn't be done the easy way, then it would have to be done the hard way. And if these Kapos couldn't manage it, they would have to lose their armbands and special caps and dig themselves. Other prisoners were itching to take their place. The SS couldn't be responsible for what would happen to these Kapos once they lost their protective status and had to rejoin the ordinary prisoners. That meant at night too. After a speech like that, the batons swung harder than ever.

It was by now the start of November 1944 and – unbeknown to Wim – a little more than 500 kilometres to the south, the Americans had just captured Aachen, the first

major German city to fall into Allied hands, while from
the east the Red Army was marching into East Prussia. In
Husum, the food was rationed even further to just one slice
of bread a day and, if that was possible, even thinner soup.
It was Griem's pocket that benefitted the most. During the
day, after the work gangs had set off, Wim watched as platters
full of steaming potatoes were brought from the cookhouse
to the farmers in the surrounding area. Griem had done a
bit of business with them and was now filling his own bank
account, rather than the stomachs of the starving men. After
Wim had drawn this to Thygesen's attention, the doctor
almost exploded with pent-up rage. He was enormously
frustrated, since how could he ever say anything about this
and hope to get off with his life?

Still, he took his chances when Griem was back in Husum
and the doctor spotted him walking past the infirmary.
Humbly, he asked the *SS-Untersturmführer* if he could speak
with him for a moment. This was already at the limit of per-
missibility and it was only because he was a qualified doctor
and belonged, as a Dane, to the Aryan race that Griem came
to listen to what he had to say. For once, he seemed to be
fairly sober. Wim had taken cover in the broom closet and
pressed his ear to the wooden wall.

'*Herr Kommandant.* May I please ask you something? Given
the many sick and the many dead – would it not be possible to do something about the food? The prisoners would
then also be able to work harder during the day and that's to
everyone's benefit, including the German Reich's.'

Griem looked at the doctor in silence and then said: 'The
prisoners who cannot be kept alive here do not have the right

to exist in the new Europe and whether they die now or later makes little difference. This is not a care centre and I will simply order new prisoner material. Do not bother me any more with your misguided humanitarian delusions.'

He turned on his heel and strode the fifty metres to the main SS residence, where he gave Klinger instructions.

At six o'clock the next morning two Kapos, one being The Extractor, tore through the infirmary barracks. Everyone had to get out of bed and stand outside for a special roll call, no matter what their condition. Those who didn't get up were beaten out of their beds. The men who couldn't move were half-dead anyway. Thygesen rushed over and made it clear to the Kapos that all of these patients had been examined by him and were in possession of a sick note. They couldn't work. The Kapos didn't even listen. The dangerously sick prisoners hung from one another's shoulders in misery on the roll–call square.

Wim watched in horror as they were forced to show their wounds to Klinger, who was standing with a grin on his face in front of the group. Suddenly, the *Rottenführer* started ruthlessly beating their wounds with his truncheon and even jabbing into them. Blood and pus squirted out in every direction.

'What do you mean you can't? Everybody can work. Either you're dead or you work!' Klinger shouted. Moaning from the pain, the sick and wounded prisoners were driven to the camp's exit and put on a transport to Ladelund to continue digging in the marshland there and so contribute to the German Reich's victory.

★

Temperatures outside were dropping quickly and the number of sick cases continued to rise. Three barracks were fully occupied already. The provisional gauze had run out and was replaced by a kind of tissue paper the doctor would wrap around the wound and stick together with a lump of flour. Together with the pot of cod-liver oil ointment, it was the only thing they still had for the patients.

The camp leadership rarely passed requests for medication on to the local pharmacy. Whenever something, for a change, was delivered, it landed in the hands of the SS. Liquid disinfectant was particularly popular with them, though not for disinfecting wounds. Thygesen was in dire need of it, but most of the time they saw the SS men, a few hours after a package had been delivered, staggering through the camp, their words slurred.

Sporadically, their tormentors too needed medical care. That presented opportunities. One evening, kitchen Kapo Müller showed up at the consultation room with a wound on his shin. Thygesen was doing paperwork in his office and called Wim.

'I do have something for that,' he said after having a look at the wound. He rubbed a thick glob of cod-liver oil ointment on it and bound it with tissue paper. 'This is to help it heal properly,' he said with the confidence of someone who had studied medicine for years. 'Leave it on there for a few days and then come back for a check-up.'

The Kapo's face showed great relief. Wim made a gesture with his fingers to his mouth and asked: 'What's the deal with the food?'

'Early tomorrow morning, six o'clock, come to the back of the kitchen,' Müller said, 'and knock on the shutter.'

The next morning, Wim got two thick marmalade sandwiches shoved into his hands.

One cold evening in November, he took an envelope containing lists to the *Lagerschreiber*, the camp administrator, for Doctor Thygesen. He'd handed it over and was shutting the door gently behind him, when a cat flew out of the SS cafeteria and up the long, empty hallway. Wim made an enticing sound and kneeled down. The animal was only too happy to walk over to Wim and let him stroke its back for a while. The cat nudged him a few times in return. From what he could feel, there was more meat on the thing than you'd have expected by just looking at it. In one motion, he grabbed the animal by the scruff of its neck and shoved it underneath his jacket.

He carefully walked further. He still needed to pass the door to a room full of SS and knew he was done for if they figured him out. A metre or two before he reached the door, he saw its handle turn. Lightning quick, he threw the cat in the direction of the *Lagerschreiber*'s office. Not a second later, Klinger appeared in the cafeteria doorway. Wim stood with his back to the wall, took his cap off and confidently stared out in front of him. Klinger didn't deign to look at him. Wim put his cap back on, by all appearances unmoved, and strolled towards the building's exit, though he felt as if the whole camp could hear his heart pounding. His breath turned to clouds of vapour in the frigid air outside. Before going back to the *Revier*, he made a lap through the camp, to bring his adrenaline levels back down.

During his absence, a huge line of patients had formed at the door to the *Revier*. A train had come in from Neuengamme with a new supply of *Häftlingsmaterial*, prisoner fodder, as Griem used to call them. Doctor Thygesen and Wim knew within ten minutes that these weren't new prisoners. They were seeing the same sick people they'd sent to the main camp, because their chances of being able to work again were zero. Now, they were back and in even worse condition because they'd made that miserable train trip twice without any further care. The majority could go straight into the infirmary barracks, but these were already overcrowded. They would just have to save themselves that night and Thygesen would try to free up a fifth barracks in the morning.

'I have a bad feeling about this,' he said to Wim after he'd examined the last patient at around eleven o'clock. 'A really bad feeling. Almost every one of them has dysentery, at least half have bloated legs, indicating oedema, but even worse: I think there might be TB cases among them.'

Wim was handed a list of nine names that Thygesen wanted to put in barracks number four. They would try to make a partition with blankets, so as to prevent further infection. Wim got to work and the critically sick patients followed his instructions without a grumble. After he was done, he washed his hands even more thoroughly than usual and used a double helping of the extremely precious liquid disinfectant the doctor had given him.

The next day, Thygesen was indeed able to set up a fifth barracks, which meant as few sick prisoners as possible stayed in the barracks with the suspected TB cases. The news that there were possible cases of the disease spread throughout the camp, with the benefit that for the time being, no SS guard, Kapo or *Blockälteste* dared to go into the infirmary.

They lacked the means to test for the disease, so Thygesen could do little else than trust his medical knowledge and intuition. Wim dived back into the infirmary barracks and did his best to make whatever life the patients still had left to live as pleasant as possible. He also told all of the new dysentery cases that there was only one way to save themselves: to stop eating for four or five days in order to halt their bowel movements and so prevent themselves from bleeding to death.

To convince starving, sick prisoners that they shouldn't eat for days was an almost impossible challenge for the doctor and his helpers. It required a heroic self-control that few patients could muster. Many of the straw mattresses grew redder and redder for days on end until that, too, stopped and the lifeless body was worked over the edge by its neighbour. All Wim could offer them against diarrhoea were pieces of wood charcoal, which he took from the stove in the consultation room on a daily basis with permission from the doctor.

The doctor also used the stove for disinfection. It happened quite regularly that abscesses needed to be cut open so as to prevent blood poisoning. Sedating the patient was impossible, so a few men were drummed up who still possessed some kind of muscle strength. They held the victim down on the writing desk, which doubled as an operating table. Thygesen would wash an old, sharpened straight razor in a tray with water and hold it, a wet towel wrapped around the handle, for half a minute on either side over a wood fire until it was glowing red. He then cut the wound open and, if the patient was lucky, they fainted from the pain. When they regained consciousness a short while later, the wound was already wrapped in tissue paper and they could lay for a while in a bunk to themselves. The luxury never lasted for more than a few hours. With this medieval treatment, Thygesen saved the lives of countless prisoners.

Wim had his own issues with his left leg. An infection in his knee, thought Thygesen. There was nothing to do except hope it would go away on its own. Besides that, he had small wounds on both legs. Wim rubbed the same ointment onto them that he had used for hundreds of others. If anything, they didn't get worse. He managed to keep his weight at around forty kilos. His knee and wounds stayed the same. By keeping busy every day and making himself useful, he held his sights on the future, no matter how miserable the circumstances.

Thygesen let him carry out more small medical procedures, usually with satisfactory results. Even the *Lagerälteste*'s secretary landed in the chair with Wim for his clogged ear. Thygesen gave Wim a makeshift syringe to rinse out the ear and that went brilliantly. He was dumbfounded by his own abilities. The patient gave him a piece of bread with sausage as thanks. That's how Wim scraped together just enough food to stay alive. Within the camp he heard the horror stories about Russians slurping up their puking fellow prisoners' stomach contents from the ground, but he tried to block them out as much as possible. Just as he did the stories about sorry prisoners being forced to spend the whole day crowing like a rooster on the fire hydrant until falling to the ground literally dead from exhaustion. His world was mainly limited to the consultation room, the attached office, the infirmary barracks and the broom closet.

Jean, who had given him the tip about the job in the *Revier*, was now lying with severe dysentery in the first barracks, where Wim took him something extra to eat from time to time. Jean told him the camp cat hadn't survived in the end. It was only good that Wim hadn't been caught at the SS barracks that time, since the animal had belonged to *Blockführer* Georges, a man from the Elzas. Two French prisoners had been shirking the *Kommando* and lying flat on their stomachs under a bed when they overheard Georges talking about his pet with a colleague. After they found out where he kept it hidden, the fat creature was no longer safe. At the first opportunity they had, they snapped its neck, gutted it and roasted it on the pot-bellied stove in the barracks where they were hiding. Not a single bone was left and the SS guard searched for his cat for days.

17

No food, no doctor

Husum, November 1944 –
Neuengamme, December 1944

Thygesen had been ordered to prepare a report for the camp management with a run-down of all the sick cases and an estimate of how long it would take before each patient could return to work. A few days earlier, another train with severe cases had been sent to Neuengamme and multiple transports had also come back to Husum from Ladelund. There were now about a thousand prisoners left and it was clear the camp leadership was deeply worried about the progress on the anti-tank traps. They were two weeks past the six Griem had originally promised to the Nazi leadership and the work's end was still not in sight.

The doctor walked with Wim and a few other helpers through the infirmary's five barracks, a piece of paper and pencil in his hand. On most days, Thygesen hardly showed his face here and didn't know what was wrong with many of the patients. Because Wim and his colleagues wandered among them daily, they could provide the doctor with extra information where needed.

The tour took nearly all morning. The doctor went to

work out the lists back at his office. He asked Wim to walk with a French pastor, himself also a prisoner, to one of the Frenchmen in the infirmary. The man was dying and had asked for the last rites.

After coming back, Wim found the doctor sunk in thought, his head in his hands and the report in front of him on the table. Thygesen pushed the list towards him in silence:

Arbeitslager Husum, 25.11.1944
The Revier currently holds 734 sick prisoners.
Specifications:

I Bowel diseases: 125
1) 45 severe cases of bloodied diarrhoea, from which one presently cannot expect recovery and for a large portion of whom it may not at all be expected that they are curable.
2) 80 average-to-severe cases of general diarrhoea, from which recovery is possible between two weeks and a month. (Many prisoners with less severe diarrhoea are working in the Kommando.)

II Other internal diseases: 139
1)
12 Cases of lung infection
6 Cases of pleurisy
6 Cases of bladder and kidney infection
4 Cases of kidney infection
11 Patients likely suffering from heart disease
2 Cases of rheumatic fever
3 Cases of gastric ulcers
9 Cases of facial erysipelas

1 Case of gall bladder infection

1 Case of vein inflammation

4 Cases of diphtheria

6 Patients likely with tuberculosis

9 Patients with severe oedema

2)

35 Cases of general weakness and emaciation – not at all able to work

30 Cases of general fever. These patients are likely to be able to work again in the course of fourteen days.

In addition, there are numerous cases of general rheumatism and many cases of oral mucosal inflammation, likely caused by vitamin deficiencies. All of them are working in the Kommando.

III Open wounds: 470

1) 242 Severe cases of soft tissue infection, abscesses, deep festering wounds, etc., who, for the time being, should not under any circumstances work and of whom a large portion will die.

2) 228 Cases of lighter wound issues, of whom a portion will possibly be able to work again after fourteen days of rest and wound treatment.

To date, 188 deaths have been recorded.

At the crack of dawn the next morning, just around the corner from the first infirmary barracks, something occurred that, despite its miserable end, at least gave them all a laugh. The report that Thygesen had turned in naturally hadn't pleased Griem and his henchmen. Thygesen wondered whether it would actually be passed on to Griem's superiors or disappear into his desk drawer. In any case, there were far too few prisoners at roll call to set off with the outside *Kommando*. The SS hit upon the idea of supplementing them with prisoners from the infirmary, but fearing infection themselves, they sent the Kapos in. Wim quickly hid himself in the broom closet. Within no time, they'd swept the five barracks clean and directed everyone who could still walk to roll call. The Kapo with a face like a clothes iron shouted that they all had to strip. They were standing there naked, extremely sick and underfed, shivering in the winter cold and waiting for what the SS now had in store for them. One of the guards asked the patients what was wrong with them and parroted their answers.

'I have a fever,' said the first one.

'I have a fever too,' said the SS man. He pointed to the pile of clothes on the ground next to the patient-prisoners and to the gate: 'Clothes on and get to work.'

He went through all of them like this until he reached an ascetic-looking Danish inmate, one of the oldest in the camp. The man had been a teacher and spoke multiple languages fluently.

'And what's wrong with you?'

Without batting an eyelid, he answered: '*Ich bin ein Idiot.*' 'I am an idiot.'

Without thinking, the guard started parroting back '*Ich bin auch ein Idi . . .*' before finally catching on that he was being made a fool of. He exploded with rage, while the other prisoners did everything they could to avoid bursting into laughter.

'*Fünfundzwanzig am Arsch!*' 'Twenty-five lashes!' he bellowed.

Two Kapos set the vaulting horse ready and the Dane had to hang over it on his belly. The clothes iron Kapo gave him twenty-five lashes with a riding crop on his back and rear end. The man had to count them out himself. After just the first five, his back was ripped open and by the end, only his mouth still moved, making barely a sound. He was helped up by a few friends, completely covered in blood and more dead than alive, and ordered by the Kapo to join the *Kommando*.

In passing, he softly said to his friends: 'His temper seems to be getting the better of him.' He pointed with his eyes to the SS guard. It was a miracle, but the Dane came back alive that evening. He was given a hero's welcome.

With seven hundred prisoners admitted, the situation in the *Revier* had become so acute that on 4 December, a transport was sent to Neuengamme again, this time with another three hundred sick men on board. They now had some more space, but it was only a matter of time before it would be just as overcrowded again. Wim wondered how the Germans were ever expecting to finish that damned Frisian Wall this way. When he'd first arrived in the camp, they'd still been reasonably fresh and healthy and with eleven hundred men. Now, a group of three hundred utterly emaciated and sick prisoners went to work each morning, only to come back with another four, five or more corpses. This could never go on for long. The farm boy on the cart slowly rode out of the camp at least three times a week with a full load of paper sacks. The remaining prisoners had lost their minds and now robbed and stole from one another. It had become extremely dangerous to save a piece of bread for the next day, because it was highly likely that you'd be beaten up during the night by thieving fellow prisoners. The general sleeping Blocks had descended into total anarchy. Even the *Blockälteste* and the *Stubendienst* had lost control over them.

In the camp's underground economy, everything was expressed in cigarettes, the most popular medium of exchange. They were scarce and sought-after but still sufficiently available. If you had them, it wasn't hard to get extra bread, sausage or warm clothing. A thin sweater cost you five cigarettes and a warm one seven. Every once in a while, a new supply would arrive in packages from the Red Cross, which also contained food. Only the Danes and Norwegians received these with any regularity. The Dutch Red Cross didn't send anything to Neuengamme or its satellite camps, as it focused itself exclusively on military prisoners of war.

Anyone who had cigarettes traded them as soon as they could for something to eat. This led to an incident that had the whole camp talking in horror and even found its way into the infirmary barracks. Two Frenchmen and a Pole had been exempted from working in the outside *Kommando* and had been ordered to clean the toilets and washing facilities. You could ask yourself where they were better off. They complained bitterly to one another about the dirty work but above all about how hungry they were. One of the Frenchmen still had a few cigarettes and told his compatriot he was planning to swap them for something edible. The Polish prisoner pricked up his ears when he heard the word cigarette and made them a proposal. His best friend worked in the SS kitchen and very occasionally smuggled some meat out.

That was, of course, strictly forbidden and incredibly dangerous, but he could sound out his friend to see whether he was open to a trade. The Frenchman nodded and half an hour later, the Pole came back with good news. That night he would bring the Frenchmen a piece of meat in exchange for the cigarettes.

The three men met each other at the agreed-upon spot, behind the tailors' and shoemakers' workshops, about fifteen metres from the latrine with the piled corpses. They looked onto the doctor's consulting room, on the other side of the camp street. There was no light inside. Nearly the entire camp was shrouded in darkness. The only light was a sliver that came from the cookhouse window, allowing them to see where they were walking. In the watchtower at the very back of the camp, they spotted a cigarette glowing red now and then.

The howling wind made it freezing cold outside and a thin layer of drifting snow covered the sandy yard. The men shivered from the cold and from suspense too. The Pole handed them a packet, wrapped in paper, and received the cigarettes. They didn't exchange a word. Then he disappeared into the night.

The Frenchmen opened the packet in a hurry. They found, as they had agreed, two small pieces of meat. Liver, by the looks of it. As they were starving and had no means of cooking them, they each dug into their portions and within several minutes, they'd taken the edge off their hunger.

The next day they saw each other again while cleaning the latrines. This time another Pole had joined them. The Frenchman who had traded the cigarettes made it clear to his trading partner that the pieces of meat had been awfully small. The Pole laughed it off and went back to whispering with his compatriot, after which the Frenchman kept insisting and started arguing. The Pole then said he'd never had a friend working in the kitchen. Just as they were about to come to blows, he opened the door on the side of the latrine. He pointed to a half cut-open corpse, draped over a pile of bodies.

'Look at what you ate.'

The remains of a roughly cut-out liver hung from a gaping wound.

The prisoners who could no longer muster the effort to look after themselves, who had stopped washing themselves and let themselves become filthy, were mentally already at death's door. That's why Wim washed himself thoroughly every morning, despite the cold, and took care of his clothes as best he could. He would trade a piece of bread to have a tailor repair holes and tears. He'd been able to take over a pair of shoes from a dead Dane that were still in reasonable condition.

It grew colder and colder and not a day went by without it raining or snowing. As December wore on, more and more of the general barracks were added to the *Revier* until even the last barracks, the eighth, was designated as an infirmary.

The powerlessness and frustration were becoming too much for Thygesen. He sometimes lay for a few days on his mattress apathetically staring into space and trying to get his thoughts in order. He himself had recently caught a few cuffs from Griem only for saying that a group of older prisoners and men with large, open wounds could in no way work in the anti-tank trenches. Griem had accused him of sabotage and said he was trying to deprive the German Reich of man-power. The camp commandant had threatened to have him join them in the trenches.

And then, on the morning of 21 December, the remaining prisoners didn't have to stand at roll call in the dead of night and march out a few hours later. Seven o'clock then eight o'clock passed and still nothing happened. It was around nine o'clock when finally the Kapos stormed the barracks with a lot of noise and everyone, sick or not, had to get out of bed and line up in rows of five. They put their caps on and took them off and directed their eyes to the left and right one last time. It was a surreal sight. The prisoners who were mortally sick clung to one another in little pathetic piles in the yard, their bones held together only by a piece of shriv-elled skin. Their clothes hung like wet potato sacks around their skeletal figures. Within half an hour, the command 'Abmarschieren' 'March out' sounded. The whole company moved itself slowly in the direction of the railway track. It took several hours before everyone had been lifted into the wagons and found a spot. The Kapos could rant and rave as much as they liked, but it didn't have any effect on the men, beaten numb as they were. Only a small clean-up crew stayed behind.

Wim had found a spot in the next to last wagon and like everyone else was sitting with his knees pulled up behind the prisoner in front of him. No one was able to lie down and those with rotting leg wounds suffered terrible pain in this position. The guards were more comfortable, sitting between the two sections of prisoners with a thick bundle of straw under their backsides.

The train left around noon and arrived at Neuengamme's railway yard forty hours later.

The camp orchestra had struck up 'Alte Kameraden' – as they would on many such occasions – a lively German marching song that only heightened the prisoners' torture. By now, the SS men of the reception committee had seen just about everything, but there was little honour to reap from this collection of human wrecks. The majority had to be helped out of the train and could no longer stand on their own legs. The Kapos sent an unsuspecting group of French hostages into the wagon. They encountered conditions that went far beyond the imaginable. Dozens of corpses had been hung by their clothes on hooks along the walls so that the living could have a little more room to move.

One of the hooks held Albartus Dokter, with his skull bashed in. He'd stepped into the wagon the picture of health, but when he'd fallen asleep it had all happened very fast. For months he'd been exploiting his position at the *Revier* door. You'd had no chance of being let in without a piece of bread he thought was big enough and, preferably, a few cigarettes thrown in. Blood might have been flowing from your mouth or anus, you might have been dying right in front of him – it didn't matter: no food, no doctor.

There hadn't been any buckets on board the trains. Nearly all of the prisoners were covered in urine and excrement and the stench was unbearable. Wim only regained con-sciousness as he was standing naked on the roll-call square in minus-ten-degree weather. The new load was being sorted by SS doctors, led by camp commandant Pauly. The severest cases were allowed to continue, for so-called recovery, on a transport to what the SS cynically dubbed 'Recreation Camp Bergen-Belsen'. Another portion, sick but not yet completely emaciated, was admitted to Neuengamme's *Revier*. The group that wasn't critically sick but still too weak to work outside was assigned to the *Schonungskommando*, a kind of indoor labour camp where they were meant to convalesce.

It was now time to take stock of the three months at satellite camp Husum-Schwesing: 297 prisoners had died on site. Eighty per cent of them were Dutch. The vast majority had ended up in a mass grave at the back of Husum's cemetery. Sheathed in just a paper sack. Dozens more had died on the journey to Neuengamme. Roughly seven hundred and fifty prisoners had returned to the main camp dangerously sick. Many of them would die in the days, weeks and months afterwards.

And the Frisian Wall? In the months of November and December 1944, the Nazi high command came to the conclusion that its actual strategic value was too minor to have it completed. The whole operation was called off. Many of the sections weren't even half finished. The planned fourteen kilometre stretch in Husum was nevertheless the only section to be completed. Griem received compliments and was rewarded with the command of a number of satellite camps in the area surrounding Meppen.

After the war, it turned out that the Allies had never even considered carrying out an invasion of northern Germany similar to the one in Normandy. The Wadden Sea was completely unsuited and the swampy marshland in East Friesland wouldn't have been able to support their tanks and other heavy material. They'd have sunk into the mud before even reaching the first trap.

18

Back in Neuengamme

Neuengamme, December 1944

Adolf Hitler had big plans for Hamburg. He'd already visited the Free and Hanseatic City on the banks of the Elbe
in 1935. Together with its mayor, Carl Vincent Krogmann,
he'd made a trip by boat along the Elbe and become en-
thusiastic about the city's future prospects. Hitler had even
personally designated Hamburg as one of the Third Reich's
five 'Führer Cities'. Berlin was supposed to become the new
world capital of Germania. Linz, in Upper Austria, where
he'd spent a large part of his childhood, was going to be the
cultural capital. Munich would be capital of the Nazi movement and Nuremberg the city where the Reich's NSDAP
party conventions would be held.

Hitler ordered his chief architect Albert Speer to develop
plans for the new Hamburg as '*Tor zur Welt*', or 'Gateway to
the World'. Thinking small wasn't a term in his vocabulary.
In 1937, Speer presented megalomaniacal plans for the Hamburg of 1965, set out in a mock-up of the new riverbank that
was to be a model for the new centre of German shipping.
The suspension bridge over the Elbe, with a span of seven
hundred and fifty metres and a height of a hundred and eighty

metres, would be the largest in the world and overshadow the recently opened Golden Gate Bridge. Hamburg's entire road network would need to be redirected and renovated.

The *Gauhaus*, the local NSDAP headquarters, was to be two hundred and fifty metres tall. The *Volkshalle*, the people's hall, was designed to hold fifty thousand visitors, next to a parade square for another eighty-five thousand. The old fishermen's port was to give way to a new presentable harbour promenade, where the ships belonging to the National Socialist leisure movement *Kraft durch Freude*, 'Strength Through Joy', could moor. The costs were estimated at 1.6 billion Reichsmarks, 1.3 billion of which the city was supposed to cough up itself.

In April 1939, the urban planner Konstanty Gutschow was appointed as *Architekt des Elbeufers* 'Architect of the Banks of the Elbe', to realise these plans. He diligently got to work and developed city plans for what were intended to be the most iconic structures. The SS helped him to source the tremendous amounts of construction materials that were needed. In 1938, under his company name Deutsche Erd- und Steinwerke GmbH, he'd bought four hundred thousand square metres of ground from the city of Hamburg, close to the small village of Neuengamme. On it was an old stone factory, shut for years already, where clinker bricks, so typical for northern Germany, had once been made. In particular, the seemingly inexhaustible supply of suitable clay ground made the location interesting.

The first forced labourers were taken to Neuengamme from concentration camp Sachsenhausen, near Berlin. Production was slowly started up again but would fall far short of meeting the immense demand once the projects' construction began.

That changed with a visit by *Reichsführer-SS* Heinrich Himmler in January of 1940. Within a few months, Hamburg's administration closed a deal with the SS venture for the construction of a new and ultra-modern stone factory, the most advanced of its kind in Europe, good for a yearly output of a minimum of twenty million stones, with the possibility of up to even forty million. The city invested a million Reichsmarks and would bear responsibility for a suitable infrastructure, including a canal from the Dove Elbe, a tributary of the river, to the stone factory and a harbour on its premises.

The SS committed themselves to supplying enough cheap labour, meaning prisoners, and their supervision by an *SS-Totenkopf* regiment. They rented out the inmates for four to six Reichsmarks per day. Neuengamme became an independent concentration camp.

In the years that followed, the prisoners were increasingly rented out to commercial and private companies, which in several cases established themselves on the camp premises itself. That's how, in 1944, the weapons factory Walther produced twenty thousand guns a month for the German army on the north side of the camp. No fewer than a thousand prisoners were put to work there. Outside the camp, inmates worked for companies such as Krupp, Continental, Volkswagen, Varta and Borgward.

The prisoners who were lucky ended up in a dry, heated factory, where they still had to work hard but at least had a roof over their heads and sometimes got an extra slice of bread. The less lucky ones ended up in one of the roughly ninety satellite camps of the largest concentration camp in northern Germany, or in one of the many city *Kommandos*. The latter were dreaded among the prisoners, since they then had to help rescue victims of Allied aerial bombings in Hamburg's city centre and clear away rubble, which was extremely dangerous because of dud bombs and the risk of building collapse. During new attacks, they were forced to keep working while the SS trained their guns on them from where they themselves were taking cover.

The stone factory's output depended on a sufficient supply of clay, which was dug up by hand in the surrounding area. Roughly six hundred prisoners, dressed in thin, striped uniforms or old rags, would stand up to their knees in mud and water the whole day, shovelling the heavy clay into rail carts, while the Kapos hounded them with truncheons and riding crops. They struggled to push the filled carts along the loose narrow-gauge track to the factory entrance. Even with five or six men, they were barely able to get the colossus moving. And once it started rolling, it constantly threatened to derail. An ideal reason for the guards to lay into them.

Near the stone factory's ramp, the cart could be lifted with a winch – that is, if the Kapos didn't choose the alternative method and force the prisoners to push the cart, which weighed a few tonnes, up the ramp themselves. All it took was a moment's inattention for the cart to come right back down just as quickly, straight over the bodies of the prisoners who had fallen on the ground and couldn't get away in time.

Once the bricks were fired, a whole other form of forced labour began: the loading by hand of the flat barges that were waiting in the harbour mouth, also dug by prisoners. The only way to get the heavy stones on board was across a small gangway that frequently became slippery from the mud, snow and ice. With kilos of bricks in their arms, the power-less skin-and-bones prisoners then also had to dodge the Kapos' blows and lashes, as their work was always too slow. Their terrorisers' ultimate goal was, of course, to make a poor wretch fall from the gangway, smack into the icy water. That person would then get an extra punishment for wasting a load of bricks and had to carry on working for the rest of the day in his wet get-up in temperatures far below zero. For a prisoner, a few weeks in the clay *Kommando* at Neuengamme meant almost certain death.

Inmates who were as good as on their last legs, but not far enough along to look forward to a highly likely and usually slow death in the *Revier*, were assigned to a *Schonungs-kommando*. There, hundreds carried out handwork in the basement of a newly built stone barracks for ten to twelve hours a day. Weaving camouflage nets from leftover scraps of fabric and old car tyres was one of the most common tasks. Others had to peel potatoes for the whole day.

The basement was dark and stuffy, and stank terribly be-cause of the lack of ventilation and the body odours of the many men who were packed on top of one another. But at least it was dry and if you were lucky, you could do your work sitting.

Wim was assigned to the *Schonungskommando*. He staggered with the rest of the group to his barracks. The rags he'd been given might have been dirty and he could only guess at how many prisoners had worn them before him, but they were warmer than the striped pyjamas.

The snow reached their ankles as they walked across the empty roll-call square in the direction of as many as eight or nine large wooden barracks, which formed a neat row and were each roughly eight metres wide and at least fifty metres deep. Again, every Block consisted of two sections, each with its own number. Stepping out of the train wagon, Wim had immediately noticed that pungent, nauseating smell and the closer he got to the barracks, the more penetrating the stench became.

It was six o'clock in the morning, though under the flood-lights it could have been the middle of the day. The icy wind was blowing exactly in their direction and, even at this early hour, the crematoriums were already burning at full capacity. They stopped at barracks number six. The Kapo understood there was little point in taking roll call an extra time. He handed the group over to the *Blockälteste*, who immediately bellowed '*Ausziehen und waschen!*' 'Undress and wash!' Despite the cold, it was the most welcome order Wim could have been given; he felt so dirty and miserable.

In the middle of the large barracks was a row of zinc sinks. For every two prisoners they were given a small piece of soap. They would have to dry themselves with their own shirts. The ice-cold water took Wim's breath away but immediately made him alert enough to see that he needed to steer clear of the new *Blockälteste*. A small, flabby man with a large green triangle on his coat and a grimace like the kind Wim had seen in a movie about the criminal underworld a long time ago. Judging by the man's figure, he wasn't going without. He yelled his commands in German, but Wim detected a Dutch accent.

On their first day back in Neuengamme, they were allowed to stay in their barracks to recover. It may have been one of the camp leadership's few remotely humane moments. Or was it because the number of available newcomers needed to be counted and categorised before a make-up could be prepared for the work details in the different *Schonungsblocks*? It made little difference to Wim. He was still here, he had survived the hell of Husum and was dead set on not giving in at Neuengamme either. It helped a little that in this Block they could sleep with only two men to a bunk. As these were just sixty-five centimetres wide, this was still no luxury, but Gait, the young Dutchman from Drenthe with whom he shared his bunk, couldn't have been heavier than thirty-five kilos, just like himself. Lying head to toe, with two such underfed bodies next to each other, it all just barely worked.

Gait told him that he, too, had tried escaping the mandatory *Arbeitseinsatz*. His father needed him on the farm, but the local *Landwachters* had seen things differently. Wim told him how he'd wound up in Neuengamme and how he'd fared in Husum.

After half a day in his bunk, Wim felt strong enough again to check out what was going on outside. Just as he was about to walk to the barracks' door, the *Stubendienst* turned up with the afternoon meal. To his surprise, everyone in the *Schonungsblock* got a *Zulage*, a supplementary ration of two thin slices of white bread with a sliver of sausage. Not something that would immediately be putting kilos back onto him, but a world of difference to the situation in Husum.

Wim, who hadn't gone further than the quarantine block during his previous stay in Neuengamme, now saw what a massive area the roll-call square occupied. The eight wooden barracks had been built side by side, their narrow faces opening onto it. On either side were stone barracks that looked recently built. On the far side stood three hospital barracks; entire groups of prisoners from Husum had been brought there that morning as well.

Not only had double barbed wire fences, nearly three metres high, been raised around the camp, but the area outside them was also patrolled by armed SS guards with German shepherd dogs. There were a lot more watchtowers than he'd been able to see from the quarantine block. At least seven or eight, and not just at the camp's corners, but also far beyond them, equipped with large searchlights and machine-gun mounts. You'd have to be clever as hell to escape this place. Wim immediately pushed the thought from his head. Surviving would be hard enough, but trying to escape was pure suicide here too.

Towards evening, the first *Kommandos* came back from their back-breaking work in the clay, fields and factories. For a moment, just for a moment, it had looked as if he'd landed in a more humane world. But when he saw how the SS guards and the Kapos pitched into the exhausted prisoners, he understood it had been an illusion to think that things here went any differently than in Husum. The main motto 'Vernichtung durch Arbeit' was practised on a daily basis. Corpses were carted off, sadistic guards beat prisoners to mush and it was the same shouting and bellowing as always. From a distance you could hear the camp orchestra and for once they were playing that damned 'Alte Kameraden' again.

On his second day, Wim was introduced to his new work-place. You woke up at five o'clock and if you didn't get out of your bunk quickly enough, the fat, lazy Kapo showed up, baton in hand. His name was Felix and the prisoners called him 'Van Vught', as he'd been active at Vught concentration camp in the Netherlands before coming here. He was known for being barbaric and sadistic, completely irrational in his behaviour and unpredictable in his actions. It was the day before Christmas, but he couldn't care less. As long as he could swing his truncheon.

At roll call, Wim was standing neatly in line, as usual some-where in the middle of the group. To his left was a large Christmas tree, put there by a group of prisoners under the camp leadership's orders. They looked at the tree as though it were their great redeemer. Wim didn't like it, this kind of sentimental stuff. He saw it as one of the Nazis' conscious strategies. They were trying to weaken you, make you soft and sensitive. And when, consumed by homesickness, you exposed your weaknesses, they would be merciless.

After roll call, they went in quick time into the Schonungs-block's basement, where they had to make camouflage nets, shoulder to shoulder, with hundreds of prisoners at the same time. It was slow going. Near the end of the day, some of the prisoners undid everything they'd spent hours braiding

– sometimes to their regret, since the Kapos were unrelenting. Those who were caught were beaten. Brutally beaten. Still, there were prisoners who were prepared to take the risk. Many of them struggled with being responsible for camouflage nets intended to hide German artillery.

Wim pretended to work hard but, in reality, his fingers did little. Seated work was naturally a lot easier than digging ditches, but in the *Revier* at Husum he'd been free to move around. He'd spent all day trying to organise things that made his life in the camp easier, from extra food to a new straw mattress and from small personal belongings to warmer clothes. That was much harder here, though he would worry about it later. He first needed to regain some strength.

They stopped at five o'clock and within an hour and a half, roll call was done. The Kapos seemed to be hitting and screaming just a little less. Perhaps they were also thinking of home, like the more than twelve thousand other prisoners. How would things be there now? What were they doing in the heated and lighted homes of Denmark, Russia, France, Poland, Belgium and the Netherlands?

Wim was given two ladlefuls of swede soup in his metal bowl and a hunk of bread. He began eating, perched on the edge of his bed. Gait had already finished his dinner and started reminiscing about the tastiest meals his mother would be serving at home that day. But Wim refused to listen: 'That won't help you, Gait. It'll only make you weak – just like the SS want.'

Gait looked at him, not understanding. On that Christmas Eve in 1944, he had tears in his eyes.

★

Around nine o'clock that evening the *Stubendienst* ordered all of the prisoners out, to one side of the roll-call square, not far from the cookhouse. The large Christmas tree was standing there, adorned with some thrifty ornaments that had been on hand in the camp. Braided tissue paper served as streamers, blocks of wood wrapped in red cloth as Christmas baubles. From the other barracks, prisoners were streaming in as well, thousands at once.

Everyone was standing there with their own thoughts, their mood turning sentimental as these drifted home. To their parents, their wives or their children. Many let their tears flow. The swirling snowflakes completed the Christmas scene. No one felt the cold any more, the harsh easterly wind, the horrors, the hunger and the pain. For a moment, the thought of peace on earth and the memories of home overpowered everything.

From out of nowhere, he was suddenly there: Francis Akos, a young and incredibly gifted violinist from Hungary, his head shaved like the rest of them. He'd been given a violin from the *Effektenkammer* and slid the bow over the strings. The melody of 'Silent Night, Holy Night' filled the square. It cut straight through the men's souls; even the hardest prisoner broke. The men sang along, each in their own language, as if they'd become innocent little children again.

It was a tiny piece of happiness that wasn't allowed to last. Wim saw them coming. A large group of SS had let dozens of bloodthirsty dogs out of the kennels and frenzied them further with pistol shots into the air. All hell broke loose on the roll-call square. Thousands of people raced in every direction, searching in sheer panic for safety. Older and weaker prisoners were trampled, crushed by wooden sandals and beaten afterwards. Those who couldn't get away in time were bitten by the bloodhounds, who smelled their Christmas prey and ripped the clothes from the stragglers' bodies. For dozens of prisoners, this was to be the last Christmas Eve of their lives.

Outside the barracks' doors, the chaos was, if at all possible, even greater. Everyone was trying to get inside as quickly as they could. That is, five hundred men were all trying to wriggle their way through a single door at the same time, with wildly swinging SS men and a pack of bloodhounds at their backs. This led to another bloodbath. Only the strongest and sharpest got off unscathed. Wim was one of the first to make it into his bunk, where he lay shuddering.

After an hour or two, peace finally returned, but it was short-lived. *'Raustreten! Raustreten!'* 'Get out! Get out!' Van Vught shouted. Everyone now had to stand at roll call, but the counting was all wrong.

Amid the chaos, many prisoners hadn't reached their barracks in time. Some prisoners were carried off to the *Revier*, others lay in the morgue. They were forced to stand at attention for at least an hour and a half, the temperature fifteen degrees below freezing and the camp Christmas tree in the background. The guards, dressed in long, warm leather coats, looked on from a distance. It was past midnight when everyone was finally allowed back inside. Christmas 1944 had come. Finally, rest.

Half an hour later, the scene repeated itself, supposedly because prisoners were missing. Wim knew this was pure harassment by the camp leadership and obediently followed the commands. *'Mützen ab! Mützen auf! Augen richten links! Augen richten rechts!'* 'Caps off! Caps on! Eyes left! Eyes right!' After a hundred times, the guards still weren't satisfied. It was the middle of the night when their sadistic appetites were finally sated. Everyone returned to their bunks, broken.

A quarter of an hour later, Wim heard violin music coming from the barracks next to them. The *Blockälteste* had given Akos permission to continue playing. He played Christmas songs until his fingers gave out. His last piece was the 'Capriccio' by Fritz Kreisler. After the final notes had died away, prisoners sang Christmas songs in their native languages. Back in his own barracks, and as a former choir singer, Wim softly sang along, unnoticed.

The next day, the *Blockältesten* plucked the best singers from their barracks to sing at the SS Christmas party. They were celebrating with their wives and loved ones. The wine flowed freely and an abundance of exquisite dishes filled the tables. Dishes of which the singers could only dream.

Their mouths were watering, it all smelled so delicious, but after the last song they were driven back to their barracks without so much as a bite. There, all of the prisoners were given a cigarette as a Christmas gift. That meant food. Wim traded his cigarette for a piece of bread and shared it with his bunkmate Gait.

19

A close shave

Neuengamme, December 1944 – January 1945

In the *Schonungskommando* barracks, Wim had slowly but surely found his place. As long as he kept himself out of *Blockälteste* Felix's sight as much as possible, life there was bearable, though he did have to watch his step to make it safely through the nights. Russian prisoners regularly went scavenging and so to save food for the next morning was to put your life in danger – you were guaranteed to lose it. Prisoners who took that risk were regularly found in the mornings with their skulls bashed in. It was for the same reason that Wim kept his shoddy sandals on while sleeping, tied with a few extra strips around his feet. At the morning roll calls there were always a few unlucky prisoners forced to stand barefoot in the snow for two hours because they'd been robbed during the night.

Wim also never skipped a meal, no matter what they got to eat. Most of the time it was that same damned swede soup, but several days after his arrival in the *Schonungsblock*, they had a real feast of an evening meal. Offal, originally intended for animal food, had been thrown into it. In the soup were also a few pieces of fodder beetroot leaves, a welcome change.

Wim really needed this extra food, since his time in Husum had left its mark. Despite his iron will, he couldn't prevent himself from feeling sick and weak and losing even more weight in those first days. One evening, he went to his bunk after a long day of weaving nets in the basement utterly exhausted. He immediately fell into a deep, nearly comatose sleep. After a while, he thought he saw his coat being unbuttoned and a fellow prisoner writing his camp number on his chest with a thick marker. This was customary in the camp to make identifying the dead easier. He dreamed on, about a farm in Baarsdorpermeer and a walk with his sister, Jo, along a canal.

When he awoke the next morning, he felt reasonably well-rested. He no longer remembered whether everything he'd seen had been a dream or reality. He grabbed his worn towel and trudged to the washroom. Using a corner of the cloth, he washed his face. The cold water did him good. Just as he was about to button up his coat, his eyes fell on a black stripe on his chest. He now undid the button below it and saw '49019' written in large characters.

Whenever Wim didn't have to weave nets, he would wander through the camp and each day meet new people in the other barracks, most of them Dutch. There were people among them who had already spent three or four years in Neuengamme. They'd managed to secure jobs somewhere in the administration or in a *Kommando* that was less taxing and offered higher chances of survival. Often they'd had to fight hard for years to get to that position. One or two of them could tell him something more about the course of the war, but Wim had his doubts about whether they actually knew what the situation was or were just dreaming it up to impress him.

The oldest prisoner in the *Schonungsblock* next door, a middle-aged Dutchman from Brabant, told Wim the Germans had started a counteroffensive in the Ardennes. If the Allies could repel it, they'd be able to advance further with a renewed attack from the south. He'd heard this from another prisoner, who himself had overheard it from a pair of SS guards.

On New Year's Eve, a Belgian prisoner with two broken legs was brought into the *Revier* from the outside *Kommando Deutsche Werft*, the 'German shipyard' detail, which had been clearing away rubble in a shipyard used for building submarines. The Allies had dropped bombs with timers attached, allowing them to explode at the most unexpected moments. It was perilous work and that day even fatal. When the air raid siren had sounded, the SS guards had forced a group of three hundred prisoners to take cover in the basement of a nearby apartment building, while they themselves had dived into a concrete bunker. The building had suffered a direct hit and the basement had been devastated. Only twenty men had survived. The Belgian sitting in the *Revier* was now deaf and blind. He repeated his story over and over to a French doctor and couldn't hear that by now they'd understood. In that way, the whole hospital got to hear in graphic detail what had happened and not thirty minutes later, half the camp knew enough to talk about it. It was how concentration camp Neuengamme saw out the old year.

★

After the morning roll call, Wim walked with the few hundred men of the *Schonungskommando* into the basement. He'd slept badly that night and reluctantly got to work. It was about nine o'clock in the morning and he was already having trouble keeping his eyes open. While retrieving another bundle of old fabric strips, he saw that towards the back of the room, straw bales had been stacked to separate their work area from the nets that were ready to be taken away. This gave him an idea. When later that morning he had to pick up new strips of fabric again, he slipped past the straw bales and nestled in a pile of nets, where he fell into a deep sleep.

The club smashed half against his head and half against his right shoulder. Wim sprang up and automatically stood at attention. He reached for his cap but had lost it. Standing in front of him, a Polish foreman snarled: '*Heute Abend fünfundzwanzig am Arsch!*' 'Twenty-five lashes – this evening!'

He beat Wim back to his work spot with a few hard strikes. The Pole had wanted to count nets and had stumbled upon the sleeping prisoner. Because a Kapo was waiting for the foreman's answer, he didn't pay any further attention to Wim. Dazed, Wim sat on his stool and made weaving motions with his hands. His neighbour whispered that he'd missed the midday soup. It was already three o'clock. Slowly, Wim came to his senses. He realised that he'd staked his life. Now, his back was going to be ripped open that evening by a Kapo or the foreman who had caught him and naturally felt fooled. If Wim was lucky, the wounds wouldn't be too deep and he would get the chance to recover in the *Revier*. But he'd also seen men never get up again after a thrashing like that. He'd been an idiot.

The afternoon had never taken so long. During the evening roll call, Wim carefully checked whether he could spy the Polish foreman or the Kapo. He'd anxiously manoeuvred himself into the middle of the group on the roll-call square. He was so tense he didn't feel the cold. He peered through the rows of prisoners but didn't see their dreaded faces anywhere. Nor did the tormentors show themselves when food was served. Wim forced himself to eat the soup; maybe the lashes would hurt less on a full stomach. Despite his hunger, he struggled to get the liquid down. Time and again he looked at the barracks' door over the edge of his bowl. It stayed shut.

He told the whole story to Gait, who listened in disbelief and kept shaking his head. He said a prayer for Wim on the spot. Instead of wandering through the camp, Wim stayed in the *Schonungsblock* that evening, terrified that he'd still run into either of the men. But no one came to get him. He didn't sleep much that night. Over and over again, he awoke with a start, his back soaked with cold sweat.

The next day went like all the rest. He worked hard, by his standards, and the foreman didn't pay him any attention. Because of the restless night, he still felt dead-tired, though he didn't even dare to look in the direction of the straw bales. His neighbour took care of their supply of old rags. That evening in the barracks, he could laugh for the first time with Gait, who was convinced his prayer had worked.

Just after eating, the men heard a terrible racket coming from the barracks next door. Through a window they saw that a section of the *Schonungsblock* was being beaten empty and the prisoners driven onto the roll-call square. Food had been stolen and no one knew who the culprit was. In any case, no one opened their mouth. Six hundred men paid the price. It was freezing cold and there was a layer of snow, but it didn't make the perpetrator any more talkative. Around midnight, the men had to undress. The next morning, when Wim looked out of the window, eighteen were still standing. The others had frozen stiff, were dying or were not far from it. In the days that followed, the crematorium's ovens burned day and night.

SS doctors submitted the prisoners in the *Schonungsblock* to periodic examinations to determine whether they'd regained enough strength to return to a regular *Kommando*. It would mean losing their *Zulage*, the extra slices of bread, and having to work hard. No one wanted that. The men who had been in the camp for some time had already warned them about what to expect during the examination. They weren't kidding.

An SS doctor was waiting at the door to the washroom. No one could leave the barracks unseen; each prisoner had to stand three metres in front of him, naked. Those who looked a little too well were removed, had to get dressed and were hauled off to another Block by the *Stubendienst*.

It felt strange to be lucky for still being skin and bones and be labelled a *Muselmann* – the camp term for prisoners who still barely clung to life – by the camp doctors. In that case, you walked ahead into the washroom, still without clothes. The windows had been opened on opposite sides and it was freezing cold. The prisoners huddled together for warmth.

After a few hundred men had passed the doctor, it was Wim's turn. He guessed that he weighed somewhere between thirty and thirty-five kilos and stood before the doctor, his back slightly curved. With a gesture of his hand, the SS man referred him to the washroom. He could now stand there, freezing to death, and they'd only just made it halfway. When everyone had been assessed, they were finally allowed to put on their clothes. If you hadn't been sick already, you were sure to have caught a lung infection or some other disease.

It was the end of the afternoon when Wim finally felt somewhat warm again. He resolved to get out of the *Schonungskommando* as quickly as possible. Things had gone well this time, but at the next inspection he'd be running the risk of becoming mortally sick from the cold or landing in some outside *Kommando* or other; a death sentence anyway.

He'd had enough of sitting the whole day in a dank basement. He wanted to be outside, wander around the camp, organise things, feast his eyes and ears, but he didn't get a single opportunity to do so. His optimistic mindset was being put to the test and very occasionally his frustration got the better of him. One morning, he'd neatly made up his bed yet again in the semi-darkness when at around five o'clock, a member of the *Stubendienst*, one of Felix's subordinates, made his rounds. Amid a lot of cursing and ranting, he dealt out orders and beatings at complete random. Coming to Wim's bed, he pointed to a bit of straw on the floor. Just as Wim went to look, the man swung, catching him under his chin. Out of reflex, Wim punched the criminal at least as hard in the face. The man was caught off guard and recoiled. He furiously marched off to grab Felix.

Wim was still dazed from the blow and realised too late that Felix was standing next to him. He grabbed hold of Wim, gave him two thumps and flung him over two rows of beds to the other side of the barracks. Wim lay there, stunned. A few fellow prisoners helped him onto his feet. By then, Felix was already after his next victim. Wim suffered from a nagging headache and a feeling of nausea for the rest of the day. He had to force himself to eat and, after the evening soup, immediately went to lie in his bunk.

By the next morning, he felt reasonably better. At about ten o'clock, a foreman came into the basement. Most of the prisoners didn't even see him and were braiding as if in a trance, staring into space. '*Gibt es hier ein Maler?*' 'Is anyone here a painter?' asked the foreman. Wim immediately raised his hand and stood up.

'*Ich bin ein Maler!*' 'I'm a painter!'

20

Cakes from an SS guard

Neuengamme, January 1945

Together with the other prisoners who had raised their hands, Wim walked to the stairs. They marched behind the foreman across the roll-call square and between the hospital barracks to a small opening in the barbed wire behind the crematorium. The SS guard who was standing there glanced at the papers the foreman gave him, stepped aside and let the men pass. After two hundred metres, the foreman stopped in front of a number of passenger train carriages that had been shunted onto a side track. Wim was the first to go inside. He couldn't believe his eyes. The carriage had been converted into accommodation. To the left was a table with two chairs and on the wall hung a small painting; to the right was a bed and against the back wall a large closet. In the middle, hugging the wall, stood a sink and on the gleaming wooden floor was a lovely woollen rug. Wim had to varnish the panelling, which had been installed on all sides and rose a metre and a half from the floor.

He'd once painted his kayak but had never worked with white varnish. He patiently waited for his guard to leave and instruct another painter, but the foreman calmly stood

there with his hands in his pockets to see Wim at work. So
he dipped the brush in the pot and smeared a big glob of
varnish onto the wood. He brushed over it a few times and
threw another load on top. The foreman shook his head as
he watched.

'*Und du bist ein Maler?*' 'And you call yourself a painter?'
he asked.

He grabbed the brush from Wim's hands and demonstrated
how to work a large surface area with a small amount. Brush
first from top to bottom, then from left to right, and go over
it all again from the upper edge down to the floor.

'No problem,' Wim said and varnished the wood exactly
as the foreman had showed him. After a few minutes, the
foreman left him alone and went to instruct the others. Wim
soon heard him jump out of the train again. He stopped a
short distance away, to make sure the prisoners stayed in the
carriages. Wim enjoyed the work and was happy just to be
out of the basement.

That evening, he roamed through the camp and tried to
sniff out what the carriages were for. After asking around, he
found a Dutchman in one of the barracks who had been in
the camp for three years.

'Those are for the railway *Kommando*,' he said. 'I had to
work there for a few weeks about a year ago – dangerous as
hell is what it is. They make you repair these wrecked railway lines, you see. And the Allies just keep bombing away,
so if you're unlucky then one lands on your head. The guards
sleep in the carriages, which they have brought out to the
worksite and parked somewhere on a side track nearby. It's a
temporary home for an SS guard.'

★

Towards the end of the following afternoon, the occupant of the carriage where Wim was varnishing suddenly appeared behind him and looked over his work. A little later, the SS man said something that would stay with Wim for a long time: '*Du bist ein richtiger Maler.*' 'You're a real painter.'

He left the carriage and came back fifteen minutes later with a packet of egg cakes. Wim couldn't believe it and thanked him enthusiastically. A packet of cakes from an SS guard! When the man disappeared again, Wim savoured them. It was better not to walk back across the camp carrying these and it wouldn't be easy to explain to the other prisoners. His best option was to eat everything.

That evening, he lay in his bunk without an overpowering feeling of hunger for the first time in months. It was wonderful to fall asleep like this, but his joy wouldn't last. In the middle of the night, there was a beastlike bellowing that could only be one person: Felix van Vught. One of the boys from Putten had taken his chances at relieving himself on the *Blockälteste*'s personal toilet; a mortal sin in the German's eyes, given all the cases of dysentery in the barracks. Still groggy with sleep, Felix had walked into his private domain at just the wrong moment. He beat the prisoner out and dragged him to the front of the barracks, where the vaulting horse was set up. There, he dealt out twenty-five strikes with a truncheon. It was excruciating to hear and Wim stuck his fingers into his ears. The next morning, he would find out that, miraculously, the young man had survived.

Wim didn't sleep for the rest of the night. He thought about what he should do. The paint job would be finished in a few days and he needed to make sure that he found somewhere new that was safe.

During the lunch break the next day, he struck up a conversation with the foreman. He'd now been painting for three days in two carriages and was about to start on the third and last one. The foreman had seen that Wim was eager to learn and not afraid to work. In any case, he wasn't the most horrible guy, otherwise he would have thrashed Wim when it turned out he had little painting experience.

Wim knew that he needed to get inside the *Arbeitsamt* office. Apparently, an experienced Belgian prisoner worked there as a *Funktionshäftling* and allocated prisoners to the work details. He could decide whether you lived or died; whether you were ground down in the clay *Kommando* or got a comfortable job as a tailor or kitchen assistant. There were rumours among the prisoners that the man belonged to a special committee, a resistance group within the camp walls. They swapped the numbers and clothes of dead prisoners with those of *Torsperre* candidates, saving various men from certain death. But would he also be able to help Wim?

Wim asked the foreman if he could take fifteen minutes out of his lunch break to report there and offer his services. The man granted him permission and walked him to the small gate in the barbed wire. He exchanged a few words with the SS guard and, turning to Wim, snapped: '*Nur eine Viertelstunde!*' 'Fifteen minutes – no more!'

Wim hurried down to the office and announced himself at the entrance. After waiting for a few minutes, which seemed like an eternity, he was allowed to enter the labour service secretary's office. Fortunately, the Belgian was a Fleming and so could speak Dutch. Wim told him that he'd worked in Brunswick for six months as a metalworker, exaggerating the actual work he'd carried out there. He was standing outside again five minutes later. The Belgian would see what he could do but was dependent on SS approval.

Wim still had a day's worth of painting left, then his *Kommando* would be disbanded. Every so often he gave the foreman an inquiring look, but the man pretended not to see him. At five o'clock in the afternoon, they marched back at a steady pace, past the SS guard at the barbed wire and on to the roll-call square. Twenty metres from the labour service office, the foreman told Wim to report there.

He was assigned to the metal *Kommando* and given work in the metal fabrication workshop at the back of the camp premises. Various businesses had built halls there to take advantage of the cheap workforce. Forced labour or not, Wim was happy just to have made it out of the *Schonungskommando* for good. An added benefit was that he'd been delivered from Felix van Vught. He moved from Block 6 to Block 12, in the middle of the row of nine barracks. The Polish *Blockälteste* there was no ray of sunshine either – otherwise the Nazis wouldn't have thought him suited for the job – but worse than Felix was impossible.

Nevertheless, the SS soon found a way to torment them all during the nights. Towards the end of January 1945, the Allies began intensifying their air attacks and the camp leadership decided air raid drills were needed. When the alarms sounded, the prisoners had to race into the basements of either of the two stone barracks on opposite sides of the square. Wim hated this with a passion. At one or two o'clock in the morning, you were wrenched out of your sleep and then hundreds of people tried squeezing themselves through the barracks' door to get to the basements as quickly as possible. If you were too late, you stood among thousands of people who needed to make it through an even smaller door. And if you weren't careful you were trampled or clobbered by the SS who, grinning widely, crashed their batons on the prisoners at the back. All of the prisoners then waited, packed in like sardines, for bombs that would never fall. The Allies knew perfectly well that there was a concentration camp near Neuengamme.

After a few hours of nearly suffocating in the stone-cold basements, the signal was given for them to return to their barracks and the same scene repeated itself, but now in reverse. An hour and a half later, when Wim had made it back to his flattened straw mattress and wrapped himself in his thin blanket, he didn't feel warm again for the whole night. If they were unlucky, or rather, if the SS felt like it, then there were two of these air raid drills per night.

Wim got the knack, at hearing the first alarm tones, of immediately sliding out of his bunk and going outside, so that he reached the basement in time and could sit on a ledge in a corner, protected by the walls behind him from thieving fellow prisoners.

A week after Wim started as a metalworker, everyone had just finished eating their evening meal, when they were shouted out of the barracks and driven onto the roll-call square. The experienced prisoners knew what was coming. A mobile wooden gallows had been set up in the middle of the yard.

The guards forced the men to line themselves up around it. As many as ten thousand men were standing with the guards at their backs, looking at the wooden colossus and waiting for something they didn't want to see. Wim had managed to end up in the rows at the outer edge, though not all the way to the back, since the guards there had aggressive dogs.

Two shackled Russian prisoners, not even twenty years old, were standing next to the gallows. As the first one climbed the stairs, the camp orchestra struck up that hated 'Alte Kameraden' again. He had attempted to escape and had been wounded in his shoulder. His right arm was bandaged and he walked, bent double with pain, onto the scaffold. As he did so, he cursed the SS men to high heaven with words whose literal meaning the vast majority of the public couldn't understand but could surmise. The guards listened impassively. All that mattered to them was the standard pay they'd be getting for an execution: twenty cigarettes and half a litre of genever.

Even after the noose had been placed around his neck, the Russian kept cursing and raging until one of the guards had had enough and yelled '*Mach Schluss mit dem Schweinhund!*' 'Put an end to that swine!' before pulling out the hatch. Wim tried to look away, but the Kapos, foremen and members of the *Stubendienst* forced everyone to watch.

The second Russian had been standing right beside the platform, horrified, and had to watch his comrade fall. For at least ten minutes, the tormentors let the lifeless body hang in the glare of the floodlights. It turned on its axis, chin at its chest as if the victim had fallen asleep. Slowly to the left at first, then just as slowly to the right. By the time they finally lowered the corpse, the other prisoner was trembling all over. It was dead silent. Wim didn't feel the cold; rage and powerlessness overwhelmed him. The body was carried away on a stretcher and a little while later, a shot rang out over the frigid square. Certainty over everything.

The gallows were readied again and the trapdoor put into position. The young man shouted a few indistinct words in Russian as he was pushed up the stairs. Once the noose was around his neck, he directed himself to his executioners and yelled something Wim didn't understand. The prisoners whispered the translation to one another while his body slowly turned.

On the stairs, he'd shouted: 'Farewell, comrades, I'm innocent.'

To the SS guards, he'd yelled: 'You wait, my father will get you soon enough.'

In the metal workshop, Wim spent the whole day die-cutting and point welding. Sometimes he found pieces of metal he could use to fashion things, like a spoon or what was supposed to be a screwdriver. He smuggled them out and traded them for an extra sandwich or other things to eat. On occasion he was offered vegetables, but he scrupulously stayed away from them. In the SS's section of the camp, the guards had access to a *Lagergärtnerei*, a camp vegetable garden and several greenhouses, where they cultivated vegetables, herbs and tomatoes for their own use. Naturally the work was done by prisoners, who gratefully took advantage of the opportunity. They organised vegetables that they would then trade for cigarettes. It sounded nice, but Wim had heard something from a *Funktionshäftling* in his new barracks that had stayed with him. The prisoner knew Leichen Heini, literally 'Corpses' Heini, who was in charge of the crematorium. He'd spoken of more than eighty cremations a day, day after day. And he'd said that a portion of the ash was regularly picked up by members of the garden *Kommando* and used as fertiliser for the vegetable garden and greenhouses. Wim preferred to stick to the bread and sausage he arranged himself.

At the start of February 1945, he was given new work in the sheet metal team and that was when things really started going wrong. Together with a Frenchman, Wim had to furnish cabinets with rivets. He got to work in high spirits, without having experience of any kind, and while his colleague handled the rivet gun, Wim had to hold the two plates against each other at the right point and make sure they didn't move. At the same time, he needed to apply counter pressure, so that the device could do its work. This wasn't so easy and occasionally he burst into laughter when the French worker cursed because something had shifted again or the rivet was completely crooked. His partner, however, didn't see the humour in it, probably fearing for his job, and kept growing angrier.

By noon, the man was at the end of his rope and stomped off to the other side of the hall; a short while later, he was standing with the Kapo next to Wim. He showed the failed rivet work and pointed at Wim. The Kapo gave Wim a surly look and Wim expected at any moment to get a bash on his head with the truncheon, but it never came. Instead, he got a broom shoved into his hands and the order to sweep the entire workshop.

After a number of days there was nothing left to sweep or tidy up and everything outside the workplace was clean too. The Kapo clearly didn't know what to do with him and wanted to be rid of him.

'You're going to the outside *Kommando*,' he said. 'You won't be able to screw up anything there. Report tomorrow morning to the *Arbeitsamt*.'

Wim stood rooted to the spot. The outside *Kommando*? He knew as well as anyone else what that entailed. The Kapo had long since turned around and was letting loose on another prisoner, while Wim, the blood having drained from his face, processed the news.

After the evening meal, Wim reported to the *Revier*, where he encountered a Russian doctor. In German, he explained what the matter was: 'The outside *Kommando* means certain death. Would you be able to admit me until the *Kommando* leaves?'

The doctor thought it over for a moment and then made a gesture with his head: 'Walk through to the back. There will be some patients lying there with a bunk to themselves. Find yourself a spot and for now make sure that no one sees you. As soon as the *Kommando*'s left, I'm kicking you back out, though. If the SS doctor carries out an inspection, I'm finished.'

In the *Revier*, Wim was engulfed by an unbearable stench. Carefully, he walked between the corpses and buckets filled with excrement. To his left and right people were moaning and hollow eyes stared into space. At the end of the aisle were two bunkbeds with just one or two people per berth. Wim crawled into the top bunk, so as to make sure that anything that could flow out of another body did not find its way down by way of his own. His bunkmate had an H in his red triangle but was barely capable of uttering a word. Wim stretched himself out and stared at the ceiling. At that moment, surrounded by thousands of people, he felt lonelier than ever.

The next morning, the man beside Wim was ice-cold. After the sun had risen, the corpse *Kommando* came to take away the newest collection of rotting bodies. Multiple times in the hours before, Wim had heard the muffled thud of cadavers being worked out of their bunks by fellow prisoners. He just couldn't bring himself to push out the dead man's body and so he helped lay his neighbour on the cart in as dignified a way as possible.

Two piles of corpses, thirteen in total, were the harvest of one night in this one hospital barracks. From the foremost barracks they'd already reaped fifteen bodies and the furthest barracks was next in line. Wim made himself as useful as possible by helping to hand out food and clean the floor.

On his fourth day, one of the nurses approached Wim. Could he report to the Russian doctor? Carefully, he peered through a split in the door to make sure there wasn't an SS man in the doctor's room. You never knew if it was a trap to have him hauled off after all.

'The outside *Kommando* has left,' the doctor said. 'You can go.'

Wim gave a sigh of relief.

'You were lucky. The day before yesterday, those poor wretches were loaded into wagons and left to stand there for forty-eight hours. The train only left this morning. I have no idea whether they got anything to eat or drink.'

Wim knew the answer but preferred not to think of it. He thanked the doctor warmly and walked to his barracks. He washed himself as thoroughly as he could and resolved to organise new clothes for himself that evening, since he still had a small supply of cigarettes. He spent the rest of the day inside, so as to take as few chances as possible.

The next morning, in clean clothes, Wim simply walked along with the metal *Kommando* to the workshop and, putting on a poker face, reported to the Kapo.

'What are you doing here? You were supposed to be on the transport!'

'I know, Herr Kapo, but I was declared unfit.'

The Kapo was at a loss with him. The concept 'unfit' didn't exist in the camp. You were either alive or dead. If you'd landed at death's door you went to the *Schonungskommando* and if you were as good as dead then the *Revier* was the right place for you. But unfit? The Kapo gave Wim a broom and ordered him to sweep clean everything around the building. It took Wim the whole morning. After the noon break, he had to measure machines in the workshop with a tape. In the course of the afternoon, the Kapo walked over with an SS member.

'*Holländer!*' he called.

Wim went over to him, stood at attention at the mandatory distance of three metres and took his cap off.

'*Häftling nr. 49019 meldet sich gehorsam,*' 'Prisoner number 49019 reporting obediently, sir,' said Wim.

'*Holländer*, why are you in the camp?'

Wim still wasn't wearing a red triangle on his clothes, just his number and the letter H.

'I don't want to work for you,' he said. 'That's why I was arrested.'

'Then you're a stupid *Holländer*. We liberated you from the British.'

This time Wim wisely kept his mouth shut.

'This Kapo wants to get rid of you,' said the SS man. 'Do you know where you'll be going?'

'No, sir, no idea.'

'To the clay *Kommando*. And do you know what that means?'

'Yes, sir, that'll be the end of me.'

'Right, that'll be the end of you. Do you want to work?'

'Yes, I do want to work.'

'Then follow me.'

Ahead of Wim, the SS man walked across the outdoor area, passing in front of the metal factory. They walked past buildings Wim had never seen until they came to a number of wooden barracks lined up beside one another, each more than forty metres long and about ten metres wide. Their entrances looked onto a brick building with a pair of large wooden doors. These were the workshops and garages where the vans and freight trucks from the companies collaborating with the SS were serviced. The SS guard walked over to the Kapo in charge, pointed at Wim and announced that Wim was coming to work in his garage.

21

Rabbits in a concentration camp

Neuengamme, February – March 1945

In the garage, Wim started thriving again. He was responsible for it being clean and tidy both in and around the workplace and he made sure no one could fault him. After a short while, it was as if he were part of the interior; he no longer stuck out. For the guards and SS men who walked in and out, he was air. No one said anything when he left for a moment to make a lap through the camp. Wim had some of his freedom back – behind the barbed wire.

He was busy collecting oil cans to store in a corner, when an SS guard called him. The officers were sitting at the back of the garage, eating lunch. Wim had smelled a while ago that they'd heated up something tasty in a small pan now standing in the middle of the table.

'*Drecksack! Sauber machen!*' 'Shitbag! Get cleaning!'

He didn't immediately understand what was expected of him and went to pick up a dustpan. The order came again, harder and more forceful now.

'*Drecksack! Sauber machen!*' 'Shitbag! Get cleaning!'

He cautiously walked over to them and just as he was about to stand at attention and take off his cap, the oldest of the group shoved the pan into his hands. He gestured with his head to the small kitchen.

Wim mumbled '*Danke*,' 'Thanks,' and disappeared behind the partition. He ran the tap over the sink and was about to hold the pan underneath it, when his eyes fell on the bottom. The brown sludge was almost unnoticeable against the black enamel, but there was still a layer of food at least two centi-metres deep. Wim grabbed his metal spoon from out of his trouser pocket and carefully scraped it over the bottom, as he was scared of making too much noise. Goulash! With pieces of meat! A meal fit for a king. He couldn't remember the last time he'd eaten so well. His mother was certainly a magnificent cook, and all the food while hiding on the farms had tasted great, but this beat everything after more than four months of bread and swede soup. He took a deep breath to calm himself down and, when he was sure nothing was left, cleaned the pan thoroughly. He dried it off with a kitchen rag, after which he put it back with the other pans. In the garage, he picked up where he'd left off with tidying. From out of the corner of his eye, he saw the SS men were gone.

This wouldn't be the last time he had to clean a pan and it meant he was able to save slices of bread, which he then traded. Within no time, he was wearing a warm sweater un-derneath his coat and he arranged a pair of trousers in the right size and without holes.

Where he worked bordered on a small camp, partitioned off from the rest, with mostly prominent French prisoners whom the Nazis treated less harshly as a result of their political or social status. In the scarce moments when it was dry and not freezing cold, the prisoners interned there came outside for some fresh air. Wim would sweep a bit outside the garage and at the edge of the double barbed wire and try to strike up a conversation, whispering so the guards couldn't hear. Some of the prominents spoke German. Wim mainly wanted to hear that the war was almost over. Very occasionally, the Frenchmen granted him a word or two; that it was going slowly but steadily and that the Russians were making good progress from the east. These were no more than rumours and fragments, nothing was certain. However, he was handed a few cigarettes now and then.

One day, at the end of the afternoon, he was walking along the edge of the roll-call square, when he ran into Drees from camp Amersfoort. He still looked relatively decent. Happy to see each other again, they talked about their experiences since losing sight of each other. As an accomplished carpenter, Drees had been lucky. After arriving in Neuengamme, he'd been assigned to a factory *Kommando* in Hamburg. He'd been back for about ten days now, because the factory had been bombed out one night. The food had been reasonable and the beds better than the ones in his current barracks. From then on they saw each other regularly and, whenever he could, Wim saved a slice of bread for Drees.

Not long afterwards, on a sunny Sunday afternoon in the middle of February, the temperature hovering close to zero, the roll-call square was abuzz. A real international football game had been organised: France against Russia. It was wasted on Wim. He preferred to scavenge around the camp. Outside the cookhouse, two members of the kitchen *Kommando* were trying to push a cart loaded with cans into the kitchen. The guard was already inside. One of the prisoners was holding the door open, the other pulled the cart as hard as he could to get it over the threshold. Before Wim knew it, he'd snatched two cans and shoved them underneath his jacket. He walked away as calmly as possible, as though nothing were the matter. He knew that if they caught him, he was screwed.

In his barracks, he first went around to make sure that no one else was inside. From his trouser pocket he pulled out a spoon, sharpened on one side in the metal workshop. He prised the cans open and it turned out to be corned beef inside. They were empty in a heartbeat. He put them back underneath his coat; now, he had to get rid of them some-where. Behind the large stone barracks an oil drum served as a rubbish bin. He walked past it once to be sure no one saw him and a few moments later, both cans were lying inside it. In high spirits, he sauntered along the temporary football field, where the spectators enthusiastically cheered on the teams. The guards stood several metres behind them, their hands on their guns. He sat down on the steps at the entrance to his barracks, savouring the meal with satisfaction. He looked around, relaxed. It was only then he noticed that he didn't see any birds. Very strange. He'd been in the camp for almost two months and only now he realised that he hadn't seen a living animal in all that time, barring the guards' trained German shepherd dogs. No crickets, no mice, no other in-sects and certainly no birds. Of course, anything that moved was eaten by the prisoners, but the birds no doubt sensed there was nothing for them in or above the camp. Would they have recognised the smell of the crematorium?

At a table a little further on, a group of men were scraping the toppings from their sandwiches and tossing them onto the ground. They all wore a purple triangle on their camp clothes. Throwing away food in a concentration camp was unheard of and he wanted to find out more. He was warmly greeted. In German, someone asked him what his name was, after which a Dutchman in the group took over. He asked Wim how long he'd been in the camp and in a few sentences, Wim told them what he'd experienced.

'Why are you guys throwing those toppings on the ground?' he then asked. 'That's fine to eat, isn't it?'

'It's blood sausage,' said the man who had greeted him. 'Because of what we believe, we don't eat anything with blood in or on it. We're *Bibelforscher*, Jehovah's Witnesses.'

'That's a shame about the food; prisoners would murder for that,' said Wim. A passing Russian inmate had already picked up the slices of blood sausage and popped them into his mouth.

'Is that why you guys wear those purple triangles? And why are you in the camp anyway?' he asked.

'I've been here for two years now, but some of my German brothers were picked up before the war; they've been in different camps. We feel closely connected to God and don't accept any command contrary to God's principles. There is nothing greater than Him and that's why we won't swear allegiance to Hitler or the Nazi Party. My brothers here refuse to do the Hitler salute and refused their mandatory service, too, just like thousands of others with us. That's why a large part of our religious community has been arrested and shut away in camps. We help one another and as many other prisoners as we can with our unshakeable faith in God. Are you a believer, too?'

'I believe in food,' Wim said. 'If you guys find any more blood sausage on your bread, then you let me know.' And then he started to get back up. His curiosity won out over his lack of interest in matters of faith. 'In which *Kommando* are you, then?'

'Well, that varies quite a lot. We have *Funktionshäftlinge*, who are in administration, but one of us works in Pauly's housekeeping.'

The commandant lived with his five children and his sister-in-law in a house in the middle of the camp premises, between the Walther factory and the harbour.

'They know we'd never hurt a man, regardless of who he is or what he does,' said the man. 'That's what it says in the Bible. I myself work with these two brothers in the Angora *Kommando*.'

He pointed to the men sitting next to him.

'Angora *Kommando*? Is that in another country or something?'

The brother burst into laughter at so much ignorance.

'You really don't know it? We work over there, behind the cookhouse and right next to those watchtowers.'

Between two barracks, Wim could just see a corner of the building behind them that the man was pointing at.

'That's the rabbit farm. There are at least two thousand Angora rabbits in pens. They give off a fine wool – it's used to line pilot jackets.'

For a moment, Wim couldn't make sense of the world. They'd got a measly cigarette at Christmas, while a stone's throw from the camp kitchen were thousands of rabbits for the taking.

The Jehovah's Witness saw him thinking and said: 'We keep our hands off what's not ours. Always.'

Wim was patching a bike tyre for an SS man who had loudly barged into the garage. The Kapo had referred him to Wim, who knew what to do after having patched the tyres on his racing bike countless times. He personally delivered the bike to the large barracks about five hundred metres away. As he was wandering back, a window went open at the back of the small camp reserved for prominent inmates. A man stuck his head halfway out and said softly, but loudly enough so that Wim could hear him: 'Hey, *Holländer.*'

Through the barbed wire he gave a bowl of pudding to Wim, who was happy he always kept his spoon in his pocket. He was just getting the pudding down when, less than ten metres from him, a guard with a German shepherd dog passed. Wim pretended not to see him and was lucky. The SS man and his dog went on their way and disappeared from sight again. Wim breathed a sigh of relief.

He knocked on the window and gave the empty bowl back to the man, who wore an H in the red triangle on his coat too.

Wim reckoned that he now weighed about thirty-five kilos. Since working in the garage, he'd gained a little weight and felt much better than he had in the *Schonungskommando.*

A group of about a hundred Dutch prisoners from the provinces of Groningen and Friesland had arrived in the camp.

Many of them wore the *Torsperre* armband and they were kept apart from the rest of the prisoners. Every day, Wim would make conversation with them and sometimes he took a few slices of bread with him. He wondered whether they knew what awaited them, since nobody seemed to be especially worried about their unusual armband. He didn't bring it up.

One day the entire section wearing the *Torsperre* armband disappeared. The wildest rumours went around, but no one knew the finer details. Someone said they'd been put on a transport to an outside *Kommando*, while others adamantly claimed they'd been murdered.

It was after the evening roll call when Wim finally heard what had actually happened. In his barracks, a few bunks further on, slept a Dutchman who had been assigned to the corpse *Kommando*. The previous night he'd been drummed up for an extra shift. In groups of seven, the prisoners with a *Torsperre* had had to go into the detention bunker. Normally, prisoners were locked up in cells a metre wide and three metres long for a period of several days or sometimes up to several weeks.

To reach the cells, you went through a door on the side of the building. A long, narrow hallway ran along the cell doors. There were seven beams along the ceiling. The prisoners first had to undress, after which their hands were bound behind their backs. A rope was laid around their neck and thrown over a beam. Then they were hoisted up, so that they were slowly strangled. *SS-Obersturmführer* Thumann was in charge of the executions. He ordered his accomplices to smoke a cigarette outside and about ten minutes later, they inspected the result of their work. The corpse *Kommando* had to free the heads from the nooses and carry off the bodies to the crematorium, where Leichen Heini had fired both ovens. None of it mattered to that tub of lard.

Before taking the corpses away, they'd first had to tear any gold teeth from the prisoners' mouths and transcribe the numbers shown on their clothes onto their foreheads. Everything had to be gone by the time the next group of seven walked in.

It took at least a week before Wim had somewhat got over these horrifying murders. He kept seeing the face of the man from Groningen for whom, the night before, he'd brought two slices of bread without knowing it would be his last evening. It strengthened his will to survive, so that he could tell this story to everyone in the Netherlands after the liberation.

Only a couple of days later, a remarkable incident helped to take his mind off things. He had to walk with the garage's Kapo to the cookhouse to fetch old potato sacks for the mechanics to lie on when tinkering away under the trucks. They walked past a shut barracks. Wim thought the building wasn't being used, as he'd never seen people inside it. As they were walking past, the door opened and a pretty young woman waved to the Kapo.

A woman – a woman in the concentration camp! Wim squeezed his eyes shut. Was that what he'd really seen? That couldn't be, could it? But the Kapo acted as if it were the most normal thing in the world and kept marching.

Wim asked some of the more experienced prisoners about

it. They told him the building was called the *Puff*, the brothel. The dozen women were, in part, sex workers who had been picked up by the Germans because of their work and classi-fied as antisocial, the black triangles. But most of them came from other camps, like Ravensbrück, which was situated near the border with Poland, north of Berlin. They'd been told they could buy back their freedom by working in the camp brothel for six months. They had it good there. Enough to eat from their own kitchen and more comfort than the other prisoners in their barracks. After the six months had passed, they were assigned to the *Himmelfahrtskommando*, literally the 'journey to heaven' *Kommando*. Wim hadn't asked any further but could guess what that entailed. Afterwards, new women filled their places.

The clientele consisted mainly of *Funktionshäftlinge*, Kapos, foremen, *Blockältesten* and other members of the *Stubendienst*. They were allowed to visit the brothel as a reward for excep-tional achievements. One of the Kapos, Frederich, arranged it all like an actual pimp.

In March, it was still freezing outside in northern Germany and Wim didn't have a single indication that the war would soon be over. Rumours went around that the Americans were trying to cross the Rhine roughly five hundred kilometres to the south, by Remagen, between Bonn and Koblenz, but whether or not they'd succeeded, no one could say. He just made the best of it in the garage, tried to take as good care of himself as he could and made sure Drees got extra food as often as possible. Every day that passed like this was another one closer to liberation.

One afternoon in the garage, he went to grab the besom broom from the corner, when he saw his Kapo stretched out on the bonnet of a broken-down freight truck, fast asleep.

'What's the matter with him?' he asked one of the mechanics.

'There's a load of methylated spirits just come in again,' was the answer.

He saw the metal jerrycan standing next to the front wheel of the freight truck and knew enough. Wim spent the rest of that afternoon searching for empty bottles or other items to transport liquid in. In the rubbish bin behind the garage, he found two bottles with caps, which each held about twenty centilitres. As soon as the mechanics were finished working and there were no SS men in the area, he filled the bottles and shoved them underneath his clothes. That evening, after eating, he strolled over to the *Klinkergebäude*, the stone Block at the back of the camp. A *Blockälteste* resided there who, for a fee, could get you a better place to sleep. He was sitting at a table at the entrance, staring out with a surly expression.

'I've got methylated spirits,' Wim said and put a bottle on the table. The man unscrewed the cap and sniffed. His face cleared up instantly.

'You got any more?' he asked.

'I can get my hands on some.'

'You're sleeping here,' said the man.

He stood up to lead Wim to his new sleeping spot. Quick as a flash, Wim snatched a small brown bag of sugar from the table and stuck it underneath his coat. He was given a glorious spot in the back, all to himself, but before installing himself there, he reported the move to his old *Blockälteste*.

In a quiet corner, he ate the sugar. He folded the bag into a wad, tossing it into a rubbish bin in his old barracks. Each week, he brought his new *Blockälteste* a bottle of methylated spirits and didn't have to fear being beaten any more in his new accommodation.

22

Oil lamps and pink triangles

Neuengamme, March 1945

Several times each week, Wim would have to fetch materials from the metal workshop for the mechanics. Because he'd worked there himself, he knew exactly where he needed to go and, no less important, where not. The Kapo still had it in for him, so Wim intentionally avoided the man.

This time he had a box with him for carrying the steel plates the mechanics needed to weld underneath a freight truck. He walked to where the materials were issued, on his guard. The Frenchman who had ratted on him to the Kapo wasn't there; Wim hadn't seen him for some time now. The smells of welding fumes, heated steel and poured aluminium reminded him of Brunswick where, in hindsight, he really hadn't had such a bad time. He tried to avoid thinking about how he would have fared if he hadn't escaped.

The materials manager had filled his box and was already walking to the back again. Wim looked around. His eyes fell on a group of oil lamps, lined up against the wall in a corner. About twenty of them were looking at him invitingly from a ledge just under the stretch of windows. When the coast looked clear, he put two in the box. Back in the garage, he hid them in a metal locker under the sink. He still had no idea what he would do with his bounty but would worry about that later.

Sweeping outside the garage, Wim spotted a pair of Frenchmen from the prominents' barracks standing near the barbed wire. He remembered the total panic and dismay when, during the air raid alarms at night, the prominents had to take cover in the pitch-dark basement.

Wim started chatting with a tall man who spoke German and asked what a lamp was worth to him. He saw the Frenchman's eyes light up. He had him! After going back and forth for a bit, they agreed on a whole Red Cross package.

After darkness had fallen, the first trade took place. Many more would follow. Wim feasted on foods that in some cases he hadn't seen for over six months. Drees and his neighbours in the stone barracks shared in the luxury too.

Drees got the news he'd been assigned to an outside *Kommando* and that he'd be leaving for Meppen the next day. Wim spent hours that same evening working on him. He told him about his experiences in Husum and how he'd only just escaped certain death: 'Others weren't as lucky. Go into hiding. Disappear. It doesn't matter how, just so long as you don't go.'

He also told Drees about the prisoners who hadn't survived digging the anti-tank trenches and about the way the Germans had worked them to death. But Drees's experiences in the carpentry factory in Hamburg had been very different and he didn't want to listen to Wim. He only promised to think about it. Wim gave him a piece of sausage and said goodbye. In his heart, he knew it was for good. Drees was lost – a dead man with a beating heart.

The next day, a line of train wagons loaded with prisoners was standing in the yard. They stayed there for three days, without food or anything to drink, waiting for the engine that would take them to Meppen.

After a few weeks in the *Klinkergebäude*, Wim discovered a door behind the hedge growing along the back of the building. He pushed against it and the door opened with a creak. Inside, his eyes needed a moment to adjust to the darkness. He could hear piano music in the distance. With two steps, he was down the stairs and found himself in a part of the basement that must have bordered on the room where he'd woven nets. After about twenty metres, he stumbled on several straw bales. He crouched, looked between two bales and saw, to his astonishment, prisoners dancing to the music one of them was playing on a full-sized piano in a corner of the room. In another corner, men were kissing one another. On a pair of little tables were bits of sausages and cheese. He watched them for a while, fascinated. All of them wore the number 175, written large on a yellow stripe or a pink triangle on their coats. Even in the most terrible environment, where they'd been imprisoned for their orientation, they'd found a way to express their feelings. And without the SS knowing. Wim recognised two Kapos wearing green triangles who were having the most fun. He couldn't resist the temptation to nab two sausages for himself and left the party as quietly as possible. Once outside, he walked a few laps through the camp to recover from what he'd just seen.

It hadn't been intended for his eyes. It was better to keep silent about this and not needlessly put himself in danger.

During the last days of March, the prisoners became increasingly desperate. The long winter and harsh conditions were taking their toll. No one could say whether they would be liberated this month, this year, or perhaps ever. How often had Wim heard that the Allies were practically at their gates? They clutched at every straw, but it wasn't enough to keep everyone going.

Each morning at roll call, Wim saw the corpses of the prisoners who had been freed from their suffering by 15,000 volts hanging in the barbed wire. Others intentionally stepped into the five-metre-wide forbidden zone and waited for a delivering bullet from a gun barrel high in one of the watchtowers.

The guards were always prepared to lend a helping hand. If you attracted attention, they would just pick you out and throw your cap into the prohibited area. You then had to fetch it at gunpoint because you couldn't 'obediently' greet SS members without headwear. In the end, the guard training his gun on you didn't have to do anything; it was done for him from ten metres above.

In the work details outside the camp, the leadership had come up with a way to shoot as many 'fleeing' prisoners as possible. They called it the *Postenkette*, the cordon. The guards would draw an imaginary line between one another along the edge of the worksite. Whenever a prisoner walked over it, they were shot. The guards were very creative in driving you across it. With truncheon blows or a lie about grabbing something – it didn't matter – just as long as they could collect the reward for shooting a fleeing prisoner: fifty cigarettes, a cash bonus and four days off. The *Kommandos* came back with corpses on a daily basis. Sometimes up to a hundred bodies were burned in a day.

There seemed to be no end to the misery. The prisoners were then astonished when at the end of March, a column of white buses painted with red crosses suddenly turned up at the camp entrance.

At the start of 1945, the vice chairman of the Swedish Red Cross and nephew of the Swedish king, Count Folke Bernadotte, had entered into negotiations with Himmler in the utmost secrecy. Himmler was trying, behind Hitler's back, to set up real peace talks with the Allies. Bernadotte himself flew multiple times to Berlin and Lübeck.

Himmler wanted to arrange a ceasefire on the Western Front in order to continue fighting against the advancing Russians, and used the concentration camp prisoners as bargaining chips to force concessions from the Allies. Bernadotte was supported in the negotiations by the Norwegian government in exile, the Swedish government and the Swedish Red Cross. He managed to have all of the Scandinavian prisoners who were in the concentration camps and prisons still under Nazi control brought to Neuengamme, where they could be transported to Scandinavia at a later stage.

A massive relocation got under way. In order to be able to receive the seven thousand Scandinavians at Neuengamme, barracks were made available. The prisoners who were housed there – mainly Poles, Russians, Dutchmen, Frenchmen and Belgians – needed to be rushed to other camps.

Only this wasn't said to them.

They were driven out of their barracks in the middle of the night. Those who couldn't get out of bed caught a blow from a baton or a kick against their head from a Kapo's boot. The dead were left behind and when a Kapo was unsure whether someone was actually gone, he jabbed a glowing poker into the man's face. A horrible smell of seared flesh filled the barracks.

Outside, the prisoners were lined up as usual in rows of five and had to undress. After an inspection by an SS doctor, in which the sickest were violently carted off to an undisclosed location, it was off at a march to the *Kleiderkammer*, the clothing depot. Everyone was given clean clothes and driven back into their barracks.

At daybreak, they were led to the white buses in groups of a hundred, full of hope and visions of freedom, which was now within reach. They thought. Two thousand prisoners left Neuengamme, only to be welcomed the next day in another camp by Kapos and SS guards with the same truncheons, riding crops and dogs.

The barracks they'd left behind in Neuengamme were cleaned by specially formed *Kommandos* and separated from the rest of the camp with endless amounts of barbed wire. From that moment on, the Red Cross had access to the *Skandinavienlager*, the Scandinavian camp, to supervise the proper care of the seven thousand Scandinavian prisoners. For Wim, who watched it all happen, this confirmed his belief that the British and Americans couldn't be far away now.

★

In Wim's barracks, they were regularly asked whether there were prisoners who wanted to help work on what was termed 'the improvement of the medical situation'. They were very cleverly promised better food in return. Dr Heissmeyer was leading the operation and Wim was happy he never took the Nazis up on their offer.

He heard from more and more prisoners what these so-called improvements involved. The doctor was conducting experiments to discover a remedy for TB. He injected some of the prisoners with bacilli or applied these to an open wound. With others, he used a probe to introduce bacilli directly into their lungs in order to then observe how the disease developed. Hunger drove some of the prisoners to volunteer, but most were simply forced. Wim never saw these men again. The story went around that the same doctor was also conducting similar experiments on children. Wim couldn't believe anyone might be capable of such things and dismissed it as one of the many camp rumours, so as to mentally shield himself. However, it wasn't just a rumour.

Increasingly, prisoners came into the camp without their heads shaved or the usual camp attire. Wim then knew enough. Behind the workshop was a shooting range for the SS, where a large heap of sand about two metres high served as a bullet trap. Whenever he heard the bursts of gunfire, Wim made sure to stay in the garage so as to hear as little of that misery as possible. Still, he couldn't escape occasionally having to face mountains of up to hundreds of emaciated corpses, neatly stacked each day beside the crematorium, where a fatty yellow smoke constantly billowed from the chimney.

Everything was telling Wim that the end of the war was in sight. The SS were behaving differently, increasingly argued with one another, were extremely nervous and even more frequently drunk. Transports carrying the sickest and weakest Scandinavians left daily, escorted by the Red Cross. From the satellite camps, more and more prisoners came back to Neuengamme. They said their camps had been disbanded – if they could still speak, anyway.

Wim was just grateful for his one-person bed in the *Klinkergebäude*, since by now the camp was bursting at the seams. The condensation that formed on the ceiling from so many people in a small stone room sometimes dripped onto his bed and froze instantly, but he was only too happy to put up with it. He faithfully arranged the weekly bottle of spirits to keep his spot.

Midway through April, he overheard a conversation between SS men who were eating lunch in the garage. The Russians were apparently already just outside Berlin. He had to restrain himself from cheering and suppressed a large grin. He only clenched his fists even tighter around the besom handle and continued sweeping. If they caught Hitler, then he'd soon be back in the Tweede Oosterparkstraat in Amsterdam.

23

Covering your tracks

Neuengamme, April 1945

On 19 April 1945, Count Bernadotte reached an agreement with Himmler allowing for the transportation of all Scandinavian prisoners from concentration camp Neuengamme to Sweden and Denmark. The next day, Wim's world was in uproar. He watched one whitewashed bus after the other appear at the *Skandinavienlager*'s gate. Over a hundred would follow that day. In six convoys, they carried off more than four thousand Scandinavian prisoners, straight to a reception station in Denmark that had been specially set up.

Roughly two hundred prisoners were assigned to a special clean-up *Kommando* to tidy the Scandinavians' barracks. Under the watchful eyes of the Swedish Red Cross, the Danes and Norwegians hadn't gone short of anything; the remnants of their packages were strewn throughout the building. The *Kommando* had to carry the food to the cookhouse and this offered an excellent chance to eat and hide underneath their clothes as much of it as possible, even under strict supervision by the guards. They shared the loot that evening. As long as the *Blockälteste* and the *Stubendienst* got a large portion, many prisoners could enjoy some extra provisions for the first time in ages.

The members of the clean-up *Kommando* were easily recognisable by the twinkling in their eyes and the new socks they'd organised. Wim watched it all happen, contented. He hadn't gone without in the last few weeks and joined them with just a few crackers from a white packet he'd been allotted.

What the prisoners in Neuengamme didn't know was that a few days earlier, on 14 April, Himmler had sent out an order to all of the concentration camp commandants. As the Nazi leadership were scared of their atrocities being discovered, he commanded the following:

> *Order from the SS-Reichsführer*
> *14 April 1945*
> *To all concentration camp commandants:*
> *'A handover is out of the question. The camp must be evacuated immediately.*
> *No prisoner is to be allowed to fall into enemy hands alive.'*
>
> *Heinrich Himmler*
> *SS-Reichsführer*

Camp commandant Pauly was at a loss. After the Scandinavians' departure, there were still ten thousand prisoners in his camp and he had no idea what to do with them. In the autumn of 1944, during a visit to Berlin, he'd received a similar message from Himmler via Oswald Pohl. As *SS-Obergruppenführer* and *General der Waffen-SS*, Pohl was Himmler's right-hand man and had been made responsible for directing the concentration camps. He had instructed every camp commandant to consider how they could rid themselves of their prisoners in the case of an enemy invasion. That also went for Pauly, though it was now out of his hands.

The German troops in the Ruhr valley about three hundred kilometres to the south-west had surrendered; the Allies were at the banks of the Elbe near the town of Lüneburg; and the Red Army continued advancing from the east. Pauly was given the order to evacuate the camp on the double and to transport the prisoners to Lübeck, a Baltic port city about a hundred and fifty kilometres to the north-east and part of a small corridor to the sea that the Nazis still had in their hands.

The order came from *Höhere SS- und Polizeiführer* Georg-Henning Graf von Bassewitz-Behr, the highest commander of the SS and police in northern Germany, and from *Gauleiter* Karl Kaufmann, the leader of the Nazi Party's regional branch in Hamburg. Under pressure from Hamburg's elite and the big industrialists, the pair wanted to deliver the city and its surroundings scrubbed clean and to hand these over to the Allies without further fighting. Hamburg's reputation needed to be held aloft. They were also afraid that after the Allies' arrival, prisoners would be out for revenge, plundering and reprisals. It was better that they disappeared.

After the announcement that the camp was being evacuated, Wim had no idea what this would mean for him. A work detail was being formed in double quick time – a clean-up *Kommando* would be staying behind to make sure the Allies didn't encounter anything indecent. Wim was in two minds. What was wise? What should he do? He tossed and turned the whole night. He expected the Allies to reach Neuengamme sooner than the prisoners would reach their unknown destination. He understood there would be nothing more to organise once he was in one of those cramped train wagons. This was the deciding factor. He would do everything he could to try to stay.

The *Kommando* was put together at the morning roll call. Through the chaos and excitement among the prisoners, Wim managed to bump himself up a few sections unseen and join those prisoners selected to remain. A short while later, the group was driven away with loud bellowing to another area. After an hour, the camp leadership had gathered six to seven hundred prisoners, a mix of nationalities, with noticeably few Poles and Russians. The remaining nine thousand prisoners were transported to the port of Lübeck. Fifty men in one wagon and twenty wagons per train.

Wim was assigned to a team that had to dismantle machines in a factory belonging to the Deutsche Ausrüstungs Werke, the DAW, where boots, uniforms and other pieces of equipment had been made for the Eastern Front. He was also assigned a new barracks to sleep in. He was back to square one and had to share a bunk with two other men again and lay, to make matters worse, in the bottom berth.

But he wouldn't see much of his bunk. He had to work like the devil, chased by the Kapos, the foremen and the SS. The end of their heyday now being in sight, they didn't miss a chance to properly live it up.

With limited tools, Wim had to partly dismantle and prepare the machines for transport. He was somewhat skilled at this because of his metalworking background, but he could never work fast enough. All day long the guards shouted '*Schnell! Schnell!*' 'Quick! Quick!' and the threatening atmosphere was back in full. The prisoners got barely any food and even less sleep. The camp had to be completely empty.

'*Schneller! Schneller!*' 'Faster! Faster!'

Wim toiled, hauled and heaved for his life. Anyone who let up for a moment was thrashed – not long enough for him to lie there dead on the ground, as the prisoners were used to, but just enough of a beating to be dying from pain and yet still be able to work. The dismantled machines were put on flat carts, which they pushed to the readied freight train. It was heavy work and Wim tried to shirk whenever he could.

That nearly cost him his life. Together with three fellow prisoners, he was pushing a machine, weighing at least two thousand kilos and loaded onto a cart, along a paved path next to the factory. Wim largely pretended to be pushing. An SS guard saw right through him and gave him a hiding. His eye black and shoulder hammering, Wim had to keep pushing under the guard's watchful eyes.

During one of the rare evenings when they were allowed some rest, the men swapped stories about their experiences. A few teams had been put to work in the barracks. That was a reasonable *Kommando*. Others had to clear out the *Revier*; they told the most horrifying stories, mainly because the sick prisoners had been left to their lot for a number of days. In turn, the stories about the detention bunker were characteristic of the Nazis' sanctimony. Led by *SS-Unterscharführer*

Dreimann, one of the camp's most merciless tormentors, the prisoners had to remove all of the overhead beams from the hallway lined with cell doors. After the war, it turned out that more than two thousand men had been hanged there or, more precisely, hoisted. Now, the prisoners had to neatly whitewash the walls again, as if nothing had ever happened.

Even the vaulting horse, on which so many innocent young men had been thrashed to death and which Wim had barely escaped, was burned. A special *Kommando* destroyed the camp administration. They mixed all the paperwork with the dirty straw sacks from the barracks. The burning combination of straw, paper and jute would ensure that nearly all of Neuengamme concentration camp's readable documents were lost.

Fear now took hold of Wim. If the Nazis were erasing their traces so thoroughly, what would they do to him? He knew way too much. What would happen when they were done here and the camp looked as if it had been a vacation spot for the last few years? Unknown to him, plans had in fact been made to have the last *Kommandos* disappear. He was lucky that the Allies were advancing so quickly that the Nazis no longer had time to carry them out.

The camp's leading SS officers took good care of themselves. All the kitchen supplies were stowed in freight trucks by the kitchen *Kommando*. This included the food supply. The men spoke at night about the thousands of Red Cross packages they'd had to load. The SS had just been withholding them and letting the prisoners die. The inmates' valuable belongings in the *Effektenkammer* were also loaded into large freight trucks. These were ordinary thieves; the remaining prisoners agreed on that. Wim didn't know whether he had to laugh or cry when a few days later, he heard that even the 2,300 Angora rabbits were taken away, with the utmost care, alive and well. Many of these transports were headed to Wesselburen, Max Pauly's place of residence.

Most of the prisoners had now left. On 23 April, the commandant had personally escorted the *Torsperre* candidates away after an hour's long nerve-wracking roll call. Nobody knew to where.

More than anyone, Thumann let himself go to his heart's content with the prisoners on the departing transports. In the seven years in which concentration camp Neuengamme had existed, no one had successfully escaped and he would personally make sure this wasn't going to happen now. He snarled at the departing men that as long as the British weren't there, he was still in charge. That they would remember *SS-Obersturmbannführer* Thumann forever but never catch him. In the meantime, he quickly found a pair of victims whom, as a goodbye, he worked over with his truncheon until they bled.

The German criminal and antisocial prisoners got the 'choice' between fighting with the SS for the Fatherland or a bullet. In that way, hundreds of men were recruited and hauled off to the north. The camp emptied out.

For Wim, the last days in the camp passed in a daze. It was getting harder to stay on his feet and keep going. He wondered how long he could hold out if the Allies didn't show up soon. Maybe he'd made the wrong choice after all.

On Saturday, 28 April, together with a few fellow prisoners and using his last ounce of strength, Wim loaded the final machines onto a waiting train. He was completely exhausted. Burned out and emptied. He didn't know where he was any more, what time it was and what now awaited him. After getting the command to ready themselves to leave, he collected some remaining bits from a Red Cross package, tied his metal bowl to one of the loops at his waist with a cord and reported to the roll-call square. After the counting, the Kapos drove his group with a heavy hand into a freight wagon. Wim dragged himself to one side, sat on the floor with his back against the wooden wall and closed his eyes. He could just hear the guards slam the door shut with a loud bang. He felt light-headed and it seemed as if he were floating above his own body. Then came oblivion.

24

Prisoners at sea

Bay of Lübeck, Germany, 29 – 31 April 1945

A day later, the door opened with a lot of noise and he gradually came to his senses. The sunlight initially blinded him, but the picture slowly came into focus. Wim didn't know whether he'd slept or for how long, whether he'd been conscious or survived the journey in some kind of slumbering state. In any case, he guessed it must be afternoon and as he looked around, he realised that the man next to him was never getting up again and that there were many more like him.

Judging from the Kapos' and SS guards' bellowing and shouting, little had changed. He clambered out of the wagon and landed on the stone quay of the Lübecker Industrie-hafen, Lübeck's industrial port. What he saw was total chaos. Marines, Kapos and Wehrmacht soldiers were swarming around one another, though order was nowhere to be found. What was clear was that the SS were still in control and that's why the Kapos were still running and hitting three times harder than usual.

They were unloaded like freight. The SS had the prisoners and the dead hauled out by their ankles. With a dull thud, their remains smacked the quay and they were then dragged down the street to a large pit serving as a mass grave. After half an hour, the grave was full and the bodies were piled high against an enormous grain silo. For good measure, a visibly drunk SS man with a small body and an elongated head put a bullet in each skull. '*Ordnung und sicherheit müssen sein.*' 'There must be order and certainty.' The prisoners who rolled onto the quay more dead than alive and didn't get up quickly enough were shot in the back of the head. The SS then kicked them into the waters of the Baltic Sea.

The roll call on the quay took over an hour. Wim's lips were scabbed and torn from thirst. The little bit of water he'd been able to bring was long since finished. They finally got something to eat from out of a large cauldron. Swede soup, naturally. Although it didn't taste of anything, the warm liquid did him some good. He was determined to save the bits of bread and dried sausage from the Red Cross package. After all, you never knew what would happen.

Evening fell. The few hundred prisoners were sitting on the quay, underneath one of the granary's awnings. SS guards and marines kept a sharp eye on them, their hands on their guns. The other SS members withdrew into the giant complex and Wim could soon hear singing and shouting. Boxes filled with wine and food disappeared through the loading dock. Outside, it quickly grew colder. It was about ten degrees, which was chilly, though at least it stayed dry. The grain silo towered twenty metres above them, like a majestic giant looking out over the port. In front of them, the water rippled quietly. They could do little but wait for what the Germans had in store for them.

After half an hour, an enormous freight ship came into the port. '*ATHEN*' was written in large black capital letters along its front. Near the ship's bow and stern were tall masts and in its middle a white superstructure around four storeys high. Wim reckoned the length to be at least a hundred metres.

This was what the Kapos had been waiting for. The prisoners had to line up in rows of five. Wim didn't manage to get himself in the middle. He was standing close to the front and had to be one of the first to go aboard. One of the Kapos made a scene when driving him over the gangway to the upper deck and Wim barely had time to think, since he could already feel the next prisoner coming up behind him. They were led to an opening in the deck, barely a square metre in size and the entrance to one of the four cargo holds.

Wim descended the metal ladder into a dark hole. After about fifteen rungs, he could feel his trousers being tugged by people below him in the hold. A fraction of a second later, he lost his footing and was pulled down further. For a moment he feared he might fall and injure himself, but the many hands that were groping him wouldn't let him. Instinctively, he hit and kicked out around him and landed with a smack on the floor. The men threw themselves on the next victim. As he got up, slightly dazed, he saw that he'd lost his jacket and also that his food and spoon had disappeared. Luckily, he'd tied his metal bowl to his waist and they hadn't been able to get it loose. He also still had his shoes. Held together with laces and extra cord, they were firmly on his feet.

All things considered, he couldn't complain; the reception committee had been favourably disposed towards him. Most of the other prisoners arrived in the hold in their underwear and on bare feet. He had soaked his trousers landing in a layer of slime and muck several centimetres deep.

The stench here was similar to what he'd been used to in the *Revier*, but many times worse. It made Wim gasp and he forced himself to stay calm, think clearly and keep looking around.

The main language was Russian, which didn't particularly put him at ease. Hundreds of Russian prisoners stole anything they could get their hands on from the new arrivals, like a swarm of bees rushing to honey. He needed to try to stay away from them. He also needed support. He was extremely vulnerable on his own with these bold, ravenous and feral creatures around him.

He approached two men who were speaking Dutch to each other. They added every other Dutchman they spotted, stumbling around half-naked, to their group. With about twenty of them, they found a spot in a corner of the hold, where a metal platform twenty centimetres wide and fifteen centimetres high stuck out from the ship's hull. You could sit on it without having your rear end in the filthy layer of mess. After an hour, the calm had returned and they sat shoulder to shoulder looking out. They didn't have much to say to one another, as they each needed time to process their new situation. Nevertheless, they could quickly agree about one thing: if they weren't liberated soon, this ship would be their ruin. Some even claimed the Nazis were planning to torpedo the vessel with their U-boats, which were waiting in the bay for instructions. No concentration camp prisoner would live to speak of the terrors of the Nazi regime.

Wim refused to indulge the thought. Of course it might

be true, but why wouldn't the Allies arrive in time? They couldn't be far away now, otherwise the camp wouldn't have been evacuated as urgently. In this way, the prisoners were living between hope and fear, ruin and liberation.

He had no idea how close he was to the truth. Just as Wim was setting foot in the *Athen*'s waste tank, the British were advancing the hundred kilometres from Bremen to Hamburg and breaking through the last German line of defence. It was just another sixty kilometres to Lübeck: the end was in sight.

On board, Wim lost track of the time. It had to be somewhere around midnight and he didn't dare go to sleep; everything was telling him that something was about to happen. They were sitting in a relatively good spot. In the other corners of the hold, most of the people relieved themselves straight onto the floor. A large proportion suffered from dysentery or other bowel diseases and as in the camp, they just let it run where they were sitting or lying down. Behind Wim, prisoners were screaming bloody murder because the Russians, who had settled on the wooden beams above them, simply crapped and pissed over them.

Wim's thirst was unbearable. He saw more and more people lying dead in the muck, on their backs or flat on their stomachs, their faces in the mess. The smell of decomposing corpses mixed with the already rotten stench. Even cattle were handled better than this. That was how the first part of the night passed. For a short while, things were much quieter and he dozed off, but it turned out to be the calm before the storm.

A group of at least eighty Russian prisoners unexpectedly raided the hold. Like a swarm of locusts, they threw themselves on the other prisoners. People shrieked and screamed like pigs. Fights broke out in various spots and Wim heard the sound of skulls being beaten in with a metal bar. The weakest prisoners didn't stand a chance. The Dutchmen huddled as close together as they could and grabbed whatever was at hand to defend themselves. As soon as the scavengers came near them, they brandished their sticks. The Russians probably knew there wasn't a lot to be had from them. They disappeared into the darkness just as quickly again.

A dark and monotonous rumble told Wim the ship's engines had been started. They picked up speed and he could hear the waves hammering against the hull.

Would they be sailing to Sweden? Prisoners were becoming seasick and spontaneously began throwing up, as if the floor wasn't foul enough. Wim dozed off to the rhythm of the waves.

He awoke from a faint early light coming into the hold. The hatch had been shoved aside and it was a new day: 30 April 1945. After a night spent on top of the metal ledge in wet trousers, a damp shirt and without a jacket, he was chilled to the bone. He itched everywhere from the lice and other vermin. He tried to scratch himself as little as possible and not damage his skin with small wounds.

The Kapos were standing on deck and shouted down that the prisoners had to haul up the corpses. The group of Dutchmen were sitting furthest from the hatch and afraid to lose their spot. They stayed put.

A macabre spectacle unfolded before their eyes. The prisoners near the hatch were thrown ropes. These were for tying around the corpses. The hollow-eyed, wasted bodies hung upside down as they were hoisted up by their ankles, their heads and shoulders banging against the walls, their arms outstretched as if slowly having to let slip from their hands the last shred of hope for survival. Other corpses were hauled up by their arms or legs. It took more than an hour before all the dead were brought on deck. If they'd wanted to hoist up all the people in the hold who were as good as dead, they'd have been busy for the whole day.

After this job was done, from their comfortable positions on deck, the guards used a rope to lower a large cauldron with a kind of soup that was closer to water. They also threw down hessian sacks filled with bread. Those with a bowl or a cup were allowed to come forwards first. A few Belgian prisoners assumed charge of the distribution. The prisoners were dehydrated and starving.

When the first twenty or thirty had received their cup of soup, the rumour went around that the pot was almost empty. The prisoners at the back of the line began pushing. The Russians played their part by aggressively working themselves forwards. Then things went wrong. The cauldron tipped over and the precious liquid mixed in with the sludge on the floor. For some of the prisoners that wasn't an obstacle at all. They threw themselves on the floor and slurped as much as they could get inside them.

Wim had seen in the *Revier* what the consequences could be. He did everything to prevent the men in his group from following their example. They were convinced and saw within several hours what Wim had saved them from. Dozens of men lay on the ground, writhing from stomach pain, fouling themselves and completely out of their minds.

A terrible sight and there was no one who could help them.

Wim had lost the ability to swallow and just barely managed to get down the lump of mouldy bread by endlessly chewing on small pieces. He couldn't dawdle for too long, since the Russian inmates were lying in wait.

They were sailing again, God knew to where. It had to have been the afternoon when they moored against a quay or alongside another ship. He heard and felt a crash. A short while later, the hatch opened and again corpses swung through the air. After about thirty bodies were hoisted up, men came clambering down. It was as if the Russians had smelled it. Within no time, the complete reception committee was standing ready and the newcomers were relieved of their clothes, belongings and food. He could hear the Kapos roaring with laughter on deck.

Hundreds more prisoners were kicked down again and the hold became overcrowded. Was that the Nazis' plan? Another few days like this and the whole ship would turn into a floating morgue. The sun blazed on the metal hull and it became unbearably warm inside.

Among the newcomers were several burly Belgians and Frenchmen. They took charge of handing out the evening meal and convinced the prisoners there was enough soup for everyone, as long as they stayed calm. That worked well. What had happened the previous day was still etched into everyone's memories.

Five large men formed a ring around the cooking pots and made the prisoners come up one by one. Because half of the prisoners didn't have a bowl or cup, the men who did were made to eat their soup first. Afterwards, the bowls were shared with the others. Even the Russians went along with the system. Wim couldn't suppress a smile. Civilisation hadn't been beaten out of them yet.

He tried to maintain some sense of time, as hard as it was. When the hatch opened again, he would have a reference point for another while. He'd been on the ship for about twenty-four hours and a new night fell. It would undoubtedly be another long one, but he didn't want to think about it too much.

That night, things were restless in the cargo hold. Groups of prisoners who had formed a secret resistance movement in Neuengamme hatched plans to overpower the guards. There were German-speaking Russians and Poles among them, Dutchmen, Belgians and Frenchmen. They went through all the scenarios but still couldn't figure it out. Maybe the next morning.

Wim shut his eyes and nevertheless was going take his chances in trying to get some sleep, when he heard a loud crack and cheering. A group of Russian inmates had removed the bottom planks from the deepest hold. They descended to the ballast tanks with cans and pots, filling them with water. Everyone could drink as much as he wanted.

Again, Wim warned as many people as he could. That water might have been sitting in those tanks for months, if not years. If you wanted to die a quick and miserable death, then by all means drink from there. But their minds were often not as strong as their weakened bodies. The moaning kept up the whole night and the next morning, the corpses were too many to count.

25

The *Cap Arcona*

Bay of Lübeck, 1 – 2 May 1945

On 14 May 1927, Hamburg's residents had flocked in their tens of thousands to the city's quays to await the launch of an ocean giant. Costing thirty-five million Reichsmarks, weighing twenty-seven thousand tonnes and measuring more than two hundred metres in length and twenty-six metres in width, the SS *Cap Arcona* dwarfed the marvelling crowds as it drifted down the Elbe. For Hamburg-Südamerikanische Dampfschifffahrts Gesellschaft – or, as the company is still known, Hamburg Süd – this was to be its definitive return to the top of the transatlantic passenger shipping industry. Nearly all of its ships had been seized as reparations for the First World War just nine years before.

In the run-up to the ship's christening, Hamburg had been awash with posters lavishing praise on the new luxury liner. The world's rich could now sail from Hamburg to Buenos Aires in just fifteen days, with stopovers in Madeira and Rio de Janeiro. With a top speed of twenty-one knots, the *Cap Arcona* wasn't simply the biggest but easily the fastest on this route.

The ship offered a tennis court on deck, a sunroom for

observing the night skies, luxurious ballrooms, a swimming pool and a cinema. Each class also had its own infirmary, mortuary, children's play area and smoking salons. The nearly four-hundred-man crew would ensure passengers had everything they could ever wish for.

Just over six months later, on 19 November 1927, the ship would embark on her maiden voyage to Argentina's capital. On board were 575 passengers travelling first class, 275 in second and 465 in third. The 84 cooks, spread across no less than five kitchens, had 15,000 kilos of meat, 6,000 kilos of poultry, 6,000 kilos of fish, 3,000 kilos of sausage and ham, 15,000 kilos of vegetables and salads, 12,000 sacks of potatoes, 40,000 eggs, hundreds of chests filled with fresh fruit and vast quantities of alcohol in every form possible. And that was just the trip out.

Over the next twelve years, the luxury liner would carry more than two hundred thousand passengers on ninety-one crossings. Then the war broke out.

In 1940, the Kriegsmarine – Nazi Germany's navy – jumped at the chance to requisition the ship. It was painted grey and used as troop accommodation in the Polish port city of Gdynia, where the Nazis had established a U-boat base. The ocean liner would lie anchored there and see little action until early 1945, when it sailed to East Prussia three times to evacuate a total of 26,000 German civilians and sick and wounded soldiers ahead of the advancing Red Army. After the last of these journeys, the queen of the South Atlantic Ocean was retired to the Bay of Lübeck, roughly three kilometres from the coastline between Lübeck and Scharbeutz, on 15 April. She was no longer seaworthy with her worn-out boilers, in part the result of sloppy maintenance during the war's chaotic final months.

Captain Heinrich Bertram had now been in command of the *Cap Arcona* for several months. After the ship had been anchored, he was ordered by *Gauleiter* Karl Kaufmann to take prisoners on board. Bertram, however, refused – a mortal sin in Nazi Germany. Kaufmann was the head of the German naval fleet and the most powerful Nazi in Hamburg. He reported directly to Adolf Hitler and Heinrich Himmler.

Each time the *Athen* moored alongside the *Cap Arcona* to tranship prisoners, Captain Bertram refused to take them on board. He had the support of the shipping company. This created an unexpected problem for the Nazi leadership and roughly 2,700 prisoners remained imprisoned in the cargo hold of the *Athen* as a result. Several days later, Bertram was ordered to shore in Neustadt. Senior SS officers, armed with machine guns, made it clear to him that he didn't have a choice. They showed him a written order; if he continued resisting, he was to be summarily executed. Bertram cut his losses: 'I have a wife and two children, so I will carry out these deranged orders.'

On 1 May, the *Athen* moored alongside the *Cap Arcona* again with a heavy bang. Wim shot backwards from the impact and landed with his hands and seat in the slime. He instantly came to his senses and when the hatch opened, he was already walking to the steel ladder, so as to be one of the first to crawl out of the hold. He had no idea what awaited him, but nothing could be worse than this cesspit where he'd spent two days and nights.

He boldly put his shoes on the ladder's bottom rung, behind two Russians who were the first to climb up. The Kapos were running the show and it was '*Schnell! Schnell!*' 'Quick! Quick!' again. He paused for a moment to take in the view of the sea and Lübeck in the distance, but a Kapo smashed his elbow with a truncheon. He screamed out, turned and only then saw the gigantic ship. He looked up along a seemingly endless grey wall that only stopped somewhere in the air high above him. Climbing onto a platform on the deck of the *Athen*, he came to a small gangway that shot steeply upwards. The thing swung back and forth as Wim desperately clung to the taut ropes on either side of him serving as railings. About eight metres below him, the seawater sloshed pleasantly against both ships' hulls, but he knew a fall would be deadly. Inch by inch, he shuffled upwards. The Kapos' batons and riding crops couldn't reach him here, in this no man's land of sorts. He could only enjoy it for a few seconds. Another few metres and the guards on the other ship would be taking things over.

From the moment he set foot on the *Cap Arcona,* he was raced along again. Here, too, Kapos, SS men and a whole army of old Volkssturm soldiers were running the ship. Behind him, a stream of hopeful men were making the same crossing. Two thousand prisoners would stay behind on the *Athen*.

Wim stepped onto the teak quarterdeck. Three massive grey-painted smokestacks jutted into the sky and two large masts stuck out high above them at either end of the ship.

The masts were fastened with cables, but before Wim could think of what they might serve, a pair of Volkssturm soldiers violently drove him to the promenade deck. They had to line up in groups of fifty prisoners. One by one, they were led past a table, where clerks took down his name and number. His name! For the first time in months, he was allowed to officially mention his name. He was Wim Aloserij again. The question was only for how long.

The Kapos drove him through a door to a lower deck. He spotted a pile of corpses against the side of the steel stair-case leading downwards. At least fifty or sixty dead bodies, stacked head to toe. In a group of about twenty prisoners, he continued descending deeper into the belly of the ship until they reached E Deck, a few metres above sea level. There, the guards beat and yelled them down the hallways. Wim simply couldn't believe what he saw there. Everything shone and glittered, the walls were covered in expensive fine wood panelling, the wooden floors gleamed. The columns looked as if they were made of solid Italian marble. How many kings, presidents, ambassadors and delegates had walked through here before him? In the cabins, prisoners now lay on thick mattresses on the floor and even in real beds. The magnificent lamps and ceiling spread a light so soft and friendly that Wim immediately felt at home. He pinched himself on his arm. This couldn't be, could it? Was he dreaming? Was he so exhausted and sick that he'd become delirious? Or was he already dead?

They walked through a dining hall decorated in Victorian style. There were even Persian rugs on the floor and the walls had been finished with luxurious gold brocade wallpaper.

The glittering chandeliers lent a surreal luxurious air to the room, where round and oval tables alternated with one another. The chairs were stacked in a corner and mattresses and blankets lay everywhere on the floor.

The dining hall looked onto a grand staircase made from dark mahogany and with brass accents. They walked past and came to a hallway. A guard shoved Wim and nine other prisoners into a cabin originally meant for four passengers.

He sat down on one of the beds. The sheets might have been used but they were still snow-white. He ran his fingers over them: real cotton, like he was used to at home. A Dutch prisoner pulled on his sleeve.

'Fresh water!'

In a small separate washroom, deliciously cold water streamed out of the tap into a sink. In a corner were white towels – used too, but still an unbelievable luxury. Wim drank no more than a few large mouthfuls. He advised the others to not immediately start drinking like crazy. Their intestines were guaranteed to protest.

They'd passed from hell to heaven. Sharing a real mattress with just one other person was a luxury they hadn't known for a long time. On the floor or in bed – it didn't matter. Before lying down, Wim splashed his face with a few handfuls of water and dried himself off with a towel that wasn't too wet. He looked in the mirror where elegant women in ball gowns had once touched up their eyelashes, put on lipstick and powdered their faces. He got a fright. He hadn't seen himself for eight months. The man staring back at him had to be someone else. A pair of hollow eyes set in a sunken face with protruding cheekbones gave him a penetrating look. It had been at least two weeks since he'd shaved and his clothes were downright disgusting.

Wim took everything off and, using the corner of the towel, began washing himself thoroughly. For the first time in ages with actual soap. After ten minutes of scouring, he felt as if he'd scrubbed off the worst of the filth from his body. He couldn't avoid putting his old rags back on, but he already felt a lot better. When bread and soup were dealt out in the hallway, Wim thought he'd landed in paradise on earth. The corpses to his left and right in the hallway immediately brought him back to reality. It was still war and he was trapped along with five thousand wrecks of men on a large cruise ship.

And yet, he was lucky. Because he'd arrived on the *Cap Arcona* among the last group, he didn't end up, like thousands of others, in the cargo holds under the engine room. The SS had stowed the Russians there en masse. The only access hatch was kept shut for a large part of the day and hundreds suffocated to death. Their bodies were hoisted up with ropes, just as on the *Athen*.

People died in the cabins too, after everything they'd had to endure, from all kinds of diseases. In Wim's cabin, two prisoners didn't make it to the next morning. They were laid by their cabin mates on a pile of other unfortunate men at the end of the corridor, a few metres past the toilets. These were dirty and stank to high heaven but still worked. Men who had lost control of their sphincters were laid nearby, mattress and all, so that the cabins didn't turn into pigsties.

The SS didn't patrol this section of the ship and instead stayed in the large sunroom above deck, where they crammed their faces and got drunk, with the knowledge that their reign would soon be coming to an end. Most of the five hundred Volkssturm and marines were fine with the prisoners walking around. As long as they kept quiet.

On the morning of 2 May, Wim left to explore the *Cap Arcona* further to see if there was anything to organise. He found it unpleasant being locked up in the middle of the ship. With a mindset focused on survival, he figured that if the SS blew up or torpedoed the vessel, he would need to be as high as possible on deck and not down below in a cabin.

On his journey, he heard rumours about Hitler's death. Supposedly he'd committed suicide, but that was of little use to Wim now. Even if the Führer was dead and the war was coming to an end, things could still end badly for him.

After wandering through E Deck, he waited for the guards to stop paying attention to him and slipped up to D Deck. The situation wasn't very different there; it only looked even more luxurious. The contrast between the glittering chandeliers and the prisoners soiling themselves and dying under them was too vast to fathom.

It was impossible to imagine that on this spot businessmen, immigrants and world travellers had once enjoyed copious meals and whiled away the time with a good glass of wine or whisky on their journey to South America.

He traded a handful of cigarettes that he'd organised for clean clothes and an extra slice of bread with sausage. After a few hours he'd seen enough and was waiting patiently in a dark corner for the right moment to retreat back to E Deck, when two prisoners speaking in German walked by in front of him. He instinctively decided to follow them. Trying not to attract any attention, he trailed them about twenty metres behind, into a hallway.

The hallway hooked sharply to the left and he lost sight of the men for a moment. By the time he went around the corner, they'd disappeared. Along the left side of the hallway, spaced every few metres, were cabin doors for passengers travelling second-class. The right wall was covered with elegant panels and lamps capped with coloured glass had been mounted beautifully to mirror the doors. He stood for a while where the men had disappeared. He carefully slid the first panel aside and found himself looking straight at the ship's hull. Rungs had been welded into the metal at intervals of forty centimetres for an emergency ladder. Wim didn't hesitate for a moment but stepped into the tight space and put his right foot onto the lowest rung. With his right arm, he held onto the rung above his head and with his left he slid the panel back into place. He climbed with large steps towards the open air and freedom.

Reaching the top, he had to make sure he didn't bump his head. His hand, groping in the semi-darkness for the next rung, felt nothing. He could only feel the metal wall curving over his head up to where it met the panels on the inside of the woodwork. He kept silent, his ear pressed against the panel. Behind it, he could hear voices speaking in German.

He waited until they weren't as close any more. Very carefully, he slid the panel a little from its place. He peered through the slit and saw a large kitchen. The men he'd followed were in the back at a stove, whispering with a few others. He could make out a number of figures at the table next to it. Bald heads, gaunt faces: from what he could see, they were all prisoners.

After he'd waited for ten minutes and still hadn't seen any Kapos, marines, Volkssturm or SS, he slid the panel further aside, enough to step into the kitchen. He greeted the men amiably and immediately opened a few cupboards, like a kid at home. They gave him a weird look and gestured with a finger at their lips that, above all, he had to be quiet.

Everywhere he looked, Wim saw shining stainless steel. Not only the supports and railing around an enormous kitchen island had been made from it, but also the rinsing basins and eight-metre-long worktop. The kitchen was strewn with bits of food. Bread, sausage, large pans with a last few mouthfuls of soup. Wim ate what he felt like. Not too much, everything in moderation.

His German was good enough to make clear to the prisoners that he was only after food and a place to hide. They told him that they'd been members of the banned German communist party and that they'd been picked up during an illegal meeting years before. They'd been in Neuengamme since 1942. They were as good as certain that Hitler was dead; they'd heard that from a Volkssturm soldier, who had read it in the newspaper himself.

Wim spent the rest of the day in the kitchen. At the back he found a suitable hiding place for the night in one of the many cupboards, where he just fit in and was well hidden, even if it was as cramped as a coffin.

As evening fell on the *Cap Arcona*, the first reconnaissance detachment from the British Army reached an abandoned

Neuengamme concentration camp. All traces of death, violence and destruction had been carefully erased. Incriminating material had disappeared, the camp records had been burned and every one of the hundred and seventy buildings and barracks were found clean. Nothing indicated that in the last three weeks sixteen thousand prisoners had died there. Several hours before, the very last SS members and prisoners had left, convinced their work was done. Unknown to them a heroic man, the German communist and hospital barracks administrator Eduard Zuleger, had mustered the courage to bury the *Revier*'s final quarterly report and the death register in a cardboard box under one of the hospital barracks, just before he, too, had to leave the camp.

That night, Wim kept being awoken by distant explosions. Each time a wave beat against the *Cap Arcona*, he feared the impact of a torpedo, but the fatal blow never came. The Nazis were blowing up their own submarines and warships. More than forty vessels were kept out of Allied hands that way.

Without the prisoners noticing, a large group of SS members left the ship. They were relieved by twenty volunteers from the *SS-Helferinnenkorps*, a female auxiliary unit, who were responsible for doing the proper paperwork. The Volkssturm and marines were given the order to remain on the ship and guard the prisoners under all circumstances.

At around two o'clock a supply ship moored alongside the ocean giant. It brought fresh drinking water and remained parked there. Wim didn't notice anything in his sleeping cupboard. He also missed the refuelling early that morning.

At Von Bassewitz-Behr's orders, a tanker pumped in just enough oil to coat the bottom of the *Cap Arcona*'s tanks, creating a highly volatile mixture of gases. The lieutenant general of the Waffen-SS had gained a lot of experience with the motorised SS, where he'd learned all about the explosiveness of oil and petrol.

26

Liberators on the horizon

Bay of Lübeck, 3 May 1945

British reconnaissance planes had discovered that part of the German naval fleet had arrived in the Bay of Lübeck. They reported that six destroyers, multiple submarines and troop transport ships had dropped anchor among the ocean steamers and freighters near Neustadt in Holstein. This confirmed their suspicion that the Nazis were moving troops by sea and fitted in with information gathered by intelligence.

Among the Allies, some were afraid the SS and other German elite troops were planning to escape to Scandinavia, so as to continue the war for as long as possible from there. Above all, Allied Commander-in-Chief Dwight D. Eisenhower was especially concerned. His staff and that of Arthur Coningham, commander of the RAF's 2nd Tactical Air Force, agreed that this needed to be avoided at all costs. For days already, fighter planes had been strafing anything that moved in northern Germany.

After British tanks and armoured trucks entered Lübeck without any resistance on 2 May, the Red Cross's local representative, Paul de Blonay, told British Major General Roberts of the 11th Armoured Division that thousands of concentration camp prisoners were on board ships off the coast. Roberts relayed the message to his headquarters.

Shortly before the city's capture, the Germans had quickly towed a large freighter, the *Thielbek*, with two tugboats and a submarine escort, into the Bay of Lübeck. Its cargo holds contained another 2,800 prisoners. Anchors were cast about seven hundred metres from the *Cap Arcona*, close enough for a proportion of the 5,000 prisoners on board to spot the ship through the ocean liner's portholes. The tugboats swung around to get back before evening. Thursday, 3 May dawned. Wim feasted on bread and marmalade. Seven German prisoners were keeping him company, or rather, they left him in peace. Wim wasn't taking any more chances and stayed in the kitchen, where he could dive into his hiding spot if needed. There was no way they'd find him. If something were to happen to the ship, he was better off here than a few decks below. He no longer had to look for any food or a trade anyway. He only took some food to his cabin mates via the safe route.

While Wim was busy with his food shuttle service, in Lübeck a Swedish doctor from the Red Cross, Hans Arnoldsson, twice informed the British that there were concentration camp prisoners aboard the ships anchored in the bay. A short while later that morning, Von Bassewitz-Behr had a misleading radio message broadcast from a panzer tank in Neustadt:

In the Bay of Lübeck, near Neustadt, three steam ships carrying German soldiers and war materials are about to leave for Sweden.

British intelligence officers were working overtime to evaluate all the incoming information. The German message appeared to confirm the Allies' suspicions. The last thing they wanted was a guerrilla war fought from Norway. Arnoldsson's message, in turn, snagged somewhere between intelligence and the British Army command and never reached the right people.

In the Allied headquarters on the Lüneburg Heath, they'd been busy negotiating from eleven o'clock that morning. On behalf of the Reich president and Commander-in-Chief Admiral Karl Dönitz, Hitler's successor, a German delegation had offered a partial surrender, so that Germany could continue fighting against the Russians, preferably with the help of the Western Allies. British general and Field Marshal Bernard L. Montgomery resolutely declined.

Meanwhile, on board the *Cap Arcona*, the tension was now so thick you could cut it with a knife. Wim heard his German companions alternately whispering about torpedoes, air attacks and even the possibility that the captain would blow up the ship himself. One of them said every German ship had explosives on board so as to prevent the vessel from falling into enemy hands in the case of an Allied invasion. None of it put Wim at ease. So close to liberation and yet still so far. It didn't matter what the situation was – he needed to get off the ship as quickly as possible.

Because of the many sea mines in the Kattegat between Sweden and Denmark, the Royal Navy couldn't intervene and the air force had to take action. Coningham didn't waste any time. At a quarter past eleven that morning, the 2nd Tactical Air Force launched Operation Big Shipping Strike with day order 71:

Hostile ships departing from the harbours at Sleeswijk-Holstein are to be destroyed by Groups 83 and 84.

Three hundred kilometres to the south, the famous squadron leader and group captain John 'Johnny' R. Baldwin readied his 198 Squadron for departure. Baldwin had already flown hundreds of missions and was a lauded flying ace with no fewer than sixteen hits to his name, most of them Messerschmitt Bf 109s, his favourite enemy aircraft. He'd marked the side of his Hawker Typhoon with a swastika for every machine he shot down.

They'd been bivouacking for about two weeks in tents at a small airstrip near Plantlünne, less than thirty kilometres from the Dutch border near the city of Oldenzaal. Each time the front advanced in a northerly direction, they followed at a safe distance. His staff would then search for a strategically placed airport or airstrip. If there wasn't one nearby, the sappers made their own.

Johnny Baldwin checked the instruments inside the cockpit of his Typhoon. He commanded nine Hawker Typhoon fighter planes, as part of the 2nd Tactical Air Force. His 198 Squadron belonged to Group 84 and was directed from the headquarters in the Dutch town of Delden.

For Baldwin and his men, Operation Big Shipping Strike would be one of their last missions over enemy territory.

For months they'd bombed German cities, dropping their explosive cargo and pulling up as fast as they could to a safe elevation, beyond the reach of the German flak guns. It was extremely dangerous work and on average just two out of every three planes returned to base. A combination of alcohol, pills and a huge amount of adrenaline enabled them to carry out these deadly missions.

The Typhoons slowly started moving, their engines roaring. At exactly two o'clock that afternoon, 198 Squadron was airborne and at a speed of about six hundred kilometres an hour, set course for the north, armed with phosphorous bombs and autocannons as well as eight RP3 rockets underneath their wings. Below them, a bombed-out northern Germany glided past and, in a little less than half an hour, the Baltic coastline came into view. Beyond the horizon, in the triangle formed by Kiel, Fehmarn and Lübeck, lay more than five hundred ships. They flew to the Bay of Lübeck, dropped to 3,500 metres and fell into attack formation.

Baldwin ordered four planes to attack the smaller *Thielbek* and dived with the four other fighters on the *Cap Arcona*. As soon as the ships were in range, they fired their rockets in salvos. On the deck they only saw shooting soldiers, while on the *Athen* and *Thielbek* the anti-aircraft guns rattled non-stop. The Typhoons skilfully evaded the deadly rain of bullets. They flew past, arched back around and resumed the attack with their 20mm autocannons. Smoke billowed from their targets and they mowed down everything on deck. They vanished as unexpectedly as they'd first appeared, leaving the ships burning and smoking. The *Cap Arcona*, hit by forty rockets, was battered but kept floating. After thirty-two direct hits, the *Thielbek* was listing, black clouds of smoke spewing from its middle. Not long after, the sea buried her with its waves.

Wim was sitting, reasonably relaxed, at a small table in the kitchen when the first rocket hit the ship's bow. Everything shook, pots and pans rattled on the stove. Anything that wasn't fastened fell to the floor with a bang. Before they could even realise what was going on, there was a second hit. And another. And another.

Wim threw himself onto the floor and shielded his head with his hands. He heard the ship's siren wailing. After a few minutes, the impacts came to an end.

His German companions fled the kitchen and Wim scrambled to chase after them. He just hoped they knew where they were going. The hallway was in total chaos and he lost sight of them. Screaming and shouting people were everywhere. The panelling and the ceiling were on fire. After all those years, the tropical wood had turned bone dry and the flames rapidly devoured everything around them. The stairwells acted as chimneys and within several minutes the entire hallway was ablaze. People stumbled over the corpses and wounded men lying everywhere. Some of the prisoners had caught fire themselves, while others were missing limbs and bleeding like stuck pigs. Whoever fell stayed down, whoever ended up on the floor was trampled and whoever didn't get up again died on the spot.

Wim had no idea where to go, since he'd only come into the kitchen using the sliding panels along the ship's hull. All he knew was that he needed to get outside as soon as possible, up on deck. But five thousand other desperate men had thought the same and a battle for survival broke out. Prisoners who tried reaching the middle deck by way of the grand staircase fell back down with bullets in their heads and chests. The SS guards weren't letting anyone up the stairs. Much of the ship was burning like a torch. With the greatest possible difficulty, Wim ran and crawled through the hall towards the ship's stern. He reached a staircase that offered access to the hallways on B Deck. Everywhere he went, he came across twisted steel plates, pieces of wood, broken furniture and torn limbs. He crawled over piles of corpses to a door that opened onto the upper deck. The chaos there, if it was even possible, was much greater. Prisoners fought with one another for life vests, a group settled a score with a hated Kapo. He oriented himself using the smokestacks and the command bridge, which spanned the ship's width. Marines were shooting at anyone who came near them. In blind panic, people jumped over the railing, many never reaching the water twenty metres below, as they smashed their heads against the ship's hull and died instantly.

All of a sudden came the throb of aeroplane engines overhead. A new attack by two other RAF squadrons with Hawker Typhoons and Tempest fighters dived on the ships. Captain Bertram ordered the white flag raised, but the pilots had no way of seeing it through the smoke and fire. On deck, the desperate prisoners watched the explosions and flashes of light on the ships around them.

The *Deutschland* and the *Athen* were also hit, the latter only by machine-gun fire. On the *Deutschland* there were no prisoners, but onboard the *Athen*, which lay in the harbour, two thousand men were anxiously hoping and praying in the cargo hold. They were spared, but the barrage mowed down the guards up on deck. The planes dived on the *Cap Arcona* again and with their autocannons fired armour-piercing, high-explosive shells. Anything that wasn't burning already now caught light. The mounted machine guns fired non-stop. Wim had found cover under a metal flight of stairs, which led to the deck above. After this wave of attacks had passed, the ship was strewn with even more corpses and body parts.

A lifeboat hung at the side of the ship, ready to be lowered. On board, many of the SS women and several SS men picked off the prisoners on deck. One of the ropes burned through, pitching the boat forwards. Amid loud screams, the men and women fell into the sea. Most of them never resurfaced and if they did, they didn't last long in water that was six degrees above freezing. People were everywhere in the sea. Swimming, floundering or floating as corpses. Those who could still move tried to grab hold of a piece of wood or anything else that was still floating. From up on deck, doors, planks and furniture were thrown down, but given the height, a lot of these items, intended as lifebuoys, transformed into deadly projectiles. Wim understood that jumping overboard in his poor condition would be suicide.

He looked around but only saw soldiers shooting blindly. Before Wim's eyes, an SS guard put a bullet in his own head. Other SS members shot their way to the last lifeboats. Their pistols drawn, they forced the marines out and made them lower the boats. One of the boats ran into trouble and became caught on one side. Everyone inside tumbled into the sea as the prisoners loudly cheered. When other boats went to pick up these SS members and there wasn't actually enough space on board, they began fighting and shooting among themselves.

As this fight to the death was taking place aboard the devastated ships, Squadron Leader Baldwin and his colleagues neatly parked their Typhoons at exactly 15:20 along the edge of the forest at Plantlünne. All except one fighter pilot had returned to headquarters unscathed and they longed for a few cold bottles of beer.

Three hundred kilometres to the north, the two other squadrons were still firing at anything that moved. A German speedboat deliberately steered itself over floating prisoners, so as to mow their heads off with its propellor. With a well-aimed rocket, a fighter pilot soon put an end to this. Several floundering prisoners struggled to two lifebuoys. The first ones there tried sticking their heads through them, but three or four pairs of hands prevented them. Everyone held on to the buoys, with the consequence that a bunch of people went down together because the ring could never hold their weight. No one came back up. Several minutes later, this spectacle repeated itself among another group of desperate drowning prisoners who threw themselves onto the buoys. In this way, the *Cap Arcona*'s lifebuoys brought about the eventual demise of many.

The supply cutter that had moored the previous night had got off scot-free. Loaded with SS members, part of the ship's crew and the violinist Francis Akos, the ship managed to pull away from the *Cap Arcona*. Smaller rescue boats had less of a chance. Floundering prisoners tried to climb in. If there were soldiers on board, the inmates were blown away without a second thought. If they were lucky enough to reach a boat that other prisoners had taken over but then stayed in one spot for too long, so many people would climb aboard that they took on water and sank. From the coast, all kinds of smaller and larger vessels rushed to help, the majority of them with SS men and soldiers on board and with explicit instructions only to save Germans. These were clearly visible in the water, floating in their life jackets.

The ocean liner's deck was now ablaze as well. Wim felt the rising heat singeing his head and he had to act quickly. It was a choice between jumping or burning alive. His eyes searched for anything that could save him. They fell on a rope that miraculously wasn't burning. He didn't hesitate for a second, got rid of his clothes, climbed over the railing and lowered himself bit by bit. Four or five metres above the waves, the rope ran out and he had to drop. He waited for a few moments until he was sure that nothing or no one was below him, pushed with his feet against the ship's hull and let go. For a moment he flew through the air, his mind blank. He no longer thought of the war, or of the hunger or of home – until his feet hit the water and he gasped for breath from the cold. He wasn't a strong swimmer. He could do it, but the last time had been one summer years ago in the calm waters near Amsterdam and it had been thirty degrees outside.

He didn't see anything to cling to. He thrashed around and kicked in the ice-cold water. He wouldn't be able to keep this up for long. He felt his strength ebbing and desperately looked around him but only saw floating corpses among the wreckage and exhausted prisoners who didn't stand a chance.

All of a sudden, not five metres from him, an empty rubber raft floated past. He tried to swim to it. It took dismally long before he could finally grab an edge. As he heaved himself aboard with his last ounces of strength, he saw another prisoner doing the same on the other side. Once they were inside, they each fished a piece of wood out of the water to paddle away from the burning wreck.

It was a few kilometres to shore, which they could see in the distance. On the way, they came across floating and swimming prisoners and after a quarter of an hour, the rubber boat was filled with ten men. To take on more passengers would have jeopardised their safety.

Wave after wave of attacks were carried out overhead. The rattling of the planes' machines guns didn't seem to end. Fighter planes from the American XXIV Tactical Air Command and the Coastal Command had rushed to the British fighters' aid in order to destroy as many ships in the Baltic Sea as possible. Wim paddled like a man possessed; his life depended on it. Now, their greatest worry was that an Allied machine gun would pierce their raft. It never occurred to him that he could also be hit.

A number of small high-hulled cruisers typical of the German navy had sailed out from the base in Neustadt with orders to fish out German soldiers. Wim watched as prisoners who desperately tried to climb aboard were mercilessly shot. It just made him paddle harder, his only means of keeping warm without clothes. After half an hour, they were a safe distance from the *Cap Arcona* but still about two kilometres from the coast. Two men lay dead at the bottom of the raft. The survivors gently slid them over the edge and handed them over to the sea; a few of them made the sign of the cross.

As they caught their breath for a moment, they heard a tremendous blast behind them. The *Cap Arcona*'s fuel tank had exploded, exactly as Von Bassewitz-Behr had planned. Flames erupted from the middle deck and it wasn't long before the ship capsized to portside, thousands of prisoners still aboard. It didn't sink but remained on its side, as it was broader than the sea was deep. Survivors who could cling to the rails or to fixed parts on deck tried to reach the keel, which still stuck out above the water. The thousands of men in the holds were like rats in a trap.

The SS had taken measures to ensure that as few people on board as possible would live to talk about it. Not only had all of the fire hoses been cut, but also the fire-fighting systems, the pumps to spray fire-extinguishing seawater and the automatic fire-resistant partitions had all been knocked out. There were only enough life jackets for the guards, as the rest had been taken to shore. Most of the SS members had left the ship in time. They weren't at all interested in what happened to their colleagues in the Wehrmacht, Kriegsmarine and Volkssturm.

While Wim was still busy paddling, the British reached the edge of Neustadt. Towards half past four that afternoon, the first tanks rolled through the streets and at around five o'clock, they reached the central market square. There, they encountered a huge chaos of refugees, prisoners, soldiers, local looters and SS members disguised in civilian dress.

Far from all of the beaches were safe. Prisoners who had managed to reach the coast with their last bit of strength were sometimes shot dead by Wehrmacht soldiers or Hitler Youth. North-west of Neustadt, towards Pelzerhaken, this was the order of the day. They also bashed in the inmates' skulls with spades.

The shipwreck survivors who came ashore to the south of Neustadt were luckier. The area was already in the British Army's hands and they were collected and directly sent to hospitals or reception centres such as the submarine school, which the British had requisitioned for this purpose.

Under British orders, the German officers and soldiers gathered themselves on the market square at six o'clock in the evening for the official surrender. The liberators now heard about the unimaginable drama that had played out at sea. At around seven o'clock, they sent a ship out to collect the survivors from the *Cap Arcona*'s keel. Hours later, the craft sailed back into the harbour carrying 314 utterly exhausted, wounded and sometimes completely naked survivors, some of whom would die in the days afterwards from previous deprivations or the sudden abundance of food.

Once everyone was counted, it appeared that only around four hundred people had survived the disaster on the *Cap Arcona*. Five waves of attacks and no less than sixty-two direct hits had laid waste to the pride of Hamburg Süd. Besides the 1,400 victims who had died on the ship in the days before the air attack, more than 4,200 further unfortunates died just hours before the liberation. The *Thielbek* had sunk within fifteen minutes, with 2,850 prisoners on board. Only fifty managed to save themselves. The luxury cruise ship the *Deutschland* went down during the attack as well. The crew had managed to get themselves to safety in time. All 2,000 prisoners on the *Athen* survived the attack.

In total, two hundred aeroplanes had taken part in Operation Big Shipping Strike. For the Allies, it was an extraordinarily successful mission. Just one plane had been hit by enemy flak; the pilot had used his parachute to land safely to the south-west of Neustadt. Twenty-three German ships were wholly destroyed and 115 so badly damaged that sailing was impossible.

The British day report for 3 May read:

In an excellently carried-out mission, nine planes of the 198th Squadron have destroyed a ship weighing 12000 tonnes, and a freighter of 1500 tonnes. According to the reports, the 12000-tonne ship burned from bow to keel when the planes left the area. Considering the weather conditions it is safe to assume that the water was very cold today.

Not a word about the seven thousand dead prisoners.

And Wim? He paddled and paddled, harder than he'd ever done in his kayak on the Amstel river or the Amsterdam canals. His thoughts faded into nothingness; he lost himself in the rhythm of the motion. With the beach in sight, he lost consciousness. He came to as someone was wrapping a blanket around his naked body and he felt sand beneath his feet.

Each wave brought new bodies ashore, a diabolical cycle. It was an image he'd never be able to forget. The sound of the sea hurt his ears. A shudder went through his starving body. Then everything went dark again.

27

Answered prayers

Neustadt, Germany – Amsterdam, May 1945

The first thing he felt when he regained consciousness was a soft hand pushing against his shoulder. The man who had wrapped him in a blanket pointed to a stone building along the coast and said a field hospital was there. He needed to go to it. He only had to cross the street.

It wasn't warm, but Wim was freezing. His whole body shook. Thinking clearly wasn't happening; violent emotions fought for priority in his head. Crazed, he walked to the emergency hospital. The Germans had equipped an old school on the outskirts of the city as a reception site for wounded soldiers who needed care but not emergency assistance.

Inside, he saw nothing but German soldiers. This didn't especially put him at ease and immediately made him more alert. A nurse gave him a shirt and underwear and led him into a ward full of bunkbeds. The bottom berths were all occupied. With some difficulty, he heaved himself up onto an empty top bunk. He had lost all sense of time, but according to the clock, it had to be six o'clock in the evening. After an hour underneath the blankets, dozing off a bit in the pleasant warmth, he already felt much better.

Two men walked into the hall and directed themselves towards several German officers. He perked up his ears. Was that English he heard? He sat up and couldn't believe his eyes. British officers were giving the Germans instructions. British! They'd been liberated. Wim couldn't believe it.

He was free. The war was over.

The German officers beat a retreat and the British soldiers took charge of the emergency hospital. He lay back to process this news too. He must have stayed like this for at least ten minutes. He stared at the ceiling and felt the doubt welling up. What would he do? Stay here to regain his strength or still try to find a way home as quickly as possible? The nurses were handing out bread to the German soldiers lying in the field hospital. Wim was ignored. When he asked if he could also get something to eat, he was told their instructions had been that the rations were only meant for soldiers. And he was no soldier.

All of a sudden, his decision was made. He wasn't going to stay a second longer than was strictly necessary in this country. He must get away from here, as fast as possible. He asked the older man in the bed below him if he could borrow his clothes for a bit, so as to get some food too. The German soldier only had one leg and mumbled that Wim would then need to come back straight afterwards. Within no time, Wim had on the grey Wehrmacht trousers and the accompanying blue sweater. A little further on, he rustled up a pair of shoes – by no means the best. There were holes in them and the soles flapped. Apparently, the Wehrmacht was no longer what it used to be either.

Still a little unsteady, he took his first steps as a free man on German soil. He walked to the street that ran parallel to the coast where he'd washed ashore. Only then did he realise that he had literally no idea where his fellow passengers had gone. A look at the beach told him, if anything, that it wasn't where he needed to be. In the distance, he saw the heavily smoking *Cap Arcona* lying on its side. On the beach, corpses everywhere lay between the flotsam.

He walked on to the city's centre. Two tanks with British soldiers drove towards him. Wim greeted them with a clenched fist and grinned from ear to ear. The British greeted him back. Soldiers on the second tank gave him Players cigarettes and chocolate. A treat! He got the chocolate down immediately, stuck the cigarettes in the pocket of his Wehrmacht trousers and walked on to the port. It grew busier and he saw more and more traces of the war. Black smoke clouds were rising from the wreck of the *Athen* too. No one paid any attention to the corpses of women and children lying along the quay.

British tanks and armoured vehicles were parked at strategic positions, but the place was still teeming with *Ordnungspolizei*, Wehrmacht, Kriegsmarine and Volkssturm, most of them with tense and ashen faces. Their bravado had vanished. In among them were cheering, laughing and singing people, mainly ex-prisoners. In a corner of the square, British soldiers were holding groups of SS members at gunpoint, the Germans' hands raised and their faces to the wall.

Shop doors were open, windows had been smashed. Prisoners and the residents of Neustadt walked around with groceries and boxes of provisions. Entire shops and storerooms were plundered and everything edible was carried off.

He saw residents running away with whole wheels of cheese underneath their arms. People spontaneously handed out bread and cheese on the street and Wim had himself a feast. Even a bowl of condensed milk came his way. He savoured it but held himself to several healthy gulps.

In the streets ahead, shots still occasionally rang out. When he came to the market square, hundreds of ex-prisoners were dancing around the British tanks. A skeleton dance in striped pyjamas. Others kneeled and thanked God. Here, too, British soldiers handed out cigarettes and delicacies. Former prisoners squeezed the hands of their liberators, crazed with joy.

Wim stumbled upon a Dutchman he'd met in Neuengamme. He asked whether Wim wanted to go with him to the reception centre at the submarine school, in the middle of the city. Wim kindly thanked him but continued his search. But what was he actually looking for? Where could he really go? He didn't have documents or a passport, he weighed barely forty kilos, he was still covered in vermin and he looked filthy and unkempt, but something was pushing him onwards. He wanted to leave this cesspool. So he kept walking, among Russians and Polish ex-prisoners, past Frenchmen and Belgians. He tensed with fear when, in a flash, he saw someone flee into a street, a Kapo from Neuengamme. For a moment, he hesitated about whether he should go after him or walk in exactly the opposite direction, but when he looked around the corner, the man was nowhere to be seen.

A car drove in his direction, a blue or green DKW, he couldn't quite make it out in the dark. It stopped right in front of him. The driver stuck his head out of the window and asked if he wanted to ride with them.

'Where are you guys going?' asked Wim.

'Home, the Netherlands.'

Wim couldn't step in quickly enough. Two men sat in the front and judging from their shaved heads, they'd also come from a camp. They introduced themselves as Piet and Peer.

'How did you guys get your hands on a car?' Wim asked when they were under way.

'A German retailer selflessly put it at our disposal,' said Peer, laughing in the passenger seat.

'Stolen from a garage, then,' said Piet. 'Brits filled her up. We're going to Hamburg first.'

After passing Allied checkpoints, they set course for the south, to Lübeck and Hamburg. The men had been *Funktionshäftlinge* in Neuengamme and had been on the *Athen* for a relatively short while. They spoke about their experiences from the previous days, but Wim didn't absorb any of it. He fell into a deep sleep.

Sometime in the middle of the night, he was jolted awake. They were in Hamburg, but Allied soldiers had stopped them before the large bridge across the Elbe. No one was allowed to cross the river and they had to hand over the car. Otherwise, the soldiers were perfectly friendly. They needed to prevent Germans or the foreigners who had collaborated with them from escaping along this route. Wim understood but was disappointed. He wanted to go home and tell everyone what had happened. What the Germans had done to him in the camps and on the ships. Everything he'd had to overcome to be able to tell his story.

The barracks where they were to stay was reasonably comfortable. They slept in bunkbeds, two high, with real mattresses, were given enough to eat and there was medical care. The next day, Wim could finally shower. He was medically examined and deloused in the days that followed.

In the displaced persons camp, he heard about the spectacular escape of a group of prisoners who were only picked up the day after the disaster of the *Cap Arcona*. They'd hidden themselves in a cabin, as they were scared of still being shot by the SS. Even that evening, when the rescue crews moored alongside the ship, they'd stayed hidden. They didn't know who the visitors were and feared for their lives. It was the next day, when they heard English being spoken at the keel of the ship, that they finally came out. Wim lapped up these kinds of stories. They gave him the strength to keep going and to try to put all the misery behind him.

On 8 May, a loud cheer sounded in the camp. The news spread like wildfire: Germany had unconditionally surrendered. The war was finally over. A party broke out and everyone who could get something alcoholic to drink eagerly put it to their lips.

A day later, Wim was chatting to the two guys he'd arrived with at a table in the lounge building, when on the intercom system a message blared in Dutch: 'This is a call for the pride of the Dutch people. Please report to barracks number three.'

'That'll be us,' said Wim enthusiastically. They jumped to their feet, but a big disappointment awaited them. A group of at least twenty Dutch military officers were standing at attention outside the barracks and being praised by a senior officer for their courage. They'd been interned in a German prisoner of war camp and were allowed to go home. All of them still looked good and had a healthy shine to their faces, as if they'd sat in a holiday camp. This was the pride of the Dutch people. Apparently, concentration camp prisoners weren't included. Wim slunk off, disillusioned.

After about three weeks in the British displaced persons camp, an officer announced the names of the men who would be going to the Netherlands. Wim was among them. They would be leaving the next morning and he couldn't wait. That afternoon, a Dutchman came to him, a postman who had worked in Germany for years. He'd heard that Wim was going back to Amsterdam and asked if he could take a kitbag with him; he would pick it up later. The man gave Wim a pair of blue postman's trousers with a red stripe down the side for the trouble. Wim was only too happy with them. Those damned Wehrmacht trousers could finally come off.

The following morning, wearing his new trousers, Wim stepped into the back of a large British army truck. Along the sides were fixed wooden benches covered with small pillows. Wim sat as close to the cabin as possible.

After half a day of driving and frequent stopping at the many checkpoints along the way, the Netherlands finally came into view. They crossed the border near Enschede after a final check; fifty metres beyond it was their destination for now. Wim feasted his eyes on the repatriation centre. It was set up in a marvellous historical building, a former Redemptorist monastery, where groups of Hitler Youth had camped during the war.

The Dutch Military Authority, which was provisionally governing the newly liberated country, had set up a special bureau for the evacuation, repatriation and care of war victims. Wim was registered and given another medical examination. His feet and legs had swollen up from oedema and his face looked unhealthily bloated. The doctor rubbed an ointment into his armpits, where unusual biological responses were taking place that were never encountered in a healthy person. The entire stream of returning Dutch people was thoroughly deloused underneath a cloud of DDT.

The police and intelligence services were working overtime to prevent collaborators from slipping into the country. He had to tell his story to an official and fill out an official document on which he could describe his experiences in the camps. The man promised they would get to work straight away – Wim would be hearing very soon when he would be able to go home. By the next day, he was transferred to another building and his name was added to the list for the Collection Point Departures. That was nice, but he was still stuck.

Wim only brightened up when it became clear he was really going to be taken home in a passenger car by two soldiers from the Netherlands Interior Forces, an army of resistance fighters formed the previous year. When the time came to leave, two young men from Putten had joined them. They were sick and completely emaciated, in terrible shape.

On 30 May 1945, after driving several hours, they arrived in the village of Putten, most of whose men had been murdered by the occupying forces. They dropped the men off and drove on to Amsterdam, to the Tweede Oosterparkstraat. Along the way, they had to stop multiple times for checkpoints and barricades. The Netherlands was in a festive mood – flags with red, white and blue stripes were hanging everywhere – but he also saw the destruction the war had wreaked. As they got closer to their destination, he also noticed the consequences of hunger and deprivation in the faces of his compatriots.

At the end of the afternoon, they finally arrived in Amsterdam. Wim stepped out in front of his mother's house. With a jovial wave, he said goodbye to his escorts.

He rang the doorbell and knocked, but no one opened, not even after ringing multiple times and pounding on the door. A few houses down the street was Jo, who did open her door right away when he tried knocking, though initially she didn't recognise her younger brother in his postman's trousers and with a kitbag slung over his shoulder.

'Wim? Is that you?' she asked carefully.

'It's me.'

She threw her arms around his neck and only let him go after a few minutes. Jo was beside herself with joy at seeing Wim again. They had so much to tell each other; she was euphoric. Wim had a harder time expressing his happiness. He noticed how unfettered the liberation had made her and decided, for the time being, to wait before telling her too much about his experiences in the camp. Jo talked his head off.

She made coffee substitute, as there was still no real coffee to be had, and started: 'We didn't know where you were. In Germany or maybe in Russia or Poland. I was convinced you were still in one piece. Hey, you did get some chubby cheeks.'

Wim just smiled and didn't mention the oedema or the pain in his chest at every breath.

'A few days after they took you away, Ger came by,' said Jo. 'He told us about the razzia and said they'd taken you to the police headquarters in Hoorn. We didn't find out until a few days later that you'd gone to the Euterpestraat. I thought they would have let you go. After that, we didn't hear anything else until we got your card saying that you were on your way to Germany. But fortunately, you're back now.'

'Fortunately. Where's Mother?' Wim asked. 'She didn't open up a second ago.'

'Oh well, of course you didn't hear about that either. She went into hiding.'

'Into hiding? Mother?'

'Yeah, in Beverwijk. A few months ago now. I just cancelled the lease and don't know who's living there. Do you remember Aunt Rita from the Kleine Kattenburgerstraat, across the street from us back then? Dirk, her youngest son, stopped by Mother's last winter with a big suitcase. He asked her for help – if he could hide at hers for a few nights from the Germans. She didn't ask any more questions and you weren't there anyway, so he slept in your room and shoved his suitcase under your bed. A few days later, suddenly all these men in uniforms turned up at the door. Mother opened up and they grabbed him by his collar right away. A little while later, they found the suitcase under your bed too and, when they opened it, there turned out to be different uniforms and papers inside. So they took Mother along to the Euterpestraat too. They kept her there for a day and questioned her. But she didn't know about anything and she speaks good German. After she was free again, we talked it over with Joop and Ger. Ger knew the address of a man who was in the oil business and only lived with his son. So she went there with Bertus. That felt safer to us.'

Wim's eyes were wide as he looked at her. She told the story as if she were ordering a kilo of apples at the greengrocer's.

'And Dirk?' he asked.

Jo shook her head. It fell silent for a moment.

'Go on and sleep here tonight,' Jo said. 'Then have a look tomorrow if you can make it to Beverwijk. I'll give you the address.'

In the end, Wim couldn't avoid telling her something about himself. He played down his time in Germany. He talked about collecting broken shovels in Husum, his job in the *Revier*, the moment when he'd pretended to be a painter and the work in the garage. Jo had to laugh at his inventiveness and in that way they chatted until late. Wim drank water as he was unwell and didn't care for any beer or wine.

In front of the house, a spontaneous party kicked off. The café just down the street was jam-packed with people in no time, but Wim didn't feel like going outside.

That night he didn't sleep very well, despite the wonderful mattress on the floor in the living room. The next day he went out to Beverwijk. He found where his mother was supposed to be living without any trouble and rang the doorbell, but nevertheless he was somewhat nervous. Her eyes went wide when she realised that her son was standing in the doorway.

'Holy Mary saved you,' were the only words she could muster.

'Well, I sure didn't see her in the camp,' Wim said.

28

Free but still captive

Amsterdam 1945 – Husum 1955

Wim ran and ran, as fast as his legs would carry him. They were coming after him. All of them. The Kapo Red Jan had beaten him with a truncheon like a man possessed, but Wim had managed to rip himself free and was now fleeing. In his striped uniform, he jumped over ditches and crawled under barbed wire. He sank up to his ankles in the marshy fields. Pauly and Griem were chasing him too. He could clearly see the bitter look in their eyes. Griem pulled out his pistol. He needed to run faster, run for his life. Then the sound of barking. They'd sent the dogs after him, the bastards. In the distance, the train to the anti-tank trenches waited, ten freight wagons in a line. He needed to try to reach them.

He was almost there, but the dogs were gaining on him quickly. The train, he had to try to get to the wagons. He kicked the first German shepherd away from him. From his left now came a whole army of SS men and Kapos. Their truncheons swung through the air. He heard the crack of their riding crops and smelled the sickly stench of the cre-matorium. The smoke blinded him for a moment. Would he make it? Just as he was about to jump onto a wagon,

Thumann and Klinger were standing right in front of him. Their eyes flamed and they were foaming at their mouths. They laughed at him satanically and pointed their pistols at his head.

'No! Stop!'

Jo lay a wet towel on Wim's forehead. He was sitting straight up in bed. His shirt was drenched.

'You were screaming again,' she said, 'just like last night. What actually happened there? What did they do to you?'

Wim took a sip of water and didn't answer.

'Thanks, but I'll be fine – really,' he said.

He didn't sleep for the rest of the night; he couldn't stop tossing and turning.

Wim had been back for two weeks and was trying to find his way in the liberated Netherlands. Every night there was a party somewhere that he could go to, but his heart wasn't in it. Wim was more worried about practical matters. He'd gone to the municipality of Amsterdam again to arrange a house for himself, his half-brother Bertus and their mother. But the rules for getting things done in the civilised world were very different than those for organising something in a concentration camp. He needed to fill in forms and had to explain, ad nauseum, why his mother had temporarily stayed in Beverwijk and he didn't have a house himself. It cost him a lot of energy every time. Energy he barely had. Wim was soon tired and out of breath, his legs and head were still swollen and the pain in his chest disseminated to large parts of his body.

★

Midway through June 1945, they were given a house at 11 Rustenburgerstraat, not all that far from the Tweede Oosterparkstraat but on the other side of the Amstel river. From family and acquaintances, they got some simple furniture and aid organisations helped to make the house a little liveable. They didn't have to worry about half-brother Henk. During the war, he'd grown from a petty thief into a more serious criminal and had been locked up again. This time in the Lloyd Hotel, the detention centre on the Handelskade.

Wim's mother noticed that he had a terrible cough and that his chest and lungs were still giving him trouble. She took him to Doctor Dasberg. Thanks to a *Sperr* – a temporary exemption, as he was the only Jewish doctor in Amsterdam who did circumcisions – he'd been able to continue practising for some time. After the last big razzia, he'd nevertheless gone into hiding with his family and they'd all survived. Now, his house was a centre for people who had come back from the concentration camps and were searching for their families.

Wim's mother had already said to Dasberg that Wim had spent a long time in various camps. The doctor examined him and referred him to a Jewish hospital on the Nieuwe Achtergracht.

'For now, just don't do too much,' said Dasberg, 'and certainly no working or exerting yourself yet.'

Wim understood. Whenever he tried doing anything, he ran out of energy. He often lay on his bed resting, but it was getting worse. Everything between his neck and his hips hurt. The doctor had given him the address of a Jewish organisation that could give him some financial help. As he couldn't work and wasn't receiving a cent from the government, this really came in handy.

A few weeks later, Wim's mother needed to go to Doctor Dasberg herself. He asked whether Wim had improved. When he found out the opposite was the case, Wim had to go back for another full examination and again Dasberg sent him to the Nieuwe Achtergracht. This time, the diagnosis was clear: a severe form of pleurisy, caused by still other lung afflictions that, according to the doctors, he was suffering from too. He would have to recuperate for between one and two years at least. Work was out of the question and for the time being, he could forget returning to butchery. With a heavy heart, Wim went to Adolfs to tell him the bad news. Through the war, the situation had also changed and at the moment, a second branch wasn't on the cards.

Much of the food was still rationed. Luckily, Ger brought fresh fruit and vegetables on his cart twice a week from Zwaag before hawking his wares in the streets of Amsterdam. Jo, too, was happy about this: she was pregnant and ate as healthily as possible.

When she was nearly due, she moved in with her mother and brothers to give birth at their house. Of course, Doctor Dasberg would be doing the delivery. Wim enjoyed having his sister around again.

On the afternoon of 21 August, Wim was resting for a moment on his mattress, which was in the living room now that his sister was using his little bedroom as a delivery room. He could hear thumping and a fuss upstairs and already had a sneaking suspicion when he heard his mother dash down the stairs. It was time, a week early. The maternity nurse whom his mother had hired some time ago was, however, unavailable for a few days and Jo needed help immediately. She hurried to the midwifery school and came back a short while later with a nurse. Her name was Miep – a nice, lively girl from Lisse in South Holland. She was to take care of Jo during and after the delivery, which was quickly approaching, judging from the sounds upstairs. From time to time, she walked to the kitchen for water or a cup of tea. Wim waited for a good moment to slip out of the living room, since he was lying in bed in just a shirt and underwear and his clothes were in another room. He managed everything without Miep seeing him. Or so he thought.

Half a day later, little Theo came into the world. Wim was an immensely proud uncle and Miep stayed a number of days to care for Jo. Several weeks later, Wim and Miep were in a relationship. A serious relationship. So serious that, after six months, they were already making wedding plans. Miep confessed that she'd indeed seen Wim slip upstairs in his underwear. Even dozens of years later, their first meeting could always give her a good laugh.

In the autumn of 1945, the young couple joined Jo on a visit to her in-laws. They were a little early and had to wait in the front room until the Bible study session was finished, said Jo.

'Bible study with whom?' asked Wim.

'A brother of the Jehovah's Witnesses.'

'Oh, but I know them. The *Bibelforscher*. They were in the camp too. I saw a lot of them and came to really respect them. I'd actually like to learn more about that.'

After the brother had finished the session with Jo's in-laws, the young people started talking with him. He mentioned all sorts of things from the Bible and with their Catholic background, Jo and Wim began discussing these with him. It wouldn't be the last time. Many conversations would follow and the new insights landed on fertile soil. In February 1946, all three were baptised and a month later, Wim and Miep were married.

The young couple immediately faced a big problem. During the war, many houses had been destroyed, meaning there was now a housing shortage and certainly in Amsterdam, it was virtually impossible to find accommodation. Wim reached out to Stichting 40-45, a foundation set up in 1944 to help war victims, but after an investigation, they couldn't be of any help. His name had been 'blocked' and they referred him to the head office of the police. An officer took Wim's details down and asked if he could wait; he needed to verify a few things. He came back with a pair of handcuffs and went to arrest Wim. Flabbergasted, Wim asked what the matter was.

'You, sir, have stolen rugs,' said the officer.

'Rugs? Stolen? Me?'

'Yes, you – a year ago now. They nabbed you and brought you in for questioning at another station, but you escaped. We won't be doing that again now, so these cuffs are going on.'

'But that's impossible,' he said. 'I was in a German concentration camp sweeping an SS garage with a besom broom.'

The officer half believed him, but after some questioning, the cat finally came out of the bag. His half-brother Henk had given a false name when they'd arrested him during a break-in. After the issue had been cleared up, the police were extremely helpful. Within several months, Wim and Miep were allocated a residence on the Tweede van der Helststraat, in the De Pijp neighbourhood.

During the first months of their marriage, Miep often had to wake Wim in the middle of the night. He was restless, trembling, sometimes even screaming and sweating.

'Wim, you were howling like a wolf again,' she said.

Eventually, he was delivered from camp syndrome through Miep's love and care, the right medication, rest and spiritual support from the Bible and his new faith. In the autumn of 1946 he was, for the first time, able to do a little light work again. He found a job as a salesman in the showroom for the Werner electronics factory in the Eerste Oosterparkstraat, where he could work part-time.

He didn't speak to anyone about his time in the camp. At most, he would mention some general things whenever Miep dug deeper. He tried to put everything he couldn't control behind him. A few times he visited Jan Kok, the man they'd made into a famous singer in Husum. He lived with his wife, a Romani woman, on a houseboat in Amsterdam. They had a pleasant cup of coffee together but didn't discuss their shared experiences in Germany. They were still young and focused themselves on the future.

It wasn't until several months after the war that the parents of Wim's friend in hiding in Baarsdorpermeer, Cor Sombeek, received the news they'd always feared. Their son was dead. Through all kinds of aid organisations, they received scraps of stories about the conditions under which it had happened. Cor's mother sent a letter to the Concentration Camps Settlement Office in Vught, declaring that Wim had cared for him and knew where he was buried. She carefully saved the draft in a small trunk in her linen closet.

When in the course of 1946 the newspapers started covering the trials of the war criminals who had wreaked havoc in Neuengamme, Wim suffered a relapse. More than anything, it brought back painful memories at night.

Of the fourteen leading SS officers from camp Neuen-gamme who were charged in the 'Curiohaus Trial', eleven were sentenced to death and hanged, including Max Pauly, Anton Thumann and Willi Dreimann. This was the first of what were to be eight trials held by the British military tribunals and named after the building in which the sessions took place.

Almost a year later, just as Wim thought he'd worked through the worst repercussions, several other announce-ments would rub salt into old wounds. The tormentors who had ruled the roost in satellite camp Husum-Schwesing were sentenced in the Neuengamme Camp Case No. 4 trial. The principal witness was Doctor Paul Thygesen. Just one man was sentenced to death and hanged: *Blockführer* Josef Klinger. The deputy camp commandant Emanuel Eichler was given five years in prison and Kapo Wilhelm Schneider four. Kapo Willie Demmer was found guilty in a later trial, but owing to mental illness was not deemed criminally responsible and was set free. In 1948, E.J. Bouwmeester, known to Wim as the Kapo Red Jan, was sentenced in Rotterdam to twenty years in prison.

Camp commandant Hans Hermann Griem escaped imprisonment under suspicious circumstances, together with Kapo Martin Tenz. The latter was shot several years later while on the run. Griem was only tracked down in 1965. He turned out to be living under his own name in Bergedorf, just down the road from Neuengamme, the former concentration camp. Everyone around him had kindly kept their mouths shut. Another investigation was started and the whole trial process, including the witness testimonies, was repeated twenty-five years after the events. Nevertheless, he would get off scot-free again. Shortly after the start of the trial, on 25 June 1971, Griem died – without ever having to take responsibility for his misdeeds.

Joseph Kotälla, the executioner of Amersfoort, and *SS-Hauptsturmführer* Ferdinand Aus der Fünten, who had been face to face with Wim at the Sicherheitsdienst on the Euterpestraat in Amsterdam, were both, after a long trial, sentenced to life in prison. That felt like justice. Both Nazis were known for decades as two of the notorious 'Breda Four', the main German war criminals imprisoned on Dutch soil and a source of national controversy for years to come.

What Wim didn't hear about in those first years after the war was the slew of awards that were conferred upon war hero and top pilot Johnny Baldwin. British distinctions covered his chest and he was allowed to receive, as one of a select few foreigners, a Croix de Guerre 1940 with Palm from the Belgian government in January 1947. Later that year, on

31 October 1947, an extremely prestigious distinction was added to his achievements. The Dutch queen Wilhelmina had the pleasure of naming John Robert Baldwin as a Grand Officer of the Order of Oranje-Nassau. With his efforts during the war and especially those surrounding the invasion in Normandy, he'd personally contributed to the Allied victory and so to the liberation of the Netherlands.

From all of the inquiries made after the war regarding Operation Big Shipping Strike, it turned out that the pilots who had taken part were in no way blamed for the huge number of innocent victims. They fully believed they'd neutralised fleeing Nazis and had carried out their orders with great effectiveness and courage.

As the worst of the traumas began to fade, Wim talked more and more about wanting to someday return to the sites where the camps had stood. He felt that he would then be able to close the book on his past for good. Neuengamme was forbidden territory; no one was allowed to enter the camp premises any more. The authorities in Hamburg had very cleverly built a prison on the site of the former concentration camp. In 1955, Wim returned to Husum one last time, together with Miep. The huts had been demolished, after serving for years as a refugee camp. Only some foundations and crumbling walls were visible now; but the *Wasserhahn*, the notorious fire hydrant, was still standing. Wim's eyes roamed over the grounds of the former camp while many mental hatches that had been closed for ten years opened. He firmly held onto his wife's hand, his mainstay and pillar of support.

To the right of the camp street, he could see for kilometres over the fields. In the distance was a farm that struck him as familiar. His thoughts went back in time and he imagined himself in the *Revier*, surrounded by starving prisoners. Then he heard a horse's hooves outside. He looked out of the window and saw a horse and cart coming closer. A young man was sitting at the front and body parts were dangling out of the paper sacks. He shuddered.

Miep squeezed his hand.

'Wim? You still here?'

'Over on that farm, there lived a boy who would come and take the corpses out of the camp and bring them to the church. Six or eight prisoners would walk behind the cart with shovels on their shoulders, guards behind them. Come on, we're going there. See if anyone still lives there who can tell us more.'

They started the car and drove to the sand path that ran to the farmhouse. Wim rang the doorbell and a woman opened it. He introduced himself, said that he'd been a prisoner at the nearby camp and asked whether the boy from those days still lived here. She asked Wim to wait at the door for a moment and came back several minutes later.

'My husband wants to speak with you,' she said.

In the living room sat a man whose expression he immediately recognised. He stood up with some difficulty to shake Wim's hand and introduced himself as Jens Erik Thomsen. Wim told him what he'd seen from the *Revier*. The man nodded: '*Das war ich.*' 'That was me.' He gave a deep sigh and asked whether Wim wanted to have a seat.

'I was seventeen at the time and actually supposed to go into military service,' he said. 'But I've got a bad leg from a congenital defect and was deemed unfit. The SS came to the door and said I had to make trips for them with the horse and cart. It was that or the Eastern Front. I had no idea what the load was and where it was supposed to go but found out soon enough. The first time, it was three paper sacks, but before long it was more. Cartloads. I couldn't sleep at night any more and became confused. After a few weeks I said I'd stop, I couldn't take it. I got the choice of continuing or putting on a striped suit myself.'

The man's eyes welled with tears. Wim put a comforting and understanding hand on his shoulder.

'Every night I make that same trip over again,' the man said, his shoulders shaking. 'Every night.'

Half an hour later, Wim gave the farmer's son a well-meant handshake goodbye and set course for the Netherlands, Miep at his side and the future ahead of him.

Epilogue

Amsterdam, April 1959

Wim walked with a feeling of satisfaction down the steep stairs and out of the house on the Nassaukade, where he'd repaired a television. He'd been an independent entrepreneur in his home town for about eight years now. A small business with a few employees. Quick, flexible and dedicated to every customer. He sold major appliances and consumer electronics, washing machines, radios and TVs, delivered the products to homes, installed them himself and only left when everything was functioning perfectly. If something ever broke, he would come over right away. His wife and four children could live comfortably.

Wim loaded his toolbox into the boot of his Ford Taunus 17M. A hulk of a car, but ideal for setting off with the whole family and spacious enough for everything he had to lug around for his business. It was wonderful weather that day in April. The sky was clear blue and the white roof of his green car glittered in the bright sunlight. He'd finished working for the week. The Saturday afternoon was almost over and Wim looked forward to a free Sunday with his family.

He hadn't driven half a kilometre, when he spotted a car

parked between two trees along the canal, its bonnet raised. A man wearing a hat was bent over the engine and he gesticulated wildly to his wife. Two children, around seven years old, were hanging around outside the blue vehicle.

A few metres before reaching the stranded car, he noticed the licence plate: white with black letters and numbers. Next to it, a sticker with the letter D. He parked his Ford behind them and stepped out. The family was happy to see someone offering help. In his best German, he made it clear that he wasn't a mechanic, but he did have a towing cable in the boot. He offered to tow the car to their hotel.

A quarter of an hour later, he carefully manoeuvred his Ford between a number of other cars and stopped in front of the Park Hotel. Wim undid the cable and helped to push the family's Opel to a parking spot. The owner introduced himself as Heinrich and thanked him several times for his help. They insisted he drank a cup of coffee with them in the lobby.

Wim asked what they'd been planning to do.

'First see Amsterdam, then off to the tulips,' the man said.

His wife Helga had been talking about them for years. She'd really looked forward to the beautiful colours that she so missed at home, but without a car, their plan had fallen to pieces. The garages wouldn't be opening again until Monday and by then the family would have to go home again. Wim saw the disappointment in their faces.

'Tomorrow morning early, nine o'clock, we'll come and pick you up,' he said. 'Right here, in front of the hotel. My wife, Miep, is from Lisse – that's right in the heart of where the tulips are grown. She knows all the nice spots and tomorrow, we'll show them to you.'

The whole German family fitted on the back seat and they rode out of Amsterdam the next morning feeling cheerful and with a full tank of petrol. It was early evening when Wim finally parked his Taunus back on the Stadhouderskade. They'd had a wonderful day. There had been childhood memories for Miep and it was just as informative for the German family as for Wim himself.

Spontaneously, Wim offered to tow the family to the border the next day. If they made sure they were picked up by family or friends, they'd be home by the end of the day. Their Opel could then go to a local garage and they wouldn't have to wait in Amsterdam. They accepted with gratitude. Heinrich called his neighbour and they agreed he would meet them at the border crossing at De Poppe, near Oldenzaal.

He must have checked the towing cable three times on Monday morning, to be sure he wouldn't lose the Opel somewhere along the way during the long journey. Then the whole affair got moving. More than a few Amsterdammers stopped to watch. It wasn't every day that you saw a Dutch Ford Taunus towing a German Opel Olympia on a rope.

It was early afternoon when they reached De Poppe, but after waiting for an hour, their neighbour was still nowhere to be seen. Heinrich called him from a restaurant and came back with bad news. Their neighbour hadn't been able to get time off from work and hadn't been able to contact Heinrich. Wim asked how far they lived from the border.

'About a hundred, maybe a hundred and fifty kilometres,' Heinrich said. 'In Wunstorf, not far from Hannover.'

Wim reattached the towing cable, said they had to get in, slid behind the wheel and joined the row of cars waiting in front of the barrier.

At half past three in the afternoon, Wim rolled the cable up again. The Opel was neatly parked in front of the German family's house and he had their eternal gratitude.

All four of them waved him goodbye.

Shortly after midnight, Wim pulled the front door shut behind him. Miep had waited for him and he gave her a big kiss. He'd travelled nearly halfway around the world, but it had all gone well. Wim told her about the misfortune at the border and how thankful they'd been. Miep asked whether he'd mentioned anything to the family that day about his time in Germany. Wim shook his head.

'That's how God intended it when He created the world,' he said. 'We're here on earth to love one another, help one another forward. Not to hate.'

Two weeks later, the Aloserij family received a thick envelope from Germany. Inside was a long thank-you letter and a newspaper for the Hannover region. An entire page had been dedicated to the story of Heinrich and Helga's adventure in Holland. How they'd been helped in the German-hating Netherlands by a warm-hearted family from Amsterdam. For a whole day, the man had showed them the blooming tulip fields and the day after, he had towed their broken-down car all the way home.

'That must have been one remarkable person.'

Acknowledgements

My first encounter with Neuengamme concentration camp was at an annual members' day in May of 2017 for the Vriendenkring Neuengamme, a Dutch foundation dedicated to the memory of the camp, its dwindling survivors and their families. Martine Letterie, the then director, had asked me to give a presentation on Joseph 'Menthol' Sylvester, the central figure in one of my previous books, who had been interned in a transit camp at Schoorl, the Netherlands. Afterwards, a spritely older gentleman approached me and we began talking. We clicked. His story grabbed hold of me and in your hands you now have the result.

While researching and writing this book, I had the full co-operation and trust of the foundation Vriendenkring Neuengamme and was allowed to be part of an extraordinary visit to the site of the former concentration camps. Thank you to the board, members, my travel companions and Martine in particular.

Alyn Bessmann at the KZ-Gedenkstätte Neuengamme was incredibly helpful while I was researching the camp. I could go to her with every one of my questions and thanks in part to her and Johannes Barth's help, I was provided access to many photos and drawings that went into the making of this book.

It is inconceivable just how much information can still be tracked down after all these years. My searching was made easier thanks to the help of the kind employees at the involved organisations. Hubert Berkhout from the NIOD Institute for War, Holocaust and Genocide Studies has to be mentioned here. Much of the detective work started with him. Thank you, Hubert, again! My many thanks also go out to the employees at the Dutch Red Cross, the Amsterdam Municipal Archives, National Monument Camp Amersfoort and the International Tracing Service in Bad Arolsen, Germany.

As the research progressed, yet more questions regarding Wim's time in hiding in Zwaag/Blokker and Baarsdorpermeer arose. What started with a photograph of four boys in a field ended with the discovery of their names and even the prayer card of Wim's murdered friend in hiding. Ina Broekhuizen-Slot from the De Cromme Leeck Historical Foundation did valuable detective work that led to important facts and details. Through Ineke Dekker-Sombeek, I was granted access to the archive made for her uncle, Cor Sombeek. Thank you very much to all.

Edwin Vrielink manages the digital archive for the Vriendenkring. His fact-checking of the chapters about Husum was incredibly valuable and I am thankful to have been able to call on his extensive knowledge about the camp. Together, we were allowed to join Wim for a memorable and remarkably powerful visit to the former site of Husum concentration camp, sixty years after his last trip. An unforgettable day.

While researching Fliegerhorst Plantlünne, I was helped by Joachim Eickhoff, thanks to whom an unknown part about the war could be written. Henry Porter (ex-RAF) helped to explain the RAF's command structure. For that I am very grateful to both.

I would like to thank Wido van de Mast, a former commander of the Volkel airbase and F-16 pilot, for his valuable advice incorporated into the chapter about the attack on the *Cap Arcona*.

I had the opportunity to brainstorm multiple times with German researcher Wilhelm Lange about the disaster in the Bay of Lübeck, with the *Cap Arcona* as the focal point. During my visit to the museum in Neustadt in Holstein, he provided access to unique records. Thank you for the constructive collaboration – the museum in that fine city is more than worth a visit.

In addition to these, there are of course many people who in their own way each helped the book to come about. For that, I am very grateful to them: Arend Hulshof, José Huurdeman, Carola Kieras, Peter Tack, Nan Kluft, Ria Jong, Bart Elsman, Jeroen Droste, Gerrit van Gils, Dick Lohuis, Ingrid Wegerif, Sietze Geertsema, Nico Spilt, Steffi Friedrichsen, Maria Jepsen, Gerhard van Dijk, Martin Reiter, Eric van den Berg, Johanna Jürgensen, Thomas Lorenzen, Marc Brugman and Janine Doerry.

Naturally, my collaborators in the Dutch publishing industry with whom I, as a self-published author, had a pleasant time working can't go unmentioned: Enno de Witt as tireless editor and conversation partner, Paul Scheurink who designed yet another extremely fine book, Paul Impens and

Ronal Rhebergen from Ef & Ef Media for the valuable advice and the book's sale. Thank you as well to Dorine Holman, Cindy Eijspaart, Jan Peter Prenger and Erik Hoekstra for all of their input during and after a very special meeting with this book's protagonist.

A special word of thanks, also, to Haico Kaashoek, who didn't solely limit himself to the translation of this book from Dutch into English but put his heart and soul into it.

Without the co-operation of its central figure, Wim Aloserij, this book would never have come about. Over the course of dozens of personal interviews and just as many clarifying phone conversations, all that had taken place before and in particular during the war slowly became clear. In the nineties, after almost fifty years of silence, Wim Aloserij began speaking about his experiences for the first time. He'd only mentioned snippets of his story until then. In the year before publishing this book in Dutch, I was able to hear his complete story for the first time – including sometimes horrific details. That speaks to a boundless trust, for which I am enormously thankful to Wim. His sister Jo, too, told me wonderful stories and so provided valuable information about their childhood on Kattenburg and the war years that followed.

It was a privilege getting to know Wim Aloserij and being allowed to write this book.

Sources

Books

Afwikkelingsbureau Militair Gezag. *Overzicht der werkzaam-heden van het Militair Gezag gedurende de bijzondere staat van beleg.* Dutch National Government, 1946. ISBN unknown.

Bästlein, K. et al. *Das KZ Husum-Schwesing, Aussenkommando des Konzentrationslagers Neuengamme.* Bredstedt/Bräist: Verlag Nordfriisk Instituut, 1983. ISBN 3-88007-121-7.

Berthold, W. *De ondergang van de Cap Arcona.* Blaricum: Bogot en Van Rossum, 1978. ISBN unknown.

Dekker, P. & Van Dompseler, G. *Van naam tot nummer, slachtoffers van de Puttense razzia.* Grou: Uitgeverij Louise, 2014. ISBN 9-789-491-536236.

Van Dijk, A. *Het concentratiekamp Neuengamme: leven in de schemering van het bestaan.* Self-published, 2012. ISBN 978-90-484-1962-3.

Eckel, C. & Garbe, D. *Konzentrationslager Neuengamme: Katalog der Ausstellungen Band I Hauptausstellung.* Bremen: Edition Temmen, 2014. ISBN 978-3-8378-4047-6.

Eckel, C. & Garbe, D. *Konzentrationslager Neuengamme: Katalog der Ausstellungen Band II Ergänzungsausstellungen*. Bremen: Edition Temmen, 2014. ISBN 978-3-8378-4047-6.

Von Frijtag Drabbe Künzel, G. *Kamp Amersfoort*. Amsterdam: Mets & Schilt, 2003. ISBN 978-90-533-0367-2.

Geertsema, S. P. *De ramp in de Lübeckerbocht: Nederlanders bij het einde van Neuengamme*. Amsterdam: Uitgeverij Boom, 2011. ISBN 978-94-6105-272-8.

Haverkate, J. & Vaanholt, G. *Twente 40-45*. Zwolle: Wbooks. 2015. ISBN 978-94-625-8075-6.

Hulshof, A. *Rijpstra's ondergang: het lot van een burgemeester in oorlogstijd*. Amsterdam: Querido, 2016. ISBN 978-90-214-0204-8.

Huurdeman, J. *Bij de beuk linksaf*. Leusden: Historische Kring Leusden, 2014. ISBN 978-90-802573-8-2.

Ineichen, S. *Cap Arcona 1927–1945: Märchenschiff und Massengrab*. Zürich: Limmat Verlag, 2015. ISBN 978-3-85791-769-1.

Kaienburg, H. *'Vernichtung durch Arbeit': Der Fall Neuengamme*. Bonn: Verlag J.H.W. Dietz, 1990. ISBN 978-3-801250-09-6.

Lange, W. *Cap Arcona: das tragische Ende der KZ-Häftlings-Flotte am 3. Mai 1945*. Eutin: Buchverlag Rogge GmbH, 2014. ISBN 978-3-942943-08-6.

Leppien, J. *Grenzfriedenshefte Jahrbuch 2014*. Flensburg: ADS-Grenzfriedensbund e.V., 2015. ISSN 1867-1853.

Van der Liet, J. *Herinneringen aan Neuengamme*. Harderwijk: Stichting Vriendenkring Neuengamme, 2013. ISBN unknown.

Lorenzen, O. *'Macht ohne Moral': Vom KZ Husum-Schwesing zum Mahnmal für die Opfer*. Heide: Verlag Boyens & Co. 1994. ISBN 978-3-804206-85-4.

Van Pée, R. *Ik was 20 in 1944: Relaas uit Neuengamme en Blumenthal.* Berchem: Uitgeverij EPO vzw, 1997. ISBN 90-6445-917-7.

Rolsma, H. *Neuengamme: de ramp in de bocht van Lübeck.* Self-published, circa 1945. ISBN unknown.

Schuyf, J. *Nederlanders in Neuengamme.* Zaltbommel: Uitgeverij Kimabo, 2011. ISBN 978-94-90920-05-0.

Shores, C. & Thomas, C. *2nd Tactical Air Force, Volume Three, From Rhine to Victory.* Hersham: Classic Publications. 2006. ISBN 978-1-903223-60-4.

Vrba, R. *Ik ontsnapte uit Auschwitz.* Utrecht: Kosmos Uitgevers. 2002. ISBN 978-94-0190-524-4.

De Wachter, E.R.M. *Maurice.* Self-published, 2013. ISBN 978-94-6203-436-5.

Wouters, T. *Opdat het nageslacht het wete.* Putten: Bureau voorlichting der gemeente Putten, 1948. ISBN unknown.

Articles

'Bulletin Neuengamme: Onder auspiciën van de Stichting Vriendenkring Neuengamme'. September 2015, 2016 and 2017.

Jorand, P. '"Here life is exterminated": The martyrdom of the prisoners of the Schwesing sub concentration camp'. Verlag Nordfriisk Instituut, 2000.

Van der Liet, J. '"Husum" een onbekend woord voor satanische wreedheid'. Lecture, 13 May 2017 in Nunspeet.

Documentary films

Andere Tijden. *De ramp met de Cap Arcona.* 22 januari 2011.
Andere Tijden. *Het laatste hoofdstuk.* 14 April 2015.
Ondergang Cap Arcona, 3 mei 1945. Broadcast 1997/1998.
Jehovah's getuigen: standvastig onder nazi-terreur. 1996.
The Typhoons' Last Storm. Lawrence Bond. History Channel.
   2000.

Other sources

ADS-Grenzfriedensbund
Amsterdam Municipal Archives
De Cromme Leeck Historical Foundation
The Dutch Red Cross – War Archive
Glanerbrug Historical Circle
Historical Blokker Association
Historical Centre Overijssel
Historical Zwaag Foundation
Husum-Schwesing Concentration Camp Memorial,
   brochure
International Tracing Service – Bad Arolsen
Kreis/Stiftung Nordfriesland
KZ-Gedenkstätte Husum-Schwesing, Lesefassung & Begleit-
   material für die Hörführung mit dem Audioguide
KZ-Gedenkstätte Neuengamme Library
National Monument Camp Amersfoort Archive

Dutch Social Insurance Bank (SVB) – Department for the
  Members of the Resistance and Victims of War
Old Hoorn Historical Association
Twente Regional Archive in Delden, the Netherlands
www.joodsamsterdam.nl

If you would like to know more about the former Neuengamme concentration camp, or need assistance:

The Amicale Internationale KZ Neuengamme (AIN) is
an international association of the national organisations of
survivors of the Neuengamme concentration camp, as well
as the families and friends of former prisoners of the Neuengamme concentration camp. For more information visit
their website at: https://www.neuengamme.international/